6/08

American Social Reform Movements

Almanac VOLUME 1

American Social Reform Movements

Almanac VOLUME 1

Judy Galens
Kathleen J. Edgar, Project Editor

U·X·L
An imprint of Thomson Gale,
a part of The Thomson Corporation

THOMSON
TM
GALE

Detroit • New York • San Francisco • New Haven, Conn. • Waterville, Maine • London

THOMSON
GALE

American Social Reform Movements: Almanac

Judy Galens

Project Editor
Kathleen J. Edgar

Editorial
Julie L. Carnagie, Madeline Harris

Rights and Acquisitions
Shalice Shah-Caldwell, Margaret Chamberlain-Gaston, Edna Hedblad

Imaging and Multimedia
Lezlie Light, Michael Logusz, Christine O'Bryan, Kelly Quin

Product Design
Pamela A.E. Galbreath and Jennifer Wahi

Cover Design
Deborah van Rooyen, DVR Design

Composition
Evi Seoud

Manufacturing
Rita Wimberley

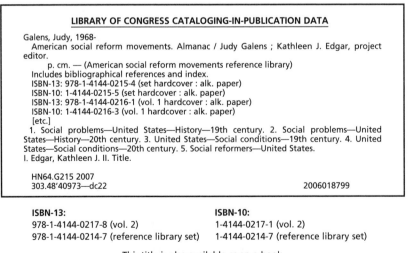

LIBRARY OF CONGRESS CATALOGING-IN-PUBLICATION DATA

Galens, Judy, 1968-
 American social reform movements. Almanac / Judy Galens ; Kathleen J. Edgar, project editor.
     p. cm. — (American social reform movements reference library)
 Includes bibliographical references and index.
 ISBN-13: 978-1-4144-0215-4 (set hardcover : alk. paper)
 ISBN-10: 1-4144-0215-5 (set hardcover : alk. paper)
 ISBN-13: 978-1-4144-0216-1 (vol. 1 hardcover : alk. paper)
 ISBN-10: 1-4144-0216-3 (vol. 1 hardcover : alk. paper)
 [etc.]
  1. Social problems—United States—History—19th century. 2. Social problems—United States—History—20th century. 3. United States—Social conditions—19th century. 4. United States—Social conditions—20th century. 5. Social reformers—United States.
 I. Edgar, Kathleen J. II. Title.

HN64.G215 2007
303.48'40973—dc22   2006018799

ISBN-13:
978-1-4144-0217-8 (vol. 2)
978-1-4144-0214-7 (reference library set)

ISBN-10:
1-4144-0217-1 (vol. 2)
1-4144-0214-7 (reference library set)

This title is also available as an e-book.
ISBN-13: 978-1-4144-0976-4, ISBN-10: 1-4144-0976-1
Contact your Thomson Gale sales representative for ordering information.
Printed in the United States of America

10 9 8 7 6 5 4 3 2

Table of Contents

Reader's Guide

An examination of the history of social reform movements in the United States reveals stunning demonstrations of courage, determination, leadership, and strength of character. Looking at this history also shows that change can be painful and difficult, whether for individuals, communities, or nations. Those agitating for change always meet with resistance from fellow citizens as well as politicians and law enforcers. They are the objects of ridicule and scorn; sometimes they are the victims of harassment and even deadly violence. They also earn considerable admiration and respect, as well as a substantial role in the history of the nation.

Social reform movements arise when a significant number of citizens organize to alter the established systems of their society: addressing social ills, changing unjust laws, achieving tolerance, easing misery. Social change does not happen overnight—securing voting rights for women, for example, required more than seventy years of activism. For most movements, the quest for change is ongoing. Such quests have led to some of the most notable instances of injustice in American history, such as National Guard troops firing into a crowd of antiwar demonstrators at Ohio's Kent State University, killing four students; police in Selma, Alabama, beating back civil rights marchers with batons, tear gas, and electric cattle prods; and militia troops and armed guards setting fire to the tents of striking mine workers and their families in Ludlow, Colorado, killing two women, eleven children, and some twenty miners. Movements for social change have also inspired acts of quiet heroism, as when nine black children in Little Rock, Arkansas, faced down hostile white citizens and gun-carrying National Guardsmen for the right to attend a racially integrated school.

Although the history of the United States is often told as the stories of presidents elected, wars fought, and industries built, that history would not be complete without an examination of the social reform movements driven by ordinary citizens. *American Social Reform Movements: Almanac* presents an overview of the reform movements that alternately tore apart and mended the fabric of American society. The two volumes are divided into thirteen chapters, with each chapter addressing a different social movement, including antiglobalization, antiwar, civil rights, education, environment, gay rights, labor, prison reform, poverty, slavery and abolition, temperance and Prohibition, women's rights, and women's suffrage.

Coverage and Features

American Social Reform Movements: Almanac (two volumes) contains numerous sidebar boxes that highlight people and events of special interest, and each chapter offers a list of additional sources that students can go to for more information. Nearly 130 black-and-white photographs help illustrate the text. Each volume begins with a timeline of important events in the history of the United States; a "Words to Know" section that introduces students to difficult or unfamiliar terms; and a "Research and Activity Ideas" section. Each volume concludes with a general bibliography and a subject index so students can easily find the people, places, and events discussed throughout *American Social Reform Movements: Almanac.*

American Social Reform Movements Reference Library

American Social Reform Movements: Almanac is only one component of the three-part U•X•L American Social Reform Movements Reference Library. The other titles in the set are:

- *American Social Reform Movements: Biographies* (one volume) presents the life stories of twenty-five notable activists and scholars, thinkers and writers, agitators and crusaders. Included are well-known figures such as civil rights leaders Martin Luther King Jr. and Malcolm X; labor organizers Eugene Debs and Mother Jones; abolitionist Frederick Douglass; women's rights pioneers Betty Friedan

and Gloria Steinem; and women's suffrage leaders Susan B. Anthony and Alice Paul. This volume also includes profiles of significant but lesser-known figures, such as poverty reformer Barbara Ehrenreich, environmentalist Jared Diamond, and gay rights advocates Harry Hay and Urvashi Vaid. In addition, *Biographies* contains sixty black-and-white photographs, sidebars, a comprehensive timeline, overall "Words to Know" section, and an index.

- *American Social Reform Movements: Primary Sources* (one volume) tells the story of social reform movements from American history in the words of the people who lived and shaped those movements. Excerpted and full-text documents provide a wide range of perspectives on reform movements. Included are excerpts from protest literature, eyewitness accounts of significant events, memoirs and other influential books, political speeches, and manifestos. Among these items are excerpts from Rachel Carson's *Silent Spring*; César Chávez's "An Open Letter to the Grape Industry"; Fannie Lou Hamer's "Testimony Before the Credentials Committee, Democratic National Convention"; Yolanda Huet-Vaughn's "Statement Refusing to Serve in the 1991 Gulf War"; Jonathan Kozol's "Still Separate, Still Unequal: America's Educational Apartheid"; Roni Krouzman's "WTO: The Battle in Seattle: An Eyewitness Account"; and Randy Shilts's *And the Band Played On: Politics, People, and the AIDS Epidemic.*

- A cumulative index of all three titles in the U•X•L American Social Reform Movements Reference Library is also available.

Special Thanks

Special thanks are due to U•X•L's American Social Reform Movement Reference Library advisers:

- Maria Barlotti, Librarian, Conestoga High School, Berwyn, Pennsylvania.

- Elaine Ezell, Library Media Specialist, Bowling Green Junior High School, Bowling Green, Ohio.

- Ann West LaPrise, Junior High/Elementary Librarian, Huron School District, Monroe, Michigan.

Comments and Suggestions

We welcome your comments on *American Social Reform Movements: Almanac* and suggestions for other topics to consider. Please write: Editors, *American Social Reform Movements: Almanac*, U•X•L, 27500 Drake Rd., Farmington Hills, MI 48331-3535; call toll free: 1-800-877-4253; fax to (248) 699-8097; or send e-mail via http://www.gale.com.

Timeline of Events

1600s Slavery begins in America with the arrival of Africans who have been forcibly removed from their homes, sent by ship to America, and sold as property to farmers and other landowners.

1775 The American Revolution begins.

1776 The Declaration of Independence is written, approved, and officially issued.

1780 The Industrial Revolution begins in the United States.

1788 The U.S. Constitution becomes law after being ratified by two-thirds of the original thirteen states.

1790 The Walnut Street Jail, the first penitentiary in the United States, is built in Philadelphia, emphasizing humane treatment and repentance through physical labor.

1792 The Bill of Rights, the first ten amendments to the U.S. Constitution, is adopted.

1798 The Alien and Sedition Acts, intending to curb protest against American war with France, are signed into law.

1808 Congress prohibits importing of African slaves.

1816 American Colonization Society is formed to gradually emancipate slaves and resettle them in Africa.

1830s–1840s Educational reformer Horace Mann travels throughout Massachusetts, inspecting schools and calling for a statewide public school system that would be free and available to all children. His efforts pay off, leading to the establishment of public schools in Massachusetts and throughout the American Northeast.

1831 William Lloyd Garrison begins publishing the abolitionist newspaper, *The Liberator,* to encourage the end of slavery.

1834 Textile mill workers in Lowell, Massachusetts, go on strike.

1836 The publication of Ralph Waldo Emerson's essay "Nature" launches the American Transcendentalist movement, which centers around the principle that there is a spiritual connection between humankind and its environment.

1836 The gag rule, forbidding the discussion of slavery in Congress, is passed.

1837 The Massachusetts Board of Education is formed, becoming the first state supervisory organization of education.

1837 The first Anti-Slavery Convention of American Women convenes in New York City.

1838 The "Trail of Tears"—the forced migration of the Cherokee from Georgia and southeastern Tennessee to Oklahoma—leaves more than 4,000 Native Americans dead.

1838 Angela Grimké, an abolitionist and women's rights advocate, delivers a speech in Philadelphia. The lecture hall where she is giving the speech is attacked by protesters and later in the night it burned to the ground.

1840s Social reformer Dorothea Dix campaigns for improved conditions for the mentally ill in prisons, hospitals, and other institutions. Her efforts lead to the establishment of separate state hospitals and more humane treatment for the mentally ill.

1840s Free blacks in the North, with assistance from white abolitionists, establish the Underground Railroad to help slaves escape from the South to freedom in the northern United States and in Canada.

1842 The Massachusetts Supreme Judicial Court decision *Commonwealth v. Hunt* asserts that unions are legal organizations and have the right to organize workers and call strikes.

1845 "The Sanitary Condition of the Laboring Population of New York City," issued by the city's Board of Health, makes some of the first convincing arguments about the link between disease and poverty.

1845 *Narrative of the Life of Frederick Douglass, an American Slave* is published.

1846 Mexican War (1846–1848) begins. Newly elected Congressman Abraham Lincoln (1809–1865) calls the war immoral and a threat to the nation's values, and writer Henry David Thoreau (1817–1862) is arrested when he refuses to pay a state tax as a protest against the war.

July 19–20, 1848 The first women's rights convention in American history meets in Seneca Falls, New York, marking the beginning of a women's rights movement that primarily sought the right to vote.

1849 "Resistance to Civil Government," an essay by Henry David Thoreau, is published. Better known as "Civil Disobedience," the essay argues for nonviolent resistance as a means to protest unfair laws or government actions.

1850 The Fugitive Slave Act passes, a law that makes it easier for slave owners to retrieve escaped slaves and severely punish anyone helping runaways. Under this law, even free blacks who had been living in the northern United States for years could be accused of being runaways and sent south for a life of bondage.

1852 Massachusetts becomes the first state to require all children to attend school.

1852 A 2,500-year-old sequoia from what later becomes Yosemite National Park is cut down for a carnival display, and prominent East Coast newspapers condemn the act.

1856 Bloody Kansas—a year-long war between pro- and antislavery factions—results in more than two hundred deaths over whether slavery will be permitted when Kansas becomes a state.

1857 Supreme Court rules in *Dred Scott v. Sandford* that even free blacks were not U.S. citizens.

October 1859 With the help of about twenty others, abolitionist John Brown raids the federal arsenal, a collection of weapons for the U.S. military, at Harpers Ferry, Virginia. He intends to pass the weapons along to slaves in the region and lead them into battle against their owners. The U.S. Marines capture or kill many in the raiding party; Brown is captured and, on December 2, 1859, is executed by hanging.

1860 The landmark Married Women's Property Act passes in New York, giving women the right to own, buy, and sell property; to sign contracts and file lawsuits; to share guardianship of their children in case of divorce; and to possess any money they earn outside the household.

1860 Abraham Lincoln, a northerner, is elected president of the United States.

1860 More than twenty-thousand shoemakers in twenty-five New England towns strike to prevent their wages from being cut and to gain union recognition.

1861 *Incidents in the Life of a Slave Girl,* by Harriet Jacobs, is published under the pseudonym Linda Brent. The book shows how religion was used in the South as a means for supporting slavery.

1861–65 The American Civil War is fought, pitting the North against the South. The war begins when southern states withdraw from the Union over such issues as states' rights and slavery, and it ends with victory for the northern, or Union, troops.

1862 Congress authorizes the Union Army to accept African American soldiers.

January 1, 1863 Abraham Lincoln signs the Emancipation Proclamation, a document that frees all slaves living in states that are at war with the Union. Some 800,000 African Americans remain enslaved, but the proclamation marks an important first step in the abolition of slavery.

1865 Congress passes the Thirteenth Amendment to the U.S. Constitution, abolishing slavery throughout the United States. In the ensuing years, the Fourteenth Amendment, guaranteeing African Americans citizenship and equal protection under the law, and the Fifteenth Amendment, securing the right to vote, are also passed.

1865 Henry George publishes *The Crime of Poverty,* detailing widespread poverty in America and its effects.

April 14, 1865 Abraham Lincoln is shot by John Wilkes Booth, an actor who sympathizes with the South; the president dies the following day.

1868 An eight-hour work day for federal employees becomes law.

1869 Elizabeth Cady Stanton and Susan B. Anthony form the National Woman Suffrage Association.

1869 The Knights of Labor is founded in Philadelphia. Representing workers in various professions, the Knights lobbied for an eight-hour workday, abolition of child and convict labor, equal pay for equal work, and elimination of private banks. The organization reached its highest total membership, more than seventy thousand, in 1886.

1872 Yellowstone National Park is established.

1872 Susan B. Anthony and more than a dozen other women attempt to vote in the presidential election in Rochester, New York. When stopped at the polls, Anthony reads aloud the Fifteenth Amendment, which has no wording that indicates the right to vote is restricted to men.

1874 The Woman's Christian Temperance Union (WCTU) becomes a national organization. With Francis Willard as its longtime national president, the WCTU effectively campaigns for a national ban on alcohol.

1877 Reconstruction, the period of transition for the South following the American Civil War, ends, and with it so do the limited rights and protections offered to southern blacks during this period.

1877 Declaring, "I will fight no more for ever," Chief Joseph surrenders after having led around seven hundred of his band of Nez Perce nearly two thousand miles from Oregon toward freedom in Canada, pursued by more than two thousand American troops.

1877 More than one hundred thousand workers strike for better wages and working hours. Strikebreakers kill over one hundred, and over one thousand strikers are jailed.

1879 Women lawyers are permitted to argue cases before the U.S. Supreme Court.

1881 The Federation of Organized Trades and Labor Unions of the United States and Canada, later renamed the American Federation of Labor (AFL), forms, representing mostly skilled workers. The AFL, which eventually joins up with the Committee for Industrial

Organization (CIO) to form the AFL-CIO, goes on to become hugely influential in the labor movement.

1882 Widespread resentment against immigrant Chinese laborers results in the Chinese Exclusion Act, suspending Chinese immigration for ten years.

1883 The U.S. Supreme Court rules as unconstitutional the Civil Rights Act of 1875, which prohibited segregation in public places.

1886 Eleven people die at the Haymarket Square labor riot in Chicago.

1886 The American Federation of Labor is formed.

1889 Jane Addams and Ellen Gates Starr purchase Hull-House in a Chicago slum populated with immigrants. By 1893, Hull-House had expanded to become the center of neighborhood activity, offering day care for children, a gymnasium, medical help, a playground, courses in cooking and sewing, and a boardinghouse for girls who work.

1889 The National Woman Suffrage Association unites with the American Woman Suffrage Association to form the National American Woman Suffrage Association. Elizabeth Cady Stanton serves as president of the organization.

1890 Sherman Antitrust Act describes unlawful restraints on business competition.

1890 The Wounded Knee Massacre in South Dakota is essentially the last battle in the war between the United States and Native Americans.

1892 Ida B. Wells-Barnett, a teacher and journalist, is one of the first reporters to bring media attention to the act of lynching. Between 1882 and 1930, more than three thousand African Americans were victims of vigilantes.

1892 The Populist Party, representing rural Americans, garners twenty electoral votes in the presidential elections.

1894 An economic depression, which began the previous year, leaves 20 percent of American workers without jobs.

1894 American Railway Union (ARU) members support the Pullman Palace Car Company workers in a major strike that disrupts most of the railroads in the midwestern United States.

1895 Booker T. Washington delivers his "Atlanta Compromise" speech.

1895 The Ohio Anti-Saloon League, which formed in 1893, becomes a national organization and a powerful lobby promoting a ban on alcohol.

1896 The U.S. Supreme Court issues the landmark *Plessy v. Ferguson* decision, which supports segregation and racial discrimination by legalizing "separate but equal" facilities for African Americans.

Late 1800s Educational reformers Francis W. Parker and John Dewey develop their groundbreaking theories, emphasizing creativity and individual expression rather than strict discipline.

1900 First major water pollution case, *Missouri v. Illinois and the Sanitary District of Chicago,* is argued before the Supreme Court.

1901 Carry Nation begins a crusade against alcohol, using an ax to demolish the interiors of saloons.

1902 President Theodore Roosevelt intervenes in a miners strike, marking the first time the U.S. government acts as peacemaker, not strikebreaker, in an industrial dispute. Miners win a 10-percent wage increase and shorter work days.

1903 W. E. B. Du Bois publishes *Souls of Black Folk,* where he states, "The problem of the twentieth century is the problem of the color line." Du Bois helped found the National Association for the Advancement of Colored People (NAACP) in 1909.

1904 National Child Labor Committee is formed to eradicate child labor.

1905 The Industrial Workers of the World (IWW) is formed to represent all industrial workers. The IWW was a major force for labor until the mid-1920s, representing as many as one hundred thousand workers nationwide.

1906 President Theodore Roosevelt makes his "Man with the Muck Rake" speech, chastising journalists who focus on the seamier side of American life. A group of important journalists adopt the nickname "muckrakers." Among them was Upton Sinclair, whose novel *The Jungle* (1906) exposed unsafe, unsanitary, and unfair working conditions in Chicago's meatpacking plants, and Ida Tarbell, whose exposé journalism revealed unfair business practices by the Standard Oil Company that contributed to an antitrust decision against the company.

1906 The Pure Food and Drug Act makes it illegal to make or sell food, drugs, and alcohol containing improper ingredients, or to give false information on product labels.

1909 National Organization for the Advancement of Colored People (NAACP) is formed.

1911 A fire at the Triangle Shirtwaist Factory in New York's Greenwich Village kills 146 women in less than 15 minutes, leading to a public outcry about workplace safety in garment industry "sweatshops."

1913 U.S. Department of Labor is established.

1914 World War I begins in Europe.

1914 Some twenty miners, two women, and eleven children are killed during a miners's strike in Ludlow, Colorado.

1915 Women's Peace Party is founded by Jane Addams and Carrie Chapman Catt.

1916 Helen Keller, widely respected for overcoming such challenges as blindness and deafness, emerges as a prominent peace activist against American involvement in World War I.

1917 The Selective Service Act creates the military draft.

April 1917 The United States enters World War I.

1917–18 The U.S. Congress passes the Espionage and Sedition Acts, making it a crime to express objections to the United States' participation in World War I (1914–18).

1918 Every state requires students to at least complete elementary school.

November 11, 1918 World War I ends.

May-June 1919 The U.S. Congress passes the Nineteenth Amendment, granting women the right to vote—pending ratification by thirty-six states.

January 1920 After the passage of the Eighteenth Amendment to the U.S. Constitution and the Volstead Act in 1919, Prohibition begins, outlawing the manufacture, transport, and sale of all alcoholic beverages in the United States.

August 26, 1920 Ratification of the Nineteenth Amendment is official; American women have the legal right to vote, though many lawmakers, particularly in the South, continue to bar black women from the polls.

1921 Margaret Sanger founds the American Birth Control League, the forerunner of Planned Parenthood Federation of America.

1923 Women's suffrage leader Alice Paul submits to Congress a proposal for an Equal Rights Amendment (ERA), which calls for men and women to be treated equally under the law.

October 29, 1929 The U.S. stock market crashes, marking the beginning of the severe economic downturn known as the Great Depression.

1931 Jane Addams is awarded the Nobel Peace Prize.

1933 Newly elected president Franklin D. Roosevelt launches his New Deal, an ambitious program designed to rebuild the economy, create jobs, and provide assistance to the poor.

December 5, 1933 The Twenty-first Amendment is ratified, effectively ending the era of Prohibition and making alcoholic beverages legal again.

1934 Passage of the Fish and Wildlife Coordination Act combines federal and state agencies to protect, rear, stock, and increase the supply of game and fur-bearing animals, as well as to study the effects of domestic sewage, trade wastes, and other polluting substances on wildlife.

1935 The Social Security Act provides retirement insurance.

July 1935 The U.S. Congress passes the National Labor Relations Act, also called the Wagner Act, giving workers the right to join a union and giving unions the ability to negotiate with employers.

1937 The term "greenhouse effect" appears in print for the first time in a textbook by University of Wisconsin professor Glen Thomas Trewartha.

1938 Congress passes the Fair Labor Standards Act (FLSA), protecting workers by mandating a minimum wage and maximum working hours and by imposing limits on child labor.

September 1939 After Germany invades Poland, France and Great Britain declare war on Germany, and World War II begins in Europe.

1941 To ensure there will be no strikes or demonstrations disrupting the manufacture of military supplies, President Franklin D. Roosevelt signs Executive Order 8802 prohibiting government contractors from engaging in employment discrimination based on race, color, or national origin. The first presidential action ever to prevent employment discrimination by private employers, it applies to all defense contractors, but contains no enforcement authority.

December 7, 1941 Japan bombs the U.S. naval base at Pearl Harbor, Hawaii, shocking the American people. Within days, the United States is at war with Japan and Germany and has formally entered World War II.

1942 Following the Declaration of War on Japan in 1941, President Roosevelt signs Executive Order 9066 mandating that more than 120,000 Japanese-Americans are to be sent to internment camps.

1944–47 The World Bank, International Monetary Fund (IMF), and General Agreement on Tariffs and Trade (GATT) are established to promote international economic development, paving the way for a rapid increase in globalization during the late twentieth century.

August 1945 The United States drops atomic bombs on the Japanese cities of Hiroshima and Nagasaki, bringing about Japan's surrender and the end of World War II. A massive, international antinuclear movement arises in protest of the use of nuclear weapons.

1946 The U.S. government seizes coal mines and railroads to avoid labor strikes and business practices that might contribute to inflation.

1948 President Harry S Truman issues Executive Order 9981, desegregating the U.S. military.

1950 The U.S. Census Bureau changes its rules to recognize that some women keep their maiden name after marriage.

1950 The U.S. becomes involved in a police action to protect South Korea from invasion by North Korea. The conflict escalates into the Korean War, which ends in 1953.

May 17, 1954 The U.S. Supreme Court issues a decision in the case *Brown v. Board of Education of Topeka, Kansas,* declaring school segregation unconstitutional.

1954 The Army-McCarthy hearings are held. Wisconsin Senator Joseph McCarthy presents accusations that the U.S. military and Department of State are deeply infiltrated by communists. McCarthy is disgraced when most of his allegations prove groundless. Anti-communist sentiments also fueled the House Un-American Activities Committee from 1947 to 1954, when many writers and activists were "blacklisted" and denied work because of alleged communist sympathies.

1954 France abandons its former colony in Southeast Asia called Indochina to fighters named the Viet Minh, followers of rebel leader Ho Chi Minh. The United States, through aid and military advisers, becomes the main backer of a democratic government in South Vietnam as the Second Indochine War, better known as the Vietnam War, begins.

December 1955 The Montgomery bus boycott begins after activist Rosa Parks refuses to give up her seat to a white passenger and is arrested. For more than one year, the black citizens of Montgomery, Alabama, boycott the city bus lines to protest segregation.

1957 President Dwight D. Eisenhower sends troops to Little Rock, Arkansas, to enforce racial desegregation of the city's schools.

1959 California enacts the first law to regulate automobile emissions.

1962 Rachel Carson releases *Silent Spring,* an influential and controversial book about the harmful effects of long-lasting pesticides, such as DDT (dichloro-diphenyl-trichloroethane), which many farmers used to control pest insects, like mosquitoes and lice.

1962 Political activist Michael Harrington publishes *The Other America: Poverty in the United States,* an influential work exposing the depths of American poverty.

1962 The National Farm Workers Association (NFWA) is organized at a convention of about three hundred farm workers led by César Chávez. The organization is later renamed the United Farm Workers (UFW).

October 1962 James Meredith becomes the first black student to enroll at the University of Mississippi.

1963 President Lyndon B. Johnson announces his intention to create a Great Society and to wage a "war on poverty," efforts that involve the passage of many laws that improve education, job training, and health care for disadvantaged Americans.

1963 Feminist Betty Friedan lays the groundwork for the women's rights movement with the release of *The Feminine Mystique,* a hugely influential book exploring society's image of the ideal woman and the resulting depression for many women when they fail to live up to that ideal.

April 1963 Led by Martin Luther King Jr., civil rights activists stage a series of demonstrations in the thoroughly segregated city of Birmingham, Alabama. King gets arrested and writes the "Letter from Birmingham Jail," explaining his mission to achieve justice and freedom for African Americans.

August 5, 1963 The United States, the Soviet Union, and Great Britain sign the Partial Test Ban Treaty, banning the testing of nuclear weapons—and any other type of nuclear explosion—in the atmosphere, in outer space, and underwater.

August 28, 1963 More than 250,000 people travel to the nation's capital for the historic March on Washington, where Martin Luther King Jr. delivers his "I Have a Dream" speech and civil rights leaders call for justice and equality for African Americans.

September 15, 1963 Four young black girls are murdered when a bomb explodes under the steps of the Sixteenth Street Baptist Church in Birmingham, Alabama.

November 22, 1963 President John F. Kennedy is assassinated in Dallas, Texas. As the nation mourns, Kennedy's vice president, Lyndon B. Johnson, assumes the presidency.

1964 Fannie Lou Hamer testifies to the Credentials Committee at the Democratic Party's National Convention about violence and intimidation directed at African Americans as they attempted to register to vote. Shown on national television, the testimony provided graphic examples of brutality and injustices to a national audience.

1964 Martin Luther King Jr. becomes the youngest man ever to win the Nobel Peace Prize.

March 1964 Black activist Malcolm X breaks with the Nation of Islam, a black separatist group, and begins the Organization of

Afro-American Unity, which promotes peaceful coexistence between whites and blacks as well as equal rights for blacks.

June 1964 Three civil rights workers are killed during the voter-registration drive called "freedom summer" in Mississippi.

July 2, 1964 The Civil Rights Act of 1964 passes, marking the end of Jim Crow segregationist laws in the American South.

August 10, 1964 The U.S. Congress passes the Tonkin Resolution, giving President Lyndon B. Johnson the power to wage war against North Vietnam. The Vietnam War, which had its roots in the mid-1950s and lasted until the mid-1970s, inspired the most widespread antiwar movement in American history.

1965 Filipino American grape pickers in California strike for better wages. They are joined by the National Farm Workers Association led by César Chávez. The grape pickers strike will last for nearly five years, and Chávez will emerge as a popular national figure for labor reform.

1965 Protests against the Vietnam War and the military draft become commonplace.

February 21, 1965 Civil rights leader Malcolm X is assassinated.

March 25, 1965 Thousands of civil rights activists participate in the Selma-to-Montgomery march, after several earlier attempts were thwarted by police brutality.

August 6, 1965 The Voting Rights Act of 1965 becomes law, outlawing such voting restrictions as poll taxes and literacy tests.

1966 Congress passes the Endangered Species Preservation Act, the first of many such laws designed to protect threatened animal and plant species from becoming extinct.

1966 The National Organization for Women (NOW) forms in an effort to achieve equality for women. With Betty Friedan as president, the emergence of NOW coincides with the emergence of the women's rights movement.

1967 Protests against the Vietnam War escalate with a march on the Pentagon and the issuing of "A Call to Resist Illegitimate Authority," which deems the conflict illegal and encourages young men to destroy their draft cards.

1967 Muhammad Ali becomes the most notable figure to refuse induction into the U.S. Army when he proclaims that he is a conscientious objector. Ali is charged with draft evasion and found guilty of violating the Universal Military Training and Service Act. Ali was sentenced to five years imprisonment and fined $10,000, but his appeal was finally resolved in 1971 when the U.S. Supreme Court reversed his draft evasion conviction.

April 4, 1968 Civil rights leader Martin Luther King Jr. is murdered by an assassin.

August 1968 At the Democratic National Convention in Chicago, thousands of demonstrators protest the war. The police and Illinois National Guardsmen respond aggressively, and a riot erupts. A number of protesters are beaten and arrested.

1969 The Woodstock Music and Art Fair draws more than a half million people to share their musical tastes and antiwar sentiments.

1969 The National Environmental Policy Act is passed, requiring the federal government to assess the environmental impact of its land development plans.

1969 Riots at the Stonewall Inn in New York City mark the beginning of the modern gay rights movement.

March 21, 1970/April 22, 1970 The first Earth Days, organized by two separate groups, are held, designed to celebrate the wonders of the natural world and to warn of abuses to its fragile ecosystems.

May 4, 1970 After four days of student antiwar demonstrations, National Guard troops open fire on unarmed protesters at Kent State in Ohio. Four students are killed and several more are injured. The incident shocks the nation and sparks widespread protests.

September 1971 A minor disciplinary action against two inmates for fighting at the Attica Correctional Facility in New York erupts into a full-scale riot. Four days later, police and prison guards storm the prison, killing twenty-nine inmates and ten hostages. The word "Attica" has since become synonymous with prison reform.

1972 After two years of intensive lobbying by women's rights activists, Congress votes overwhelmingly in favor of the Equal Rights Amendment (ERA), a provision guaranteeing equal treatment under the law for men and women. The ERA is sent to the states for ratification, but a powerful opposition movement prevents its approval.

1972 The U.S. Congress passes a series of amendments to the Elementary and Secondary Education Act of 1965, including one known as Title IX. With the passage of Title IX, schools at all levels that receive federal funding are forbidden from excluding or otherwise discriminating against any student based on his or her sex.

1973 Congress passes the War Powers Act to more clearly define how a president can pursue military action. The act is intended to avoid another prolonged military conflict like the Vietnam War, where war was never officially declared.

1973 The Endangered Species Act recognizes the need to conserve the ecosystem of endangered plants and animals.

1973 The American Psychiatry Association (APA) removes homosexuality from its official list of mental disorders. Many gay rights activists believe that branding homosexuality as a mental illness provided a basis for discrimination.

1973 Ruling on two cases, *Roe v. Wade* and *Doe v. Bolton,* the U.S. Supreme Court legalizes abortion.

1974 Two women are among the nation's first openly gay people elected to public office: Kathy Kozachenko is elected to the Ann Arbor, Michigan, city council, and Elaine Noble is elected to the Massachusetts state legislature.

1975 The Church Committee, chaired by Senator Frank Church, reveals extensive domestic spying operations on Americans during the previous two decades as well as illegal activities committed by the Central Intelligence Agency (CIA).

1975 Congress passes the Education for all Handicapped Children Act, later renamed the Individuals with Disabilities Education Act (IDEA). This law requires schools to provide opportunities to mentally and physically disabled students.

1979 In honor of nineteenth-century reformer Susan B. Anthony's tireless work and achievements, her image is chosen for a new dollar coin, making her the first woman to be depicted on U.S. currency.

Early 1980s A deadly and mysterious disease, later given the name Acquired Immunodeficiency Syndrome (AIDS), emerges; doctors and scientists realize that this syndrome seems to disproportionately affect gay men.

1982 The Equal Rights Amendment fails to be ratified as it falls three states short of the necessary number for ratification. President Ronald Reagan was among those opposed to the amendment; earlier, he became the first major presidential candidate to voice his opposition to the ERA.

June 1982 Activists stage a massive peace demonstration in New York City, the largest protest rally up to that point in American history. Estimates of the number in attendance at the "No Nukes" rally range from 500,000 to one million demonstrators.

1983 A federal holiday is established to honor Martin Luther King Jr.

1987 *And the Band Played On: People, Politics, and the AIDS Epidemic* brings widespread coverage and information on the growing AIDS problem.

1989 Oil spilled from the Exxon *Valdez* tanker causes major environmental damage in Prince William Sound, Alaska.

1991 The U.S. leads a coalition of nations in the Gulf War against Iraq.

1992 Sections of Los Angeles erupt in riots following the acquittal of three white police officers accused of severely beating motorist Rodney King, an African American.

1994 The North American Free Trade Agreement (NAFTA) involving Canada, Mexico, and the United States strengthens rules and procedures governing trade and investment throughout the continent.

1995 The World Trade Organization (WTO) is established to set rules and resolve disputes for global trading. By 2006 there were one-hundred and fifty member nations in the WTO.

1996 President Bill Clinton signs into law a welfare reform bill that abolishes the Aid to Families with Dependent Children (AFDC) program. The new law, sometimes known as the welfare-to-work law, emphasizes the need for welfare recipients to find jobs and removes government-funded safety nets for the poor.

November 30, 1999 The antiglobalization protest known as the "Battle in Seattle" begins; it is a series of marches and demonstrations designed to obstruct the annual meeting of the World Trade Organization, or WTO.

2000 Vermont becomes the first state to legally recognize civil unions between gay or lesbian couples.

2000 California establishes a state holiday to honor Latino labor leader César Chávez.

2001 Representatives of 189 nations gather for the first Special Session of the United Nations General Assembly on HIV/AIDS. They unanimously adopt the Declaration of Commitment on HIV/AIDS.

2001 Barbara Ehrenreich issues *Nickel and Dimed: On (Not) Getting by in America,* which demonstrates the extreme difficulty of living on a minimum-wage salary.

September 11, 2001 Terrorists fly two passenger jets into the Twin Towers of New York City's World Trade Center and one into the Pentagon in Washington, D.C. A fourth plane crashes into a field near Shanksville, Pennsylvania after passengers seize control from terrorists. The administration of President George W. Bush responds to the events of 9/11 by declaring an open-ended War on Terror; as part of that war, the U.S. military invades Afghanistan in 2001 and Iraq in 2003.

2002 Passed by Congress in 2001 and signed into law by President George W. Bush in 2002, No Child Left Behind is a sweeping education reform bill.

February 15, 2003 As the U.S. invasion of Iraq looms, citizens in countries all over the world gather for historic peace demonstrations, assembling in dozens of American cities and in several hundred cities throughout Europe and elsewhere. Estimates of the total number of participants worldwide range from six to ten million.

March 20, 2003 Despite the opposition of millions of citizens and the governments of many other nations, U.S.-led forces invade Iraq on land and by air. The war officially ends three weeks later, on April 9, 2003, though the U.S. military and Iraqi insurgents continue to violently clash for years afterward.

2004 Jared Diamond's *Collapse: How Societies Choose to Fail or Succeed* explores how some powerful ancient civilizations fell into ruin by failing to perceive and solve their environmental problems. He relates the problems of the past to environmental trouble spots today.

2004 Senator John Kerry, a Vietnam veteran who later spoke against the war, runs for president against incumbent George W. Bush and loses.

2005 Jonathan Kozol's *The Shame of the Nation: The Restoration of Apartheid Schooling in America* reflects on a new kind of educational segregation in the largely non-white public school systems of many major American cities. Kozol also challenges the success of reforms of the No Child Left Behind Act.

2005 Maureen Dowd's *Are Men Necessary?* questions the gains made by women since the 1960s.

2006 Between thirty-six and forty-five million people are living with HIV, the virus that causes AIDS.

2006 Millions rally across the United States in peaceful demonstrations to protest proposed immigration laws that would affect more than eleven million illegal Mexican immigrants in the United States.

2006 Top climate scientists associated with the National Academy of Sciences issue a report warning of the imminent dangers of global warming.

Words to Know

abolition: The act of abolishing, or getting rid of, slavery by making it illegal.

abolitionist: A person who works to make slavery illegal.

abstinence: Refraining from participation in or indulgence of certain vices or activities; in terms of the temperance movement, the avoidance of all alcoholic beverages.

activist: A person who campaigns vigorously for or against a political, social, or economic issue.

AIDS: Acquired Immunodeficiency Syndrome; a disease related to a severely compromised immune system, leaving the body unable to defend against infection.

anarchist: An individual who advocates the use of force to overthrow all government.

antiglobalization: Opposition to the methods and practices of globalization, particularly the perceived emphasis on corporate profits over human benefits.

antitrust laws: Laws opposing or regulating trusts or similar business monopolies.

antiwar: Opposition to a specific war, to one side of a war, or to all war.

apprentice: Someone who is bound to work for someone else for a specific term in order to learn a trade.

armistice: A temporary agreement among warring nations to stop fighting and draft a formal peace agreement.

B

biodiversity: The diversity of plant and animal species within an ecosystem; also refers to diversity within a species or diversity among a number of different species.

bisexual: A person who is romantically and physically attracted to both men and women.

black nationalism: An ideology held among militant groups of American blacks that called for the formation of self-governing black communities that were separate from those of whites.

blacklist: A list of employees involved in union activity that was sent to employers to warn them against hiring those people, effectively preventing those workers fired for unionism from getting another job.

blind pig/blind tiger: An establishment where alcohol is illegally sold.

bootlegger: A person who makes, sells, or transports alcohol illegally.

boycott: A refusal to do business with a certain company as a form of protest; often takes the form of employees refusing to work or encouraging consumers to stop buying their employers' products.

C

capital: Assets, including money or property, used to create further wealth through investment or the production of goods and services.

capitalism: An economic system in which the companies that produce goods or provide services are owned privately by individuals or groups of people. Owners have invested funds, or capital, in a business and earn profits when the business succeeds.

civil disobedience: The purposeful and usually peaceful violation of laws or rules that are considered unfair or morally wrong.

civil rights: Personal rights guaranteed by law to all citizens.

civil union: A legally recognized marriage-like relationship, often between two people of the same sex, that offers many of the same legal rights and benefits of marriage.

civil war: A war fought by different groups within a country rather than among many countries; the American Civil War (1861–65) was fought between the northern (Union) and southern (Confederate) states.

collective bargaining: The process of negotiating a contract between an employer and the union that represents the employees.

coming out: The act of revealing to others one's previously hidden sexual orientation.

common school: A public school, free and available to all children; term used during the nineteenth century.

communism: A political system in which most aspects of social and economic life are dictated by the government. Under communism, all property is owned by the government and, theoretically, wealth is distributed evenly throughout society.

conscientious objector: A person refusing to serve in the military because it violates his or her conscience; term often used to describe those whose religious beliefs prevent any endorsement of war.

conservation: The protection and managed use of natural resources and wilderness areas.

conservatism: A political ideology based on the concept of a limited federal government, one that protects individual's freedoms by maintaining domestic order, providing for national defense, and administering justice. This ideology is generally opposed to the use of federal powers for the protection or preservation of civil rights.

convict: A person convicted, or found guilty, of a crime; term usually reserved for those serving time in prison.

cross-dresser: A person who wears clothing typical of the opposite sex; also described as "transvestite."

currency: Any form of money, generally either coins or paper bills, issued by a government or a bank and used in legal exchanges.

D

dame schools: Schools conducted by women in their homes during the American colonial era; also known as "petty schools."

depression: A severe economic downturn usually characterized by high unemployment.

desegregation: The act of eliminating laws or provisions that force segregation, which is the legal separation of people of different races or ethnic groups.

determinate sentence: A prison sentence given for an exact time period as opposed to a range of months or years.

direct assistance: Cash payments made to welfare recipients; other types of welfare include subsidized housing, paid for in part by the government, or vouchers to be used to buy food or pay for rent.

discrimination: Unfair treatment of a group of people based on prejudice, a negative opinion formed without justification.

disenfranchise: To deprive a group or person of the right to vote.

domestic: Within the borders of one's own country, as opposed to "foreign."

dove: A person who favors diplomacy and negotiation and generally objects to war as a method of resolving conflict between nations.

draft (selective service): A system by which persons are chosen for mandatory service in a nation's military.

draft dodgers: Persons who hide in or flee from a country in order to avoid mandatory military service.

E

ecology: The study of the relationship between an organism and the entirety of its surroundings.

ecosystem: A community of plants and animals that live in balance with one another.

Emancipation Proclamation: An order of President Abraham Lincoln freeing the slaves in the southern states that had not remained loyal to the Union and that were not under Union control.

environment: The surroundings of a living being that affect that being's health and survival.

ERA: The Equal Rights Amendment; a proposed constitutional amendment that would have mandated equal treatment under the law regardless of gender.

executive order: A statement written and issued by the president that uses some part of an existing law or the U.S. Constitution to enforce an action.

export: Goods or services sent out of one country for trade or sale in another country.

extinction: The state of a species that has died out.

F

felony: A serious crime, including armed robbery, arson, or murder; usually punishable by a sentence of a year or more in prison.

feminism: The theory that women should have economic, political, and social rights equal to those of men.

food chain: Sequence in which one organism is the food source for the next organism, which is the food source for the next organism in the chain; for example, grass-rabbit-fox.

foreign: Relating to another country, as opposed to "domestic."

fossil fuels: Energy sources that were formed hundreds of millions of years ago from the fossilized remains of plants and animals.

franchise: The right to vote.

free blacks: African Americans who had never been slaves, or who had escaped from slavery by fleeing to the North.

free-market economy: An economic system in which goods and services are privately owned and sold to anyone wishing to buy them at whatever price can be obtained. Prices are set by the principle of supply and demand and are affected by competition.

free trade: The international exchange of goods and services without any barriers, such as tariffs or trade quotas.

Freedmen's Bureau: An organization formed by the U.S. Congress to aid former slaves after the American Civil War.

furlough: A temporary leave from prison granted to model inmates as a tool for helping them re-enter free society.

G

gay: A man who is romantically and physically attracted to other men; term also sometimes refers to the broader gay community, including lesbians and bisexuals.

gender: Either the male or female sex; term also implies a set of traits typically associated with that sex.

general strike: A work stoppage by all organized workers—working in various industries—in a city, region, or entire country; usually a form of protest designed to halt or greatly disrupt the normal functioning of the area in question.

global warming: Theory that an increase of greenhouse gases in the atmosphere, resulting from pollution, has begun to cause a warming of Earth's climate.

globalization: The exchange of goods, services, and capital across national borders.

grassroots organization: A group or network of local citizens; term suggests a rejection of a hierarchical structure with a centralized leadership.

H

habitat: The natural environment of an animal or a plant.

halfway house: A transitional place where inmates can live after leaving prison but before living on their own; offers counseling and supervision.

hawk: A person who supports aggressive foreign policies, including declarations of war.

heterosexual: A person who is romantically and physically attracted to people of the opposite sex.

hierarchy: The classification of people into ranks indicating authority, with the leader at the top.

HIV: Human Immunodeficiency Virus; the virus that causes AIDS.

homosexual: A person who is romantically and physically attracted to people of the same sex.

I

imperialism: The practice of one nation taking control of another's government or economy through invasion or other means.

import: Goods or services brought from one country into another for sale.

incarceration: Imprisonment.

indeterminate sentence: A sentence covering a range of time, such as fifteen years to life; prisoners can be granted parole after the minimum sentence has been met.

industrial union: A union that represents all workers, skilled and unskilled, in a particular workplace.

industrialism: The social system that results from an economy based on large-scale industries.

industrialists: People who engage in profit-making enterprises that manufacture a certain product, such as textiles or steel.

industrialization: The development of industry.

Industrial Revolution: A period of rapid industrial growth causing a shift in focus from agriculture to industry beginning in the late eighteenth century and continuing through the nineteenth century. During this time, new manufacturing technologies and improved transportation gave rise to the modern factory system and a massive movement of the population from the countryside to the cities.

injunction: A court order that either prohibits an action (such as a strike) or forces action to be taken (such as striking workers returning to work).

inmate: A person serving a sentence in a jail or prison.

integration: The mixing together of racial, cultural, or religious groups that had formerly been separated; integration implies that the groups will be on equal social footing.

J

jail: An institution where people are confined for short sentences or while awaiting sentencing; term is sometimes used interchangeably with "prison."

Jim Crow: A set of laws, customs, and regulations in the American South that separated blacks from whites to ensure that blacks were kept on a lower social footing; "Jim Crow" also describes the time period during which such laws were common, from the Reconstruction era until the mid-1960s.

just war doctrine: The principle, with a basis in New Testament teachings, that outlines the conditions under which a just, or fair, war might be fought, as when a nation has been attacked and all nonviolent attempts to resolve the conflict have failed.

K

Ku Klux Klan (KKK): The most prominent of several white supremacist groups that used violence—in the form of beatings, whippings, murder, rape, and arson—to control blacks and their sympathizers through fear and intimidation.

L

labor union: An organization of workers formed to protect and further their mutual interests by bargaining as a group with their employers over wages, working conditions, and benefits.

leftist: A person promoting radical or socialistic politics in the form of liberal reform or revolutionary change.

lesbian: A woman who is romantically and physically attracted to other women.

liberalism: A political ideology based on the concept of a federal government that protects an individual's freedoms by maintaining domestic order, providing for national defense, and administering justice, but also protects and preserves the civil rights of citizens by maintaining programs to aid certain social groups.

loom: A frame or machine used to weave thread or yarn into cloth.

lynching: The murder of an individual, most commonly a black American, by a mob of white Americans, with no legal authority, usually by hanging.

M

male chauvinism: The expression or attitude of a man indicating a belief in the superiority of men over women.

Middle Passage: The trip across the Atlantic made by slaves captured in Africa; the Middle Passage came between the slaves' forcible removal from their homes and their being sold as property to slave owners in the United States.

migrant workers: Laborers who travel from place to place to harvest crops for various farmers as the crops mature through the seasons.

minimum wage: The lowest rate of pay that an employer is allowed to pay employees, as decided either by law or by a negotiated contract.

misdemeanor: A minor crime, such as petty theft, punishable by a fine or a prison term of less than one year.

monopoly: The exclusive possession or right to produce a particular good or service.

moonshine: Illegally distilled alcohol, usually whiskey.

muckrakers: Journalists who search for and expose corruption in public affairs.

N

naturalist: A person who studies nature or natural history.

New Deal: A set of legislative programs and policies for economic recovery and social reform initiated in the 1930s during the presidency of Franklin Delano Roosevelt.

nonviolence: The deliberate avoidance of violence during demonstrations or protests designed to change a law or custom.

O

oppression: The act of using power in an unjust and cruel way; also the state of being weighed down by an unjust authority.

organized crime: A specialized form of crime carried out by loosely or rigidly structured networks of gangs with certain territorial boundaries.

ozone: A form of oxygen; forms a layer in the stratosphere that filters out harmful ultraviolet rays of the sun.

P

pacifism: An opposition to war or violence; the pursuit of peaceful resolution to all conflicts.

parochial school: A privately funded religious school.

parole: A release from prison allowing the inmate to serve the remainder of the sentence outside the prison, living according to the prison's rules and restrictions.

patriarchy: A society or organization in which men possess most of the control and authority.

penitentiary: A prison, generally reserved for serious offenders; originally referred to an institution where inmates would seek to show penitence, or regret, for their crimes. In the U.S. federal prison system, a penitentiary is a maximum-security facility.

pension: A fixed sum paid regularly, usually as a retirement benefit.

picket line: A group of striking workers marching at the entrance of their workplace to inform fellow employees and the general public of a labor dispute and to influence others not to enter the workplace.

poverty: The condition of one who lacks money, resources, and material goods.

prejudice: A negative opinion or attitude about a person, race, or group of people that is not based on fact or one's experiences with such people or groups. Instead, such opinions are based on unfounded ideas about how that person, race, or group might be or act.

preservation: Safeguarding an area of the natural world from undue human interference.

prison: A correctional institution designed to confine those convicted of a serious crime; term sometimes used interchangeably with "jail."

private school: A school controlled by private agencies and funded through private means, including student tuition and donations, rather than by the government.

probation: An alternative to a prison sentence whereby the convicted person remains free but has to abide by a set of restrictions and submit to supervision for a period of time.

Prohibition: The period from 1920 to 1933 when the government outlawed the manufacture, sale, and transport of alcoholic beverages.

protectionism: Policies designed to erect trade barriers, such as tariffs, to protect domestic companies from foreign competition.

protest: An organized public demonstration of discontent with the governance of or social circumstances within a society.

public school: A school supported by taxes, free and available to all students, and run by an elected school board.

Q

Quaker: A member of the Religious Society of Friends, a religion that supports equality between the sexes and promotes peace and tolerance in its teachings.

quota: A limit placed on the quantity of certain goods to be imported from a particular country.

R

racist: A person who discriminates or is prejudiced against a group based on that group's race; racism is based on the notion that one race is naturally superior to another because of genetic makeup.

radical: Someone who supports an extreme political cause.

recidivism: The repetition of criminal behavior; term usually refers to an ex-convict committing additional crimes after being released from prison.

Reconstruction: The period from the end of the American Civil War in 1865 until 1877, when newly freed slaves were given protections under the law including the right to citizenship, the right to vote, and the right to hold political office.

rumrunner: A person who illegally smuggles liquor across a waterway or a land border.

S

secondary school: A school attended between elementary school and college.

secular: Not religious.

sedition: Actions that encourage resistance of or rebellion against a governing body.

segregation: The separation and isolation of a racial or ethnic group in schools or other facilities.

settlement houses: Places established and run by educated, and often wealthy, reformers to provide social and educational services to the residents of poor urban immigrant communities.

sex: Gender classification, either male or female.

sexism: Discrimination based on sex; usually refers to discrimination against women.

sexual harassment: Sexually suggestive speech or physical contact directed at a person, usually by a figure of authority—for example, an employer or teacher.

sharecropper: A tenant farmer who works the land for an agreed share of the value of the crop, minus the deductions taken out of his share for his rent, supplies, and living costs.

sit-down strike: A refusal to work conducted by laborers who stay at their workstations and block employers from replacing them with other workers.

sit-in: A nonviolent form of protest popular during the civil rights movement that involved black and sometimes white activists occupying seats in a segregated establishment, like a restaurant, and refusing to leave until all were served.

slavery: A system in which a human being is considered the property of another and is forced to work for the "owner" without pay and often under brutal conditions.

social services: A range of services, often provided by the government, that promote the well-being of disadvantaged or disabled citizens; can include health clinics, counseling, job training, and the like.

social welfare: Private or government efforts to help disadvantaged or disabled individuals.

socialism: An economic system in which the means of producing goods and providing services are owned by the community rather than by private individuals or corporations; all members of the community share in the work and wealth is distributed equally.

speakeasy: An establishment where alcohol is illegally sold.

species: Related organisms that are capable of breeding with one another.

straight: An informal term for a person who is heterosexual, or attracted to members of the opposite sex.

stock market: A system for trade in companies, ventures, and other investments through the buying and selling of stocks, bonds, mutual funds, limited partnerships, and other securities.

strike: A refusal by employees to work, in an attempt to gain concessions from their employer, including increased wages, safer working conditions, better job security, and the recognition of the employees' union.

strikebreakers: Workers hired to replace striking employees; strikebreakers allow business to be continued without interruption, thereby defeating the purpose of the strike. Also referred to as replacement workers or, in a derogatory sense, as scabs.

suffrage: The right to vote.

suffragette: A woman who supports the right of women to vote; the term was often used in a negative, belittling way by opponents of women's suffrage.

suffragist: A person who promotes the right to vote; the term is used particularly in regard to a person supporting the right of women to vote.

sweatshop: A factory in which workers labor for long hours in poor conditions for very low wages.

T

tariff: A tax placed on goods imported from another country; tariffs raise the prices of imported goods, making it more difficult for such items to compete with domestically produced goods.

teetotaler: A person who abstains from all alcoholic beverages.

temperance: Moderation in the drinking of alcoholic beverages; in the context of the temperance movement, it usually refers to the complete avoidance of alcohol.

tenant farmer: Someone who farms land owned by someone else and pays rent or a share of the crop for the use of the land.

tenement: Urban dwellings rented by impoverished families that barely meet or fail to meet the minimum standards of safety, sanitation, and comfort.

trade agreement: An agreement among two or more nations that establishes terms for exchanging goods and services in a manner beneficial to all parties.

transgendered individuals: A range of people, including transsexuals and cross-dressers, who express their gender in ways that differ from conventional expectations.

transsexual: A person who has changed his or her biological gender through sex reassignment surgery and/or hormone treatment.

transvestite: A person who wears the clothing and, often, adopts the manner of the opposite sex.

treaty: A formal agreement between nations.

trusts: A group of companies, joined for the purpose of reducing competition and controlling prices.

U

Underground Railroad: A network of people in the mid-1800s secretly helping slaves to escape to the northern United States or Canada and assisting them in establishing new lives there.

union: An organization of workers designed to negotiate with employers for workers' rights and to secure improvements in such areas as wages, working hours, benefits, and workplace safety.

W

Wall Street: Financial district and home of the nation's major stock exchanges in New York City.

War on Poverty: The central program of President Lyndon B. Johnson's "Great Society." This effort tried to end poverty by providing poor Americans with education, job training, food, housing, and money.

welfare: Government-funded help for the needy, in the form of money, supplies, and services.

work release: A program allowing certain convicts the option of working outside the prison during the day and returning to their cells at night.

workhouse: A facility, often run by a church, designed to provide jobs for the poor and unemployed; term also describes a prison housing minor criminals.

Research and Activity Ideas

The following research and activity ideas are intended to offer suggestions for complementing social studies and history curricula; to trigger additional ideas for enhancing learning; and to provide cross-disciplinary projects for library and classroom use.

The Antiglobalization Movement: Antiglobalization activists contend that they do not oppose the idea of globalization; they simply object to the current methods and practices associated with global trade. Pretend that you have traveled one hundred years into the future and write a description of the impact of globalization on the world in the twenty-second century. Assess the status of the antiglobalization movement's primary concerns, including poverty in developing nations, workers' rights, environmental issues, and intellectual property rights.

The Antiwar Movement: In the United States, every military conflict has had its detractors, people opposed to war in general or to a specific war for specific reasons. Assume the role of a conscientious objector, someone who refuses military participation, regarding two of the following conflicts: World War I, World War II, the Vietnam War, and the war in Iraq. In reference to each of the two wars you choose, write a short paragraph explaining why you refused to serve and a short paragraph outlining the consequences of your decision: Did you go to jail? How did your friends and family react?

The Civil Rights Movement: The 1954 Supreme Court case *Brown v. Board of Education of Topeka, Kansas* was a landmark decision that outlawed segregation in public schools. Pretend that you are a lawyer arguing on behalf of African American students and write an essay describing the unfairness of the "separate but equal" doctrine and the importance of integration.

Education Reform: The Progressive Era, covering the first three decades of the 1900s, marked a period of substantial educational reform. Pretend you are implementing a new, progressive school program in the early 1900s, a program along the lines of those advocated by John Dewey and Francis W. Parker. Create a poster advertising your program, using text and pictures to demonstrate what your school will be like and what you hope to accomplish. Bear in mind that most classrooms at that time were run by strict, authoritarian teachers who emphasized memorization and discipline over creativity and self-expression. Make it clear in your poster that your program is a radical departure from that method.

The Environmental Movement: Create a brochure for people in your community outlining ten steps citizens can take to "save the Earth": reducing waste or pollution, protecting wildlife and habitats, conserving energy, recycling, and the like. Use illustrations to enhance the text.

The Gay Rights Movement: Assume the role of a journalist who witnessed the riots at the Stonewall Inn in New York City during the summer of 1969. Write an article about the event from the perspective of one year later. Capture the sense of chaos and fear during the riots but also the joy the protesters felt over their strength in numbers. Assess the impact of Stonewall in the months following, describing the development of the gay rights movement that came in the wake of that incident.

The Labor Movement: The labor movement has a long, conflict-ridden, and sometimes bloody history, including such major clashes between labor and management as the incident at Haymarket Square (1886), the Homestead strike (1892), the Pullman strike (1894), the Ludlow massacre (1914), and the General Motors strike (1936–37). Choose one of these events and write an eyewitness report for a newspaper. Include background information, the reasons for the strike, the actions of the workers (and their families if they became involved), and the response of management.

Poverty Reform: Imagine that you are the president of the United States, and the nation has fallen into an economic depression. Examine the programs begun by President Franklin D. Roosevelt during the Great Depression of the 1930s as well as the "war on poverty," President Lyndon B. Johnson's effort during the 1960s. What programs would you implement to reduce unemployment, provide relief for the poor, and get the nation's economy back on track? Write a brief description of your ideas.

Prison Reform: One of the central issues throughout the history of prison reform has centered on the severity of punishment for those convicted of crimes. Some reformers have advocated a progressive approach to imprisonment, advocating shorter sentences and improved educational and job-training opportunities for inmates. Others have taken a more conservative approach, claiming that prison should be a miserable experience both to punish convicted criminals and to deter others from committing crimes. Conduct a debate among classmates, with one group arguing for prison as an institution of reform and the other promoting prison as an instrument for punishment and retribution.

Slavery and Abolition: Write a short story about a family that decides to become part of the Underground Railroad, a network of people who secretly helped slaves escape from the slave-owning southern states to the northern United States and to Canada. Explore the reasons behind the family's decision and the risks they take to help escaping slaves. Also address the courage and determination displayed by the fleeing slaves.

The Temperance Movement and Prohibition: With classmates, stage a town meeting, circa 1918, and conduct a debate between the two sides of the temperance movement: the "drys," who support abstinence from and a complete ban on alcoholic beverages; and the "wets," who believe it should be legal to produce and sell alcohol.

The Women's Rights Movement: With a group of classmates, create an early-1970s-era magazine demonstrating the beliefs and opinions of the women's movement. Write articles, poetry, and short stories, and use photographs and illustrations to complement the text.

The Women's Suffrage Movement: Research the differing approaches of two important leaders in the women's suffrage movement: Carrie Chapman Catt and Alice Paul. Catt's Winning Plan involved a state-by-state campaign of lobbying lawmakers to give women the right to vote. Paul's more confrontational approach involved the staging of demonstrations and protests to bring about the passage of a federal amendment guaranteeing women's voting rights. Explain which method you believe was most effective and why. Also, consider the possibility that both approaches were necessary to achieve change.

The Antiglobalization Movement

Globalization is a phenomenon that rose to the top of the world agenda in the late twentieth century. It involves the abundant exchange of goods and services, information and ideas, and technology and culture across international borders. Although globalization has significant social, political, and cultural aspects, it is driven primarily by commerce. Nations buy and sell products and services around the world more freely than ever before. A country's economy no longer depends on the goods bought and sold within its own borders. The economies of many nations are intertwined with other nations, dependent in large measure on imports, which are products brought in from other countries, and exports, which are products sold to other nations. In addition to interlinked economies, globalization has led to a greater sense of connectedness among individuals, making the cultures of the world more accessible and familiar.

Many economists have long argued that a global economic system is a key to worldwide prosperity and peace among nations. When nations freely trade with one another, these economists believe, the wealth of prosperous nations can help lift developing nations out of poverty. In addition, the increased understanding that can result from economic partnerships could minimize conflict and reduce the likelihood of war. However, some economists are critical of globalization, especially the practices that began in the late 1990s. During that time, a social reform movement often known as the antiglobalization movement began to take shape.

Although the term "antiglobalization" is the one most often used to describe this movement, many have pointed out the inaccuracy of this name. The antiglobalization movement does not object to the idea of globalization, but rather to the way it has developed. Antiglobalization activists note that contemporary globalization practices have resulted in unfair and devastating conditions in many nations. They contend that

WORDS TO KNOW

antiglobalization: Opposition to the methods and practices of globalization, particularly the perceived emphasis on corporate profits rather than human benefits.

capital: Assets, including money or property, used to create further wealth through investment or the production of goods and services.

currency: Any form of money, generally either coins or paper bills, issued by a government or a bank and used in legal exchanges.

domestic: Within the borders of one's own country, as opposed to "foreign."

export: Goods or services sent out of one country for trade or sale in another country.

foreign: Relating to another country, as opposed to "domestic."

free-market economy: An economic system in which goods and services are privately owned and sold to anyone wishing to buy them at whatever price can be obtained. Prices are set by the principle of supply and demand and are affected by competition.

free trade: The exchange of goods and services without any barriers, such as tariffs or trade quotas.

globalization: The exchange of goods, services, and capital across national borders.

import: Goods or services brought from one country into another for sale.

privatize: To take something that was once public and make it private; to take a public land and sell it or give control of it to a private entity.

protectionism: Policies designed to erect trade barriers, such as tariffs, to protect domestic companies from foreign competition.

quota: A limit placed on the quantity of certain goods to be imported from a particular country.

tariff: A tax placed on goods imported from another country; tariffs raise the prices of imported goods, making it more difficult for such items to compete with goods produced domestically.

trade agreement: An agreement among two or more nations that establishes terms for exchanging goods and services in a manner beneficial to all parties.

multinational corporations have grown in strength, power, and wealth, while developing nations continue to struggle with dire poverty. They point out that globalization has led many corporations to hire low-wage workers in developing nations, taking jobs away from people in industrialized countries. Environmental protection has also been sacrificed in the name of globalization, according to opponents. Large corporations have avoided the stricter environmental regulations in industrialized nations by relocating factories in less-regulated countries. Some critics also argue that, in addition to exporting goods to other countries, powerful Western nations have exported their cultures as well, imposing their ways on distant lands and eroding native cultures, languages, and practices.

Historical international trade

The term "globalization" came into widespread use in the 1980s. However, the practices associated with it, including financial and cultural exchanges across borders, have existed throughout human history. Wealthy and powerful nations have always traded with one another. Such nations have also established empires by seizing control of other lands to make use of natural resources and inexpensive labor forces.

During the 1400s, an age of exploration began in Europe that lasted several centuries, with nations such as Spain, Portugal, and Great Britain creating vast empires to aid trade and increase prosperity. Just as modern-day globalization has done, the colonization of distant lands gave Europeans a new knowledge of foreign cultures, including foods, religions, and farming techniques. At the same time, colonization tended to overwhelm native cultures because they were pressed to adopt the ways of their colonizers.

The Industrial Revolution brought an era of global trade that had been previously unimaginable. It began in Great Britain in the mid-1700s and spread to the United States during the late 1700s. The era saw numerous inventions and innovations that transformed American society. Previously, the nation consisted of a loosely connected group of farming states. During the Industrial Revolution, it grew into a powerful manufacturing nation.

Advances in transportation and in manufacturing technology made possible a new level of international trade. Throughout the 1800s, the United States and several European countries laid thousands of miles of railroad tracks, making it possible to send goods cross-country and across international borders. Innovations in shipping technology allowed products and people to travel more easily across oceans. Governments passed laws making it easier to buy from and sell to other nations, and many countries formed trade agreements with each other. In North America, Europe, and throughout Asia, imports and exports became a significant part of national economies. Many historians refer to this period as the first era of globalization.

By the end of the 1800s, however, support for international free trade had shifted to an emphasis on building strong national governments. Powerful central governments, which sought extensive control over their nation's industries and economies, were not compatible with the practice of freely trading across borders. At that time, a policy known as protectionism resurfaced. Under protectionist policies, many nations created barriers to free trade. These included high tariffs, which are taxes placed on imported goods, or trade quotas, which are limits set on the number of certain goods that can be imported. Rather than promoting economic interdependence among nations, many governments emphasized self-sufficiency and domestic power. The final blows to the first era of globalization came during the twentieth century, with the destruction wrought by World War I (1914–18), the Great Depression (1929–41), and World War II (1939–45).

Postwar economic development

Even before World War II ended, the United States and its allies began to plan for postwar economic recovery. The war had destroyed the landscape as well as the economies of several European nations. A number of organizations formed during the final months of the war and soon afterward in an attempt to stabilize world markets and facilitate international trade. The push for worldwide economic stability was motivated in large part by a fear of communism, a political and economic system that had taken hold in the Soviet Union and other nations. Soviet communism was a political system in which the authoritarian government controlled the economy with the intention of eliminating class distinctions and private property.

The leaders of the United States, Great Britain, and several other nations believed that a poor and unstable nation would be more likely to turn to communism than one with a healthy economy. These leaders understood that postwar reconstruction depended on financial cooperation among nations, which would be made possible by new multinational organizations, programs, and agreements. Among the most prominent of these are the World Bank, the Organization for Economic Cooperation and Development (OECD), the International Monetary Fund (IMF), and the General Agreement on Tariffs and Trade (GATT), which produced the World Trade Organization (WTO).

The World Bank includes several related institutions, primarily the International Bank for Reconstruction and Development (IBRD) and the International Development Association (IDA). The IBRD was established during the summer of 1944 at a United Nations meeting in New Hampshire known as the Bretton Woods Conference. Its initial purpose was to aid in postwar reconstruction by providing loans to member nations. To that end, the IBRD loaned nearly $500 million to European countries in the years following World War II. According to

U.S. Secretary of the Treasury Henry Morgenthau Jr. addresses attendees at the United Nations' Bretton Woods Conference in New Hampshire in 1944. The International Bank for Reconstruction and Development (IBRD) was established at the conference.
© BETTMANN/CORBIS.

the World Bank, its focus later shifted from reconstruction to economic development, with an emphasis on investments that spark growth in poor countries. World Bank loans are also intended to help the citizens of poor nations obtain social services such as education and health care. The IDA was formed in 1960 to provide interest-free, long-term loans to the poorest countries, those that could not afford to pay the interest on ordinary bank loans or those from the IBRD.

Another postwar group designed to aid in the reconstruction of Europe, the Organization for European Economic Cooperation, later evolved into a collection of industrialized nations with free-market economies. The group, renamed the Organization for Economic Cooperation and Development (OECD), expanded to include non-European nations and shifted its focus to international trade and economic growth.

The International Monetary Fund, formed around the same time as the World Bank (1944), set out to stabilize currency values of member nations and to encourage international trade. Associated with the United Nations, the IMF established a fixed value for each nation's currency in an attempt to make it easier to exchange money or to buy and sell goods from one nation to another. In 1971 the practice of fixing each currency's value was discontinued. Instead, the IMF attempted to prevent massive fluctuations in exchange rates by monitoring each member nation's economic policies. During the following decades, the IMF also began lending money to developing nations to spur economic growth. In many cases such loans came with conditions: the developing nation could borrow the money, but the IMF had a say in how the borrowed money was spent.

One of the primary goals for those interested in increasing trade among nations is reducing or eliminating tariffs. In 1947 twenty-three nations met in Geneva, Switzerland, to sign the General Agreement on Tariffs and Trade (GATT). This document refers both to the agreement and to the agency (which is part of the United Nations) that oversees the agreement. The purpose of the GATT was to loosen trade regulations by minimizing tariffs and quotas, paving the way for free global trade. Each nation signing the treaty agreed to limit trade barriers according to a schedule. The details of the GATT were ironed out through a series of eight rounds of negotiations over several decades. The first five rounds took place between 1947 and 1962. The sixth round, known as the Kennedy Round, began in 1962 and ended in 1967. The Kennedy Round created significant tariff reductions, as did the Tokyo Round, which lasted from 1973 to 1979.

The eighth GATT round was launched in 1986 in Uruguay, and thus became known as the Uruguay Round. Concluding in 1994, the Uruguay Round created twenty different trade agreements among 124 member nations. One of the notable developments of the Uruguay Round was replacing GATT with the World Trade Organization (WTO). Unlike the GATT, the WTO was granted the authority to resolve international trade disputes. At the Uruguay Round, tariffs were reduced further and protection was granted to intellectual property, which includes patents, trademarks, and copyrights. This change meant that books, films, music, computer software, medicines, and other types of intellectual property could not be copied legally when exported across borders.

The "Other" Antiglobalization Movement

Generally, discussions of the antiglobalization movement refer to the loose network of social reformers or progressives who oppose the practices of globalization that they believe benefit corporations and industrial nations while doing little to help the poorest people on the planet. This network includes labor activists, who campaign on behalf of workers and unions; environmentalists, who fear the negative impact of globalization on natural resources; human rights supporters, who give voice to the poor and powerless; civil liberties champions, who seek to protect the rights of individuals from being infringed upon by governments and corporations; and many others. For the most part, this movement is characterized by a liberal, or left-wing, political stance. These antiglobalization activists seek to change society's institutions, to banish inequality, and to provide a safety net for the most vulnerable citizens.

At the other end of the political spectrum are antiglobalization activists with different goals and objections. These critics of globalization represent a conservative, or right-wing viewpoint. They believe that globalization undermines the strength of individual nations in the global political arena. Their opposition stems from strong nationalism, an intense loyalty to one's own country and a belief in that country's superiority to all others. They object to such international institutions as the WTO and the IMF not because they are seen to ignore the needs of developing countries but because they trespass on their nation's ability to be sovereign, or independent.

Called nationalists, these critics of globalization promote protectionist economic regulations, creating barriers to foreign competition rather than removing them. Trade barriers like high tariffs and quotas benefit domestic industries while making it difficult for foreign corporations to compete. Protecting American industry, nationalists suggest, is the only way to ensure independence, prosperity, and even national security. These activists also support strict immigration policies and, in some cases, a complete ban on all immigration. According to some critics, antiglobalization nationalists use language that often reflects attitudes that are racist and xenophobic, or hostile toward foreigners. Many nationalists contend that this criticism is untrue, that they are protecting their country's interests.

Among the leading right-wing opponents of global trade in the United States is Pat Buchanan (1938–), a conservative commentator and former presidential candidate. Buchanan suggests that the United States should not focus on global trading but on protecting its status as a superpower. He believes that this can be achieved by shoring up national security and the nation's industries.

While both the right-wing and left-wing opponents of globalization criticize current practices, their reasons for doing so are very different. Tensions between the two groups run high, and confrontations are often hostile. While some right-wing antiglobalization activists have on occasion suggested the two factions band together, many left-wing activists seek to avoid any association with nationalist groups.

Developments of the late twentieth century

During the 1970s, the world's leading industrialized nations formed an organization known as the Group of Six (G6). The G6 included the United States, France, West Germany (which later became the unified Germany), Italy, Japan, and the United Kingdom. The members agreed to meet annually to discuss issues of global concern, including trade, development, terrorism, energy, and public health. The group was expanded to include Canada, becoming the Group of Seven. During the 1990s, Russia was invited to attend certain G7 sessions, depending on its financial stability. At that time, the group became known as the Group of Eight (G8).

In addition to forming such groups as the World Bank, the IMF, the WTO, and the G8, many other trade agreements were signed at the end of the twentieth century. Numerous agreements were made by smaller groups of countries wishing to ease trade restrictions with each other. For example, the Maastricht Treaty, formally known as the Treaty on European Union, was signed in 1992 by nations that were part of the European Community. The Maastricht Treaty created the European Union (EU) and established a common currency, known as the Euro, to be used in most member nations. The treaty set up a means for member nations to cooperate in matters such as law enforcement, criminal and civil justice, and immigration. In addition, the treaty created a powerful economic union that would enable the EU nations to compete with trading superpowers such as the United States, China, and Japan.

In 1994 a trade agreement between the United States, Canada, and Mexico, known as the North American Free Trade Agreement (NAFTA), went into effect. Canada and the United States had signed a free trade agreement in 1989, and NAFTA expanded the agreement's provisions to include Mexico. The agreement reduced or eliminated tariffs on imported goods and scheduled the removal of all restrictions on investment. Supplemental agreements offered some protection for workers and for the environment. Numerous similar agreements, including the Asia-Pacific Economic Cooperation and the Middle East Free Trade Area Initiative, have been forged throughout the world.

Various political and diplomatic developments during the final decades of the twentieth century helped pave the way for globalization. A civil war in China, the world's most populated nation, ended in 1949, with the Communist Party seizing power in China. For nearly three decades, China's economy remained closed to trade with other nations.

Trucks line up at a border crossing between the United States and Mexico. Due to the North American Free Trade Agreement (NAFTA), trade between the two nations has increased. AP IMAGES.

During the late 1970s, however, the Chinese government began a series of economic reforms hoping to generate enough extra income to modernize the vast nation. In the early 2000s, the Chinese government retains complete control over many aspects of society, including the media, religion, cultural institutions, and politics. However, the government no longer controls the economy, which has gradually become market-driven. In some ways, it is similar to the economies of Western nations. Beginning with the late-1970s reforms, China allowed foreign companies to sell goods in China or invest money in Chinese businesses. China also began investing capital and selling goods in other countries.

Another communist power, the Soviet Union, began making economic reforms in the late 1980s. It created a restructuring policy known as Perestroika. Under Perestroika, businesses could be privately owned, rather than state-owned, and survive not because of government bailouts but because they made sufficient profits. The Soviet Union also began easing restrictions on foreign investment. By 1991, in part because of the change in economic policies, the Soviet Union had collapsed. The former

Soviet nations were claiming their independence. While the economies of the former Soviet republics, including Russia, remained unstable for the next several years, many of the barriers to trade with other nations had been significantly reduced.

The substantial changes brought by multinational financial organizations, free trade agreements, and significant political developments set the stage for a new global economy. Other critical aspects of late-twentieth-century globalization relied on dramatic technological advances in transportation and communication. Improvements in air travel allowed for people and cargo to travel halfway around the world in a matter of hours. Developments such as fax machines, wireless phones, and the Internet significantly changed many industries, including banking. Such advances greatly improved worldwide communications. Currencies could be exchanged electronically, for example, in a matter of seconds, without any paper money ever changing hands. These technologies both fueled and were fueled by globalization. They made international commerce easier. An unprecedented exchange of information among nations allowed for further advancements and innovations.

Pressing issues of globalization

Many observers strongly opposed the vast changes brought on by globalization. Critics of globalization include labor unions, environmental groups, human rights organizations, and numerous other citizen associations. They formed a loosely connected movement to protest not global trade but the manner in which it is being conducted. The movement points out that many of the stated goals for globalization have not come to pass. These include the economic development of poor nations and business partnerships as a route to world peace. The major world organizations designed to spur global economic development—namely, the IMF, World Bank, and WTO—have been the focus of much of the criticism. Antiglobalization activists assert that these agencies wield tremendous power but are not accountable for their decisions. The leaders of these groups are not elected officials and, critics claim, do not represent the needs of ordinary citizens. Rather, they represent the needs of multinational corporations and wealthy industrialized nations. And in most cases, according to antiglobalization activists, serving the needs of these powerful entities conflicts with serving the needs of poor people and developing nations.

Third world debt The IMF and the World Bank in particular state that reducing poverty is among their primary goals. However, opponents suggest that their policies have failed to improve the economies of the world's poorest nations while at the same time enriching and empowering multinational corporations. In a 2002 essay in the *New York Review of Books,* Benjamin M. Friedman wrote: "The most pressing economic problem of our time is that so many of what we usually call 'developing economies' are, in fact, not developing." Particularly in Africa, but also in some parts of Asia, South America, and Central America, millions of people continue to live in dire poverty. They suffer from a lack of decent health care, leading to shorter life expectancies and high rates of infant mortality. Many people die of malnutrition and preventable diseases. Education is a luxury few can afford in developing nations, and millions never learn to read and write.

The reasons the economies in poor nations continue to falter are numerous and complex. Yet, many critics of globalization, including a number of respected economists, point out that the policies of organizations like the IMF and the World Bank are partly responsible. Since their inception, these institutions have loaned billions of dollars to poor nations in an effort to develop their economies. In many cases, these loans come with conditions. In order to be eligible for the loans, recipients must make recommended changes to their national economic policies. Opponents of globalization contend that the conditions attached to loans for so-called third world countries are tailored for wealthy, industrial economies and are unsuccessful in less-developed nations. Developing nations, faced with new economic policies that have failed, still have to repay their loans from the IMF or similar institution.

Often, the cost of paying interest on these loans is too burdensome. Poor nations have to borrow more money simply to continue making payments on the original loans. This cycle of ever-increasing debt makes it difficult for these countries to devote funds to basic social services, like health care, education, and poverty relief. It also makes it difficult for such nations to improve roads, increase access to technology, and make other improvements that could lead to economic prosperity. One of the primary goals of antiglobalization activists is to pressure the IMF, World Bank, and other such lenders to cancel third world debt. Activists believe that wiping out these debts is a crucial step in helping developing nations experience economic growth and stability.

U2 singer Bono (left) and Columbia University professor Jeffrey Sachs are among the well-known people who have campaigned to reduce, if not cancel, third world debt.
© WYMAN IRA/CORBIS SYGMA.

Opponents of globalization contend that the conditions attached to loans for poor nations are harmful in part because they do not take into account the unique needs of the borrowers. These conditions also present problems because they erode a borrowing nation's sovereignty, its ability to be an independent nation, free of outside control. By accepting a loan and its conditions to reshape economic policy, the government of a developing nation may be forced to implement changes that hurt rather than help its citizens. Critics of the IMF and similar institutions suggest that these lenders are guided by the needs of the wealthy industrialized

Members of the United Auto Workers (UAW) union picket in front of Ford Motor World Headquarters in Dearborn, Michigan, in 2005. The protest is in response to Ford's plans to build more cars in Mexico rather than in the United States. © REBECCA COOK/ REUTERS/CORBIS.

nations that provide the bulk of their funding rather than by the needs of the poorest countries. In the *New York Review of Books,* Friedman wrote: "There is no reason to assume that institutions that are controlled by a small group of people from one or a handful of high-income countries would adequately represent the interests of the world's poor and working people."

Workers' rights Many critics of globalization express concern that relaxing trade regulations has harmed the average worker. Free trade agreements and other means of reducing barriers to international trade have made it easier for corporations in industrialized nations to manufacture their goods and services in other countries. For example, many U.S.-based corporations have concluded that they can produce goods more cheaply in Korea or Mexico than in the United States. This occurs because the workers in those countries typically earn far less than

American employees. Many Americans have lost their jobs in this manner. Although many U.S. laborers find new jobs, they often have to settle for lower wages.

In addition, opponents of globalization fear that the practice of relocating manufacturing to another country has undermined the labor movement. In the United States and other Western nations, workers' rights in some industries are protected by labor unions. Such unions negotiate with employers to guarantee fair wages, safe working conditions, and benefits like health insurance and paid vacations. Corporations can save money by operating out of countries where workers are not unionized—where the wages, working conditions, and benefits are far less. For example, a worker in a developing nation might make $4 to $7 per day creating a product, whereas the same worker in the United States would make $50 to $70 or more. Also, laws in the United States restrict child labor. The same is not true in some other countries.

Globalization means that labor unions have less bargaining power. If they ask for too many safeguards for their workers, the company may simply choose to relocate its factory to another country. Critics point out that not only does this practice weaken unions in the United States and elsewhere, it also means that workers in developing nations are being exploited, or used to the employer's advantage.

Environmental issues One of the most pressing concerns of opponents of globalization is the threat to the environment posed by global trade practices. A number of global trade institutions, like the WTO, and free trade agreements, like NAFTA, allow corporations or countries to sue another country if their laws are seen as a threat to corporate profits. For example, if a nation's strict environmental regulations will act as a barrier to a corporation's success, that business can sue the government in question for a loss of profits. Under the provisions of NAFTA, the U.S.-based Ethyl Corporation sued the government of Canada for banning MMT. An additive to gasoline, MMT poses health risks to infants and the elderly when inhaled. Canada settled out of court, agreeing to lift the ban. The country paid millions of dollars to Ethyl Corporation for lost profits.

In addition, free trade agreements enable corporations to locate manufacturing plants in the nations with the fewest environmental regulations. In turn, other nations that want to compete and attract corporate investments sometimes decide to lower their environmental

Members of the environmental group Greenpeace are handcuffed together as they sit on drums, like those used to store hazardous waste. They are protesting a U.S. company's waste disposal facility that was set up in Mexico, a country with fewer environmental regulations. AP IMAGES.

standards. Jerry Mander, in an essay in *Globalization: Opposing Viewpoints,* described the outcome of these practices: "The result is that all laws and standards race downward to a low common denominator."

Critics of globalization also point out the heavy toll on the environment from the massive increase in international transportation that has occurred as a result. In industrial and developing nations, new highways, airports, and railroad lines have been built to accommodate increased global trade. In many cases, the construction has occurred in forests, wetlands, and other wilderness areas. As a result, the habitats of numerous species have been destroyed. And the destruction will likely continue as more transportation routes are being constructed and/or considered.

In addition, the fuel used to power ships, airplanes, trucks, and other vehicles transporting people and cargo produces substantial pollution. In *Globalization,* Mander pointed out that "a two-minute takeoff of a

747 is equal to 2.4 million lawn mowers running for twenty minutes." Plus, as globalization improves the economies of nations such as India and China, more people in these countries are buying cars and needing fuel. As reported by Michael Casey in the *Detroit News* in 2006, "the skyrocketing number of new vehicles means more air pollution, traffic jams and a big spike in oil consumption." While the emissions from the additional cars cause damage to the environment, the increased need for oil drives up gas prices worldwide.

One business that has been targeted by opponents of globalization in particular is industrial agriculture. In many areas, large, multinational farming corporations have edged out local farmers. Called agribusinesses, they rely heavily on chemical pesticides. They also reduce the diversity of crops by planting far fewer varieties than regional farmers do. Many agricultural corporations also modify crops genetically. They alter the plants' natural properties in an effort to make them more productive, more resistant to disease, or generally more profitable. Critics of genetically modified foods express concern because the long-term effects of such products on human health are unknown. Agricultural corporations are also criticized for the massive amounts of fresh water they use, at a time when one billion people on Earth cannot obtain clean drinking water. In various nations, corporations and sometimes governments have proposed privatizing the water supply. This means that businesses could own or control lakes and streams, and profit by selling access to clean water.

Intellectual property rights Many free trade agreements, as well as organizations like the WTO, offer intellectual property protection to corporations. This allows them to patent, trademark, or copyright their products internationally. In other words, a product patented by a U.S.-based corporation allows that company to have a global monopoly on production of that item. A monopoly means that no other business can legally produce that item unless the company holding the patent, trademark, or copyright will allow it.

Numerous citizens' groups have protested that these intellectual property protections can have a devastating impact on developing nations. For example, agricultural corporations have placed patents on certain seeds. Such patents force farmers to buy the seeds at far higher prices than if the seeds were not patented. Furthermore, agribusinesses have altered some seeds to prevent them from reproducing, ensuring that farmers will have to buy new seeds year after year.

Another type of intellectual property that has received tremendous criticism is pharmaceuticals. Many people are concerned about the patents that drug companies have obtained for medicines. Patented, or brand-name, drugs often come with a high price tag. Once a drug's patent expires, however, generic drugs can then be made legally, which drives the price down. But U.S. patents generally last for twenty years, according to the U.S. Food and Drug Administration (FDA). "The patent protects the investment—including research, development, marketing, and promotion—by giving the company the sole right to sell the drug while it is in effect," explains the FDA. "Because [makers of generic drugs] don't have the same development costs, they can sell their product at substantial discounts."

The high cost of patented drugs is too steep for many people who suffer from life-threatening illnesses worldwide, especially those who are unable to work and earn money. Plus, many people do not have health insurance to help cover the costs. In some cases, the citizens of developing nations, many of whom suffer crushing poverty, cannot even afford basic medicines. Many of the poor are unable to pay the high prices that pharmaceutical corporations charge.

A 1998 case sparked outrage among citizens' groups worldwide when thirty-nine pharmaceutical companies tried to sue the government of South Africa. They wanted to prevent the government from obtaining less expensive, and unpatented, medications for its citizens suffering from human immunodeficiency virus (HIV)/acquired immunodeficiency syndrome (AIDS). Although HIV/AIDS is incurable and ultimately fatal as of 2006, the development of a class of drugs known as antiretrovirals has greatly extended the lives of many patients. In Africa, as many as 20 percent of adults suffered from HIV/AIDS by the end of the twentieth century. However, few could afford to spend thousands of dollars per year on antiretroviral drugs.

When the South African government passed a law enabling it to import cheaper antiretrovirals, dozens of pharmaceutical companies tried to reverse this law. Activists from around the world protested that the drug companies were willing to sacrifice human lives to protect profits. By 2001 the pharmaceutical companies had dropped the lawsuit. At that time, the citizens' groups in developing nations began pressuring the WTO and other organizations to give a higher priority to issues of public health.

Protesters stage a rally in 2001 against pharmaceutical companies who manufacture AIDS drugs, claiming that millions of people worldwide cannot afford the expensive medications and will die earlier as a result. © RHODES MARTIN/CORBIS SYGMA.

Protest actions

Antiglobalization activists blame organizations like the WTO, the World Bank, and the IMF for many of the most harmful aspects of globalization. Because of this, many of the movement's activities have focused on meetings held by these financial organizations. Protesters have gathered by the tens of thousands at these meetings in the hope of disrupting or preventing the proceedings. These activists hail from a variety of backgrounds and represent numerous causes.

Activists also take advantage of the major press coverage at such events to publicize their grievances. One of the earliest such demonstrations took place on June 18, 1999, when antiglobalization activists in more than one hundred cities held simultaneous protests of the G8 meeting in Cologne, Germany. This event was not the first protest of globalization. Various social reform groups have spoken out against aspects of globalization for decades. But it is considered significant for its international scope. Antiglobalization groups are said to have united as a movement a few months later to protest a WTO meeting in Seattle, Washington.

The Battle in Seattle In the days leading up to the Seattle WTO conference, thousands of activists attended meetings and lectures in Seattle. They discussed the issues of globalization and planned their protest strategies. The major demonstrations began on the same day as the start of the conference, November 30, 1999. The protests were conducted by a coalition of tens of thousands of social reformers, including labor unionists, environmentalists, students, members of religious organizations, and others. Activists marched through the streets of Seattle, converging on the intersections surrounding the location of the meeting, the Washington State Convention and Trade Center. Their goal was to use nonviolent direct action to block the WTO participants from gaining access to the meeting.

The police response was swift and aggressive. Attempting to disperse protesters from intersections, the Seattle police fired tear gas canisters and shot rubber bullets into the crowds. Hundreds were arrested. Most protesters remained nonviolent, although a small faction attracted considerable media attention by breaking store windows and painting graffiti on walls and signs. The protesters were unable to prevent the meeting from taking place, but they did delay its start and bring about its early conclusion.

The "Battle in Seattle" marked the beginning of a series of substantial protests at gatherings of global trade organizations. Activists protested throughout the United States and in cities all over the world, demonstrating at meetings of the IMF, the World Bank, the WTO, the G8, and other global trade institutions.

Antiglobalization protesters clashed with Seattle police, dressed in riot gear, during demonstrations aimed to stop the World Trade Organization (WTO) meetings in late 1999. Activists from all over the globe attended the protest. KIM STALLKNECHT/AFP/GETTY IMAGES.

Genoa Protest One of the more notable demonstrations took place in Genoa, Italy, in July 2001. The protests, which coincided with a summit of the G8, included a massive crowd of activists who had traveled to Genoa for the event. By some estimates there were several hundred thousand protesters. The demonstration is not remembered particularly for the accomplishments of the activists, but for the response of the police.

Italian police raided buildings, including schools, believed to be housing activists. Hundreds of protesters were arrested, with many of them later claiming to have been treated brutally by the police. Dozens of protesters were hospitalized and one, a young man named Carlo Giuliani, was fatally shot by police. Public outcry about the police violence was strong. As a result, dozens of officers faced criminal charges for brutality. Evidence showed that some officers had planted Molotov cocktails (a type of homemade explosive) at one of the schools housing activists to justify the police raid on the facility.

Movement Strengthens

At the beginning of the twenty-first century, the antiglobalization movement was in its early stages. The movement had achieved some victories. For example, international lending institutions like the IMF and the World Bank responded to worldwide pressure and began the process of canceling some third world debt. In addition, citizens' groups in Bolivia successfully prevented corporate and government attempts to privatize the water supply. In many instances, however, the forces driving globalization (powerful industrial nations and multinational corporations) have proven to be mighty foes.

Under the umbrella of the antiglobalization movement, organizations with widely different purposes and goals have found common ground in the quest for a more humane approach to globalization. Antiglobalization activists seek to replace or reform the existing global trade agencies so that their leaders answer to citizens rather than corporations. Activists urge leaders to protect humankind and the environment rather than profits.

For More Information

BOOKS

Gerdes, Louise I., ed. *Globalization: Opposing Viewpoints*. Detroit: Greenhaven Press, 2006.

"The World Bank and the IMF in Developing Countries: Globalization and the Crisis of Legitimacy." *History Behind the Headlines: The Origins of Conflicts Worldwide, Volume 6.* Gale Group, 2003.

"The World Bank Group." *Worldmark Encyclopedia of the Nations, Vol. 1: United Nations.* 11th ed. Thomson Gale, 2004.

WEB SITES

Casey, Michael. "Boom in Auto Sales Drives Demand for Fuel in China, India: Even Middle and Lower Middle-Class Families Are Buying Cars" (May 1, 2006). *Detroit News.* http://www.detnews.com/apps/pbcs.dll/article?AID=/20060501/AUTO01/605010329/1148 (accessed on May 9, 2006).

Friedman, Benjamin M. "Globalization: Stiglitz's Case." *New York Review of Books* (August 15, 2002). http://www.nybooks.com/articles/15630 (accessed on May 7, 2006).

"Generic Drugs: Questions and Answers." *Center for Drug Evaluation and Research, U.S. Food and Drug Administration.* http://www.fda.gov/cder/consumerinfo/generics_q&a.htm#cost (accessed on May 9, 2006).

"Stop Corporate Globalization: Another World Is Possible!" *Our World Is Not for Sale.* http://www.ourworldisnotforsale.org/about.asp?about=signon=english (accessed on May 7, 2006).

"Teaching Guide for 'Globalization' Essays." *Social Science Research Council.* http://www.ssrc.org/sept11/essays/teaching_resource/tr_globalization.htm (accessed on May 7, 2006).

Weisbrot, Mark. "Globalization: A Primer." *Center for Economic and Policy Research.* http://www.cepr.net/publications/global_primer.htm (accessed on May 7, 2006).

"What Is the WTO?" *World Trade Organization.* http://www.wto.org/english/thewto_e/whatis_e/whatis_e.htm (accessed on May 9, 2006).

OTHER SOURCES

The Corporation (film). Big Picture Media Corporation, 2003.

The Antiwar Movement

For as long as nations have engaged in war, there have been those who opposed it, seeking peaceful resolutions to conflicts and an end to violence. Some antiwar activists have protested a specific war as unjust, illegal, or too costly in terms of both economics and the loss of life. Others are dedicated to pacifism in all circumstances, believing that war is always immoral because it requires people to commit violent acts against others. Pacifism often has its basis in religious belief, though many seek peace not because of biblical demands but because they believe the stakes of war are too high and the damage done to humanity too great.

Nearly every war in modern American history has been accompanied by an antiwar movement. Such movements have varied in size and effectiveness, but the goals are the same: to prevent or end a war. Wars generally arouse emotional responses on either side of the issue and usually result in deep divisions between those opposed to and those in favor of the conflict. The issue of free speech is central to any debate over a war. Antiwar activists firmly believe in their right to express their views, while many citizens and government officials contend that the expression of such ideas during wartime is harmful and unpatriotic.

Historians have debated the effectiveness of antiwar movements. Some have suggested that the regular occurrence of wars demonstrates that such movements have little impact on the decisions of governments. Wars continue to arise, and the prospect of eliminating war altogether seems unlikely. Others argue that antiwar movements have had considerable influence, shortening wars or preventing them altogether. Regardless of the prospects for success, antiwar activists have repeatedly sought an end to war and will continue to do so in the hopes of establishing a lasting global peace.

The roots of peace activism

The peace movements that arose early in U.S. history based their philosophies primarily on religious teachings. For the Quakers, a Protestant

WORDS TO KNOW

antiwar: Opposition to a specific war, to one side of a war, or to all war.

armistice: A temporary agreement among warring nations to stop fighting and draft a formal peace agreement.

civil disobedience: The peaceful violation of a law considered unjust.

conscientious objector: A person who refuses to serve in the military because it violates his or her moral standards. The term is often used to describe those whose religious beliefs prevent any support of war.

imperialism: The practice of one nation taking control of another's government or economy through invasion or other means.

isolationism: Concerned only with the defense of one's own borders and avoiding involvement in foreign conflicts.

just war doctrine: The principle, with a basis in the Bible's New Testament teachings, that outlines the conditions under which a just, or fair, war might be fought, as when a nation has been attacked and all nonviolent attempts to resolve the conflict have failed.

pacifism: An opposition to war or violence; the pursuit of peaceful resolution to all conflicts.

reparations: The payment—either in money, goods, or services—to cover the cost of damages and expenses as a result of war. Reparations are usually made by the losing side.

sanctions: Punitive actions imposed on nations violating international laws.

sedition: Actions that encourage resistance of or rebellion against a governing body.

treaty: A formal agreement between nations.

---

sect also known as the Religious Society of Friends, the promotion of peace has long been a cornerstone of their faith. They also embrace the principles of tolerance and equality. Quakers, along with other Christian denominations such as the Mennonites, the Amish, and the Church of the Brethren, have historically been known as peace churches because they promote pacifism.

Other religious faiths, including Jehovah's Witnesses and Seventh Day Adventists, have also been considered peace churches for their pacifist beliefs. During wartime, members of the peace churches, as well as other pacifists, have declared themselves to be conscientious objectors. Such individuals seek to avoid participation in any military activities because of their firm belief that war is wrong.

A number of religious denominations support the idea of peace but also believe that there are times when war is necessary. Many Christian faiths, particularly the Catholic Church, follow a principle known as the doctrine of just war. This belief acknowledges the benefits of peace, but also maintains that there are certain circumstances when a war might be justified. The doctrine also indicates the manner in which war may be waged.

According to the just war doctrine, war is an appropriate response if all attempts at nonviolent resolution of the conflict have failed. It is also permitted as self-defense against a serious attack, and if there is a reasonable chance of success. Those engaging in warfare must not create a situation that is worse than the one they are trying to eliminate. In addition, they must treat civilians and prisoners of war in a humane manner. The doctrine of just war not only formed the foundation of many antiwar movements throughout history, it also became part of international laws governing warfare.

Along with religious teachings, the concept of civil disobedience also helped establish the basis of antiwar movements. American writer Henry David Thoreau (1817–1862) gained lasting influence in part due to his well-publicized refusal to pay taxes during the mid-1840s. He strongly opposed slavery and the participation of the United States in the Mexican-American War (1846–48). Thus, he refused to pay taxes to the government for those reasons. Thoreau was joined in these beliefs by many others, some of whom formed organizations like the American Peace Society and the New England Non-Resistance Society. At this point in American history, peace activism had grown from its beginnings as a religious movement to include political motivations as well.

Thoreau was briefly jailed for refusing to pay taxes. He later wrote an essay, published in 1849, that came to be known as "Civil Disobedience." In his essay, Thoreau noted that people should follow their conscience in all matters, even if one's moral standards conflicted with the policies of the government. He also stated that, in a nation where governments are elected by the people, citizens can justifiably withhold financial support of the government as a means of expressing disagreement with its actions. Through his essay, the title of which describes the peaceful violation of an unjust law, Thoreau contributed substantially to later social reform movements, particularly the civil rights movement of the 1950s and 1960s. Martin Luther King Jr. (1929–1968), the best-known leader of the civil rights movement, gained inspiration and protest strategy from Thoreau's writings.

During the late 1800s, many American social reformers objected to the idea of a powerful nation such as the United States taking over another nation. This practice, called imperialism, involved physically invading a nation or exerting control over its government or economy. As American businesses rapidly expanded throughout the 1800s, business leaders and politicians continually sought raw materials for producing goods and new consumers to buy those goods. Many such leaders looked to other countries for these opportunities, opting to seize by force any weaker nations that resisted American business expansion within their borders.

Anti-imperialists argued against such practices. They suggested that working with other nations as equals rather than trying to dominate them with military might would be more successful and lead to a healthier economy for the United States. The anti-imperialists of the late 1800s, who objected to the Spanish-American War (1898) among other actions, formed one of the earliest antiwar movements in the United States. Opposition to imperialist practices has continued to fuel various antiwar movements in modern American history.

Pacifism in Early American History

Throughout American history, people known as conscientious objectors have refused to fight in wars due to deeply held beliefs in pacifism. During the colonial era, conscientious objectors' antiwar views stemmed primarily from their religious faith. Quakers, Mennonites, and other members of peace churches refused to participate in violent actions against Native Americans. This decision often caused them to be harassed by their Puritan neighbors. When military conflicts arose, pacifists in some colonies were allowed to withdraw from military duty. However, other colonies were less tolerant and punished pacifists by seizing their property, imposing fines, or imprisoning them.

During the American Revolution (1775–83), those colonists who refused to fight against the British were expected to contribute in other ways. For example, they were expected to provide shelter for colonial troops. However, some even refused non-military service because they objected to any contribution to war and violence. Such objectors faced harassment, seizure of their property, or forced participation in military efforts.

The American Civil War (1861–65) marked the first time the federal government instituted the draft. This made military participation mandatory for all able men in the Union between the ages of twenty and forty-five. The law did not excuse conscientious objectors from service. However, it did allow people to pay a sum of $300 to avoid military duty. This clause essentially gave wealthier citizens the option not to fight, while poor people had no alternative.

In several cities, outrage among the poor led to draft riots. A particularly violent incident occurred in New York City in March 1863. Rioters set fire to government buildings, including a recruiting station, and attacked factories and modes of public transportation. They engaged in combat with Union troops as well. Hundreds were injured and more than one hundred people, mostly rioters, were killed. Many of the rioters blamed the war, and their forced military participation, on African Americans. They believed that the war came about solely because of the issue of slavery. During the uprising, some rioters destroyed the homes of African Americans as well as attacking and killing several black citizens.

Toward the end of the Civil War, in 1864, the Quakers and other pacifists successfully pressured the U.S. Congress to exempt members of the peace churches from military service. They were allowed to seek alternative ways of serving the nation. In the Confederacy, the southern states that had withdrawn from the United States, initiating the Civil War, members of peace churches could avoid the draft. However, they had to paid a fine or offer another person as a substitute soldier. By the end of the war, the need for Confederate soldiers was so great that every able-bodied man was required to join the army, regardless of his beliefs.

World War I and the birth of the modern peace movement

World War I (1914–18), known at the time as the Great War, began during the summer of 1914 in Europe. When Austria's archduke Franz Ferdinand was assassinated by students from the newly independent nation of Serbia, the empire of Austria-Hungary sought to punish Serbia and gain more control over that nation. With the backing of Russia, an ally from a previous defensive agreement, Serbia refused to give in to Austria-Hungary's demands. Allied with Germany through another longstanding defensive agreement, Austria-Hungary declared war on Serbia on July 28. When the Russian army mobilized to defend Serbia, Austria-Hungary declared war on Russia as well.

Under treaty obligations, Great Britain and France soon entered the war on the side of Russia, and a global conflict began. Germany and Austria-Hungary, later joined by other nations, became known as the Central Powers. France, Great Britain, Russia, and other nations on their side became known as the Allied Forces. Initially the United States, led by President Woodrow Wilson (1856–1924; served 1913–21), declared itself neutral, joining neither side in the conflict.

When World War I began, the United States was in the midst of a period of tremendous social change known as the Progressive Era. During the 1800s, the Industrial Revolution had led to a dramatic growth in manufacturing and the rise of massive corporations. It had also drawn millions of American citizens and new immigrants to the nation's growing cities. The result was an increase of such social ills as poverty, overcrowding, and corruption. During the first decades of the 1900s, social reformers, known as progressives, organized to address these problems. They also sought to expand the rights of citizens, particularly by gaining the right to vote for women. These activists worked to improve access to education for all Americans.

This period was marked by increasing tensions between the nation's workers and those of the upper class. Conflicts between workers and management (those who owned and ran businesses) increased. Many labor disputes turned violent and deadly. At this time, the United States witnessed the rise of socialism, an economic and political system wherein the community as a whole, rather than private individuals or corporations, share equally in the ownership of businesses that produce goods and provide services. Socialists were among the most vocal critics of the war, strongly opposing U.S. participation. The socialists saw American entry into the Great War as the upper classes sending those of the working class to fight so that the former could gain access to international markets and increase their vast fortunes.

In addition to socialists, a number of prominent Americans urged President Wilson not only to keep the United States out of the war but to actively negotiate for peace in Europe. Social reformer Jane Addams (1860–1935) was the leader of the Women's International League for Peace and Freedom. She met with Wilson many times to enlist his aid in peacefully resolving the war. Lawyer and politician William Jennings Bryan (1860–1925), who was secretary of state at the time, also urged Wilson to work toward peace. Bryan eventually resigned his position in the government due to differences between himself and the president over the war. Wisconsin senator Robert La Follette (1855–1925) also called for peace. He felt the government should focus on domestic issues and avoid the overseas war. Former President William Howard Taft (1857–1930; served 1909–13) sought to end the war through his leadership of the League to Enforce Peace. The organization could not prevent American entry into World War I but did have influence in the postwar peace efforts.

At the beginning of the Great War, millions of Americans supported Wilson's stated neutral position. But as the fighting in Europe continued, some started to believe that the United States should join the Allies on the battlefield. The change in American sentiment was partly the result of government-initiated press reports and official documents that depicted the German government and people in an extremely negative light. Also responsible for swaying public opinion, according to historians, was the way in which actual events were presented to the people.

On May 7, 1915, a British vessel called the *Lusitania,* with nearly two thousand civilian passengers aboard, was sunk by a German U-boat, or submarine. About 1,200 passengers drowned, including more than 120

When the British ship Lusitania *was sunk by a German submarine in 1915, some 2,000 civilian passengers were onboard. The tragedy claimed 1,200 lives, including 120 Americans.* THE LIBRARY OF CONGRESS.

Americans. Unknown to the public at the time, the *Lusitania* was also in violation of international law. The vessel was carrying thousands of cases of ammunition intended for the Allies. The U.S. government presented the incident as a horrible attack by Germany on innocent people. Some Americans became convinced at that time that the United States should abandon its neutral stance. For the time being, the United States remained officially neutral. However, it continued to aid the Allied Forces, particularly Great Britain, materially, financially, and diplomatically.

In early 1917 Germany, having earlier promised that its U-boats would warn non-military ships before attacking, reversed its position and announced that it would begin attacking all vessels upon sight. German submarines sank three American ships in March, angering the American public. In addition, the U.S. government and citizens learned that Germany had made a secret promise to Mexico. If the United States declared war on Germany, and if Mexico allied itself with the Central

Powers, then Germany would help Mexico recover land it had lost to the United States during the Mexican-American War, including Arizona, New Mexico, and Texas.

Although most Americans continued to object to U.S. involvement in the war, a growing number called for the government to declare war on Germany. One month after beginning his second term as president, Wilson, who was elected as the antiwar candidate, appeared before the U.S. Congress and asked for a declaration of war. The United States entered World War I on April 6, 1917.

The campaign at home

Once the United States declared war, thousands of young men enlisted in the armed services. However, the number of American soldiers who volunteered to join the military fell far short of what was needed. To build an adequate military force, the U.S. government instituted the draft. This required all men between the ages of twenty-one and thirty to register for service. Once they were registered, these young men were randomly selected to become soldiers and sent overseas to fight in battle. Instituting the draft was a controversial step. The government understood that the people would only support the draft if they felt certain that the war was necessary and right.

The Wilson administration began an intensive campaign to rally the American people. The government attempted to unite citizens behind a war that Wilson famously declared would "make the world safe for democracy." Wilson formed the Committee on Public Information, headed by newspaper editor George Creel (1876–1953), to put a positive spin on news from the battlefields. The committee's job was also to shower citizens with pro-war propaganda, information intended to persuade people that American participation in the war was vital. The propaganda campaign included posters, pamphlets, speeches, films, and news articles that portrayed the Germans as evil and the Allies as heroic.

Many schools stopped teaching the German language, and German books were burned. Musicians wrote patriotic songs depicting American soldiers as the saviors of the Allies in Europe. Several celebrities urged the public to buy war bonds, known as Liberty Bonds or Victory Bonds. The government raised billions of dollars through the sale of war bonds, which essentially involved citizens loaning money to the government that would be repaid with interest several years later. Americans were also flooded with pleas to support the war effort by donating to scrap-metal drives and by conserving fuel and food. According to Ruth Tenzer Feldman's *World*

Although they still did not have the right to vote nationally, various women did not want the United States to enter World War I. Above, women wear hats and sashes urging the country to "Keep Out of War."
© BETTMANN/CORBIS.

War I: Chronicle of America's Wars, one slogan read: "If U fast U beat U boats—if U feast U boats beat U."

In this atmosphere, the expression of antiwar sentiments was considered un-American and unpatriotic. Although millions had opposed American entry into the war, once U.S. participation became official, it was expected that the entire nation would stand behind the troops. And most people did. The government started a campaign to discredit the peace movement and to jail activists as traitors. In June 1917 Congress passed the Espionage Act, a law that seemed intended to punish those spying on behalf of the enemy. But the law included broad, vague language that allowed for the prosecution of anyone who encouraged disloyalty to or rebellion against the government. The law also made it a crime to do anything that was perceived to interfere with the draft, including publicly supporting pacifism. A provision of the law banned the use of the postal service to spread any "disloyal" ideas. As such, it became a crime to use a newspaper, a book, or even a personal letter to express opposition to the draft or any other U.S. law.

In May of 1918 Congress passed the Sedition Act, which made it illegal to say or write anything considered disloyal to the U.S. government, the Constitution, or the military during wartime. In what many viewed as a clear violation of the right to free speech as described in the First Amendment, the government made it a crime to express objections to any aspect of the war, such as the draft. According to the Espionage and Sedition Acts, such antiwar sentiments were traitorous. Punishments included thousands of dollars in fines and up to twenty years in prison. The law also prescribed stiff penalties for anyone who refused to serve in the military.

In spite of such pressure, antiwar activists, particularly the socialists, continued to voice their opposition. They held meetings, made speeches, and published articles. These activists were determined to express their views even though it could result in imprisonment. Many people, including a number of prominent social reformers, were arrested and sentenced to several years in prison. Among those sent to prison for violating the Espionage and Sedition Acts were Eugene Debs (1855–1926), an influential labor leader, presidential candidate, and the nation's best-known socialist. Ironically, Debs received nearly one million votes in the 1920 election despite being in jail. A. Philip Randolph (1889–1979) was also sent to prison. An African American reformer, Randolph had formed the nation's first black union and would later take a leading role in the civil rights movement. Women were imprisoned as well, including Emma Goldman (1869–1940). A renowned radical, Goldman fought for the rights of women, workers, and other oppressed citizens.

Not all of those arrested were radical reformers, however. Many were simply individuals who expressed opinions that the government considered un-American. Hundreds of conscientious objectors, pacifists who refused to participate in any aspect of the war, were jailed for evading the draft. Robert Goldstein, a film producer, was also sentenced to prison. Goldstein produced the 1917 film *The Spirit of '76* about the American Revolution (1775–83). He was sentenced to ten years for depicting the British, American enemies during the Revolution but allies during World War I, in an unfavorable way.

The end of the "War to End All Wars"

After four years of bitter warfare, and the loss of nearly ten million soldiers and several million civilians, the warring nations agreed to stop the fighting. At 11 A.M. on November 11, 1918—the eleventh hour of the eleventh day of the eleventh month—an armistice (an agreement to halt warfare) went into effect. President Wilson, who had proposed a peace plan known as the Fourteen Points almost a year earlier, hoped to reintroduce his plan in meetings with the leaders of France, England, and Italy. The Fourteen Points included a ban on secret treaties among nations and a call for fair international trading rules. The key element of Wilson's plan was the creation of a League of Nations, an organization of major countries that would band together to try to ensure a lasting peace and prevent any future world wars.

U.S. President Woodrow Wilson returned home from the Versailles Peace Conference in France in 1919 and worked to establish the League of Nations, which the United States later refused to join. AP IMAGES.

Wilson met with strong opposition to his League of Nations proposal, both within the United States and among the other countries negotiating the terms of a peace agreement. Critics of the plan included several powerful U.S. senators. They feared that membership in such an organization might limit the influence and hinder the independence of the U.S. government. Leaders of the Allied nations in Europe wished to shift the emphasis of the treaty away from the development of a lasting peace. Their main priorities were to acquire disputed territory and to weaken and punish Germany.

During negotiations to draft the peace treaty, Wilson compromised on many points. The final treaty was far more punishing to Germany than Wilson had envisioned. Under the treaty, Germany lost control of a significant amount of territory and would be forced to pay billions of dollars in reparations to the Allies. To Wilson's satisfaction, however, the treaty did call for the establishment of a League of Nations. The peace treaty, known as the Treaty of Versailles, was signed on June 28, 1919, in the Palace of Versailles, near Paris, France.

The government of each nation signing the treaty then had to ratify, or approve, the agreement. This process proved extremely challenging in the United States. A number of American lawmakers and many citizens continued to oppose the provision of the treaty that would establish the League of Nations. In the midst of negotiations with Congress, President Wilson was awarded the 1919 Nobel Peace Prize for his attempts to end the war and to establish harmony among the nations. In the summer of 1921, the U.S. Senate finally ratified a different version of a peace treaty with Germany and other Central Powers, a version that kept the United States out of the League of Nations.

Several European and Asian nations, including Great Britain, France, Italy, Japan, and China, did form the League of Nations. Over the next several years, the league managed to resolve a number of regional conflicts without resorting to military action. But during the 1930s, as Adolf Hitler (1889–1945) rose to power in Germany, it became clear that the League of Nations did not have the strength to prevent a determined aggressor from waging another major war.

World War II

The American antiwar movement, which had been largely suppressed during World War I, suffered in the years following the conflict. Activists had been labeled as unpatriotic by the government. At the same time, however, millions of Americans vividly recalled the misery of World War I and dreaded the prospect of another war. Pacifist sentiments were widespread. Many also believed that the United States should maintain an isolationist position, one that concerns itself only with defense of its own borders and avoids involvement in foreign conflicts. As events of the 1930s unfolded in Europe, however, the prospect of preventing global conflict seemed dim.

Adolf Hitler gained power in Germany in 1933 as the leader of the Nazi Party. The Nazis promoted a fascist philosophy, which placed the welfare of the nation over individual liberties. A fascist system is marked by a powerful central government that is led by a dictator who eliminates all political opposition. A persuasive and powerful public speaker, Hitler appealed to millions of Germans with his passionate speeches about returning Germany to its former glory. Germany had suffered a humiliating defeat in World War I, and the nation had endured economic hardship as a result of the Versailles Treaty.

Hitler spoke of rebuilding Germany's military and economy and of restoring the nation's dignity. He angrily ranted about those he claimed were responsible for Germany's misfortunes, blaming Jewish people in particular. Hitler also targeted communists, homosexuals, people of color, and Slavic people, including Poles. Hitler repeatedly and heatedly spoke of "true" Germans as the master race. He voiced the need to get rid of any others who would "pollute" that race. In other words, Hitler advocated genocide, the systematic murder of people based on race, ethnicity, religion, or politics. His goal was twofold: to alienate and ultimately eliminate what he perceived as undesired elements within the population and to use the military to dominate as many other nations as possible. At the same time, Japan and Italy were also ruled by repressive fascist dictators. Emperor Hirohito (1901–1989) reigned over Japan while Benito Mussolini (1883–1945) ruled Italy. Both men sought far-reaching military domination.

Despite the widespread reluctance to engage in another large-scale war, many of the world's leaders came to view Hitler as a huge threat. They began to believe that Hitler's plans for world domination could only be stopped by force. When Hitler invaded Poland in September 1939, England and France declared war on Germany. Both Allied nations had earlier promised to defend Poland against invasion. Thus, World War II (1939–45) began. Germany, Italy, Japan, and others joined forces and were known as the Axis powers. Great Britain, France, the Soviet Union, and other nations were known as the Allied powers. (The Soviet Union began the war as an Axis power, but soon switched sides.) The United States, while supporting the Allies with loans as well as weapons and other supplies, initially refrained from entering the war militarily.

As Germany's massive military conquered one European nation after another, Hitler simultaneously began carrying out his objective of ridding society of Jews and others he considered dangerous, undesirable, or subhuman. In each nation Germany invaded, Jews were rounded up, arrested, and sent to large prisons known as concentration camps. In some areas, notably Poland, Jews were forced to reside in ghettos. These were small neighborhoods that were often surrounded by walls and guarded by Nazi troops. The ghettos housed tens of thousands of Jews in overcrowded, unsanitary conditions, where food was scarce and illness was widespread. Thousands died of starvation and disease, and many others were killed by Nazi guards. Periodically, groups of ghetto residents were shipped out by train to concentration camps, where many were gradually starved or worked to death.

By 1941 Hitler had devised a plan known as the Final Solution. It involved the systematic murder of Jewish people throughout Europe. To that end, the Nazis constructed death camps, which were prisons designed for efficient mass murder. As news of the atrocities committed by the Nazis spread around the world, Jews and other concerned citizens felt an urgent need to stop Hitler.

On December 7, 1941, after months of increased tensions between Japan and the United States, Japan attacked the American naval base at Pearl Harbor, Hawaii. Several important ships were destroyed, and about 2,400 Americans were killed. The following day, led by President Franklin Delano Roosevelt (1882–1945; served 1933–45), the United States declared war on Japan. The American public was shocked and outraged over Japan's surprise attack on Pearl Harbor, and the government easily justified its declaration of war to the masses. Three days later, Germany declared war on the United States. An ally of Japan, Germany hoped that the Asian nation would help it take over the Soviet Union. Thus, the U.S. military joined the Allies and became engaged in a war on two major fronts, Europe and the Pacific.

Opposition to World War II

Throughout the early years of the war in Europe, millions of Americans opposed U.S. intervention in the conflict. They were reluctant to revisit the horrors of a widespread European conflict so soon after World War I. In the fall of 1940, an isolationist organization called the America First Committee (AFC) formed in an attempt to prevent U.S. involvement in World War II. The AFC grew rapidly, attracting several hundred thousand members in hundreds of chapters. The AFC supported the idea of a strong American military, but only to defend the nation's borders. The organization contended that involvement in the war would harm rather than preserve American democracy. The AFC opposed any type of aid given to the Allies, claiming that funds would be better spent on building up the U.S. armed forces. The AFC believed that providing support to warring nations brought the United States ever closer to military involvement in the war. Members of the AFC included a number of prominent citizens, including writers, politicians, and business owners.

The best-known spokesperson for the organization was aviator Charles Lindbergh (1902–1974). For many years, Lindbergh had been a national hero for his accomplishments in aviation. During the 1930s, as Hitler was rising to power, Lindbergh had attracted some controversy when he expressed admiration for Nazi Germany and shared his views on the superiority of some races over others. In spite of this controversy, Lindbergh's antiwar speeches drew massive crowds. A speech he gave in Des Moines, Iowa, in September 1941, however, ended in disgrace. In that speech, Lindbergh contended that the forces driving the United States toward war were the British government, the Roosevelt Administration, and American Jews.

Lindbergh spoke of his belief that the Jewish people had undue influence on American policy. He alleged that Jews posed a danger to the nation because they supposedly controlled the media, the motion picture industry, and the government. Lindbergh's claims echoed those that had been made in the past, in the United States and elsewhere, as attempts to justify anti-Semitism, or hatred and persecution of Jews. Although Lindbergh stated that he was not anti-Semitic and that he condemned Hitler's treatment of the Jews in Europe, his remarks caused an outcry. The speech tarnished his reputation and that of the AFC. The AFC disbanded a few days after the Japanese bombed Pearl Harbor.

Like the AFC, most antiwar voices became silent after the United States formally entered the war. While most citizens had hoped that American participation in the war could be avoided, many came to believe there was no other choice once Pearl Harbor was attacked. To persuade those who were still unsure about supporting the war, the government generated propaganda in the form of posters, films, pamphlets, and other media. The propaganda illustrated American strength and glory as well as portraying the dangers posed by the Axis nations. Such propaganda capitalized on American fears of enemy invasion, emphasizing the importance of protecting American women and children from the brutal, oppressive dictators of Germany, Japan, and Italy.

In addition to those who objected to U.S. involvement in the war because of their isolationist views, a small but significant group of citizens protested because of the long-held belief that any war was immoral. For many citizens, their pacifist views stemmed from their religion. Members of the historic peace churches and other pacifist religions contended that any activity in support of a war violated their beliefs. Before the United States entered the war, these conscientious objectors (COs) began formulating plans to serve their nation in ways that had nothing to do with the military. The U.S. government had passed a draft law in 1940, and the peace churches lobbied successfully to amend the law with a passage allowing for conscientious objection. The law only allowed such status for those whose views came from their religious training. Objectors who opposed the war for moral, political, or philosophical reasons would still be required to register for the draft. The law provided two options for COs. First, they could be drafted into the armed services but given jobs that did not involve combat. Second, if their beliefs dictated that they withhold all support for military operations, they could be assigned a civilian job that would benefit the nation in some meaningful way.

Approximately 25,000 COs chose to join the U.S. armed forces and serve in noncombat positions. More than 6,000, most of whom were Jehovah's Witnesses, refused to perform any service for the government, military or civilian, and faced imprisonment for that decision. Approximately 12,000 COs chose to perform alternative service that was, as the draft law stated, "of national importance." To accommodate those COs, over 150 Civilian Public Service (CPS) camps were established throughout the nation. The CPS camps were funded by the peace churches, which paid the cost of maintaining the camps and meeting the needs of the workers. The workers did not receive any government wages for their work.

Although some CPS workers were assigned meaningless tasks to fill their days, others performed important functions. Several hundred CPS workers were trained as smoke jumpers, firefighters who parachuted down into isolated areas to put out forest fires. Others worked as road

During World War II, conscientious objectors cut logs and performed other nonmilitary tasks at Civilian Public Service Camp No. 21 near Cascade Locks, Oregon. The camp was designed to give COs constructive work to do rather than military service, which they were unable to perform for religious reasons. © BETTMANN/CORBIS.

builders, soil conservationists, and agricultural laborers. One of the most significant contributions came from those COs who worked in hospitals for the mentally ill. They publicized the horrendous conditions and sometimes violent treatment imposed on patients in such hospitals. In addition, they introduced new, more humane, methods of care.

The path chosen by COs during World War II was a difficult one. The families of CPS workers suffered economic hardship. They received only minimal support from the cash-strapped peace churches. The COs themselves endured harassment and sometimes physical violence from fellow citizens who failed to appreciate the pacifist stance. And many of the CPS workers wondered what their purpose was at the camps. Their religious beliefs dictated not only an avoidance of war but an active promotion of peace. Many felt they should be doing more to spread pacifist values rather than working in forests or hospitals. They also struggled with the question of how to stop a man like Hitler without using violence. In spite of the difficulties, COs persisted in their belief that using physical violence to solve problems was immoral.

As World War II came to a close, the Allies emerged as the clear victors. The leaders of the Allied nations began discussing the terms of a global peace. Out of these discussions came an agreement to form an international organization of governments that would be known as the United Nations (UN). The UN was seen as a successor to the League of Nations. Like that organization, the UN was designed to avoid future global conflicts. In the years since its formation in 1945, the UN has met with both failure and success, generating significant controversy along the way. Some critics complain that the UN possesses too much power, while others are saddened by the organization's limitations. Regardless, the UN does provide a forum for discussion and debate among the nearly 200 member nations.

The Cold War

In the months following the conclusion of World War II, tensions between the world's two superpowers, the United States and its former ally, the Soviet Union, grew rapidly. The Soviet Union lent its support to communist forces in Greece, China, and other nations. Such actions sparked fears in the United States that the Soviet Union planned to spread communism throughout the world and extend its own influence in the process. Soviet communism was a political system that had an authoritarian government, which controlled the economy. Its goal was to eliminate class distinctions and private property. In the United States, most government officials and many citizens viewed communism as a genuine threat to democracy, capitalism, and American security.

In the spring of 1947, the U.S. government passed a law known as the Truman Doctrine, named for President Harry S Truman (1884–1972; served 1945–53). The Truman Doctrine reflected the government's top priority: preventing the spread of communism through a policy known as containment. The law declared that the United States would offer its support, from funding to weapons to American troops, to any nation struggling against communist forces.

The hostilities between the United States and the Soviet Union led to an extended political and economic conflict known as the Cold War

Fear of a nuclear war between the United States and the Soviet Union prompted some families to build bomb shelters in their backyards. Such shelters contained beds, food, and a radio, among other necessities. NATIONAL ARCHIVES AND RECORDS ADMINISTRATION (NARA).

(1945–91). Unlike other "wars," this struggle did not involve direct military battles between warring nations like those present in a "hot" war. Instead, the threat of a military war loomed over both countries. And because the atomic bomb had been invented by the United States during World War II, both countries understood the massive damage that could result if a nuclear war began.

Throughout the Cold War, the United States and the Soviet Union engaged in diplomatic battles, economic fights, and intensive spying missions. They both took part in a number of proxy wars, wherein the two countries became involved on opposite sides of another nation's military struggle. The Korean War (1950–53) was one example of a proxy war. From 1910 until 1945, Korea had been under Japanese control. After World War II, the United States and the Soviet Union decided to send troops to Korea in the wake of Japan's departure from that South Asian nation. Korea was divided in half along the 38th parallel, a latitudinal line that crosses Asia, the Mediterranean, and the United States. The Soviet Union occupied North Korea and the United States occupied South Korea.

The Soviet Union installed a communist government in North Korea while the United States attempted to establish a democratic government in South Korea. The leaders of both Korean governments wanted to rule over a unified Korea. During the summer of 1949, fighting began along the 38th parallel. Not long after communist forces emerged victorious from a civil war in China in October 1949, the new leader of the People's Republic of China, Mao Zedong (1893–1976), forged an alliance with the Soviet Union. He pledged military support to North Korea. On June 25, 1950, North Korea, having received training and weaponry from the Soviet Union and China, invaded South Korea. The United States promptly responded by authorizing additional troops to attack North Korea by land, air, and sea.

At the center of the Cold War was the threat of a nuclear confrontation between the United States and the Soviet Union. The United States had developed nuclear weaponry for possible use against Germany during World War II. (Nuclear weapons are extraordinarily devastating devices that use nuclear reactions as their source of power.) Instead, the United States dropped atomic bombs, a type of nuclear weapon, on the Japanese cities of Hiroshima and Nagasaki in August 1945 in an attempt to end the war with Japan. (The war with Germany had ended earlier that year.) The bombings of those cities resulted in their near-total destruction and the deaths of several hundred thousand people. Japan surrendered a few days later. The U.S. government stood behind its decision to use nuclear weapons, stating that the bombing of Hiroshima and Nagasaki hastened the end of the war with Japan. U.S. officials noted that the bombings made a costly invasion of Japan to end the war unnecessary, ultimately saving the lives of as many as 500,000 American soldiers.

The use of nuclear weapons also served as a display of America's vast military power and its willingness to use such weapons against its enemies. Observers around the world were shocked and horrified by the devastation of the Japanese cities, with many critics describing the bombings as mass murder. Many historians argue that Japan was on the verge of surrendering even before the bombs were dropped. Others note that Japan had been warned in a statement called the Potsdam Declaration in July of 1945 that if the country did not surrender unconditionally, it would face "prompt and utter destruction."

Within a few years, the Soviet Union had also developed nuclear weaponry, detonating a test atomic bomb in 1949. From that time on, considerable military funding and research in both countries focused primarily on the buildup of nuclear weapons and effective means of launching such weapons against the enemy. Fears of communism, the Soviet Union, and the Soviet nuclear program were widespread in the United States. However, many people disagreed with the notion that a nuclear arms race would make America safer. They contended that the possession of nuclear weapons would inevitably lead to massive destruction.

The antinuclear movement

In a response to the bombings of Hiroshima and Nagasaki, an international antinuclear movement arose. A number of prominent citizens, including scientists who had contributed to the development of this technology, publicly expressed their opposition to nuclear arms. In 1955 two influential thinkers published a document that established the foundation of the antinuclear movement. Welsh reformer, philosopher, and mathematician Bertrand Russell (1872–1970) and German-born American scientist Albert Einstein (1879–1955) wrote *The Russell-Einstein Manifesto.* In the document, they pleaded with the world's leaders to abandon nuclear programs and concentrate on peaceful conflict resolution. Russell and Einstein pointed out that a nuclear war is unwinnable and would be likely to destroy the entire human race. As quoted in *The Antiwar Movement,* they wrote: "Shall we … choose death, because we cannot forget our quarrels?"

Opposition to nuclear weapons stemmed not just from the immediate danger of detonation but also from the lingering damage done to all life forms in the area surrounding a nuclear explosion. Whether occurring because of an attack, a weapons test, or an accident at a nuclear power plant, a nuclear detonation creates large quantities of radioactive fallout. This fallout, containing materials that emit harmful radiation, rises into the atmosphere and then settles back to the earth, potentially covering a large area. Radioactive fallout contaminates the water supply, soil, and plant life that is then consumed by humans and other animals.

In New York City, members of the Committee for a Sane Nuclear Policy protest the continued development of nuclear weapons in 1959. Their demonstration marks the fourteenth anniversary of the bombing of Hiroshima, Japan, by the United States.
© BETTMANN/CORBIS.

Radioactive contamination can last for hundreds, even thousands, of years, and poses a significant health risk, causing several types of cancer as well as other serious ailments.

A number of citizens' groups formed to protest the development and stockpiling of nuclear weapons. One of the largest and most influential of these organizations was the Committee for a Sane Nuclear Policy, known as SANE, which formed in 1957. SANE worked to persuade world leaders to end nuclear testing and halt the accumulation of nuclear weaponry. With such prominent members as editor and peace activist Norman Cousins (1912–1990) and renowned pediatrician Dr. Benjamin Spock (1903–1998), SANE played a significant role in convincing the government that the American public was passionately opposed to the further spread of nuclear arms.

Women activists played a major role in the antinuclear movement as well. They organized protests, made speeches, and lobbied lawmakers. Lawyer and activist Bella Abzug (1920–1998) helped form a group called Women Strike for Peace (WSP), which spearheaded a nationwide protest against nuclear testing on November 1, 1961. College students also participated in the antinuclear movement in large numbers. The Student Peace Union (SPU), which formed in 1959, had chapters at colleges and universities across the nation.

An incident in the autumn of 1962 emphasized the threat of nuclear war and the urgency of halting the arms race. The U.S. government had learned that the Soviet Union had positioned missile launch sites in Cuba that could enable it to mount nuclear strikes on the United States. Cuba, a communist nation ninety miles south of Florida, had formed an alliance with the Soviet Union. President John F. Kennedy (1917–1963; served 1961–63) convened a committee of military and civilian analysts to discuss the nation's next move. Options considered by the committee included invading Cuba, attempting to bomb the missile sites, conducting private negotiations with the Soviet Union or Cuba, and installing a naval blockade to prevent shipments of weapons from reaching Cuba's shores.

President Kennedy decided to install the blockade on October 24, a move that was greeted with fury by the Soviet Union. Over the next few days, the leaders of the United States and the Soviet Union exchanged threats. People around the world tried to prepare themselves for the possibility of nuclear war. On October 28 the two leaders reached an agreement. The Soviet Union would remove its missiles from Cuba under the supervision of the United Nations. In turn, the United States agreed not to invade Cuba. For the time being, nuclear war had been averted.

The incident became known as the Cuban missile crisis. It had brought the world's two superpowers to the brink of a nuclear war that would have led to the devastation of both nations. In the months after the crisis, both leaders softened a bit in their approach to each other, showing a desire to ease tensions. The time was right for peace activists to intensify their campaign.

A primary focus of the antinuclear movement was halting the testing of nuclear weapons. Activists sought to end testing because of concerns about radioactive contaminants spreading worldwide. In addition, many believed that a ban on testing would pose a significant obstacle to the development of new nuclear weapons. During the summer of 1963, the pressure activists had applied to politicians seemed to have paid off.

At the request of President Kennedy, Norman Cousins of SANE helped to devise a treaty banning nuclear weapons testing. On August 5, 1963, the United States, the Soviet Union, and Great Britain signed the Partial Test Ban Treaty. It has also been referred to as the Limited Test Ban Treaty. This agreement banned the testing of nuclear weapons (and any other type of nuclear explosion) in the atmosphere, in outer space, and underwater. The treaty also placed limitations on the testing of nuclear weapons underground. While the treaty was far from perfect, and did nothing to slow down the stockpiling of nuclear weapons on both sides, it was an important first step and signalled an improvement in U.S.-Soviet relations. Historians have since acknowledged the important role played by antinuclear activists. The development and testing of nuclear weapons was extremely unpopular with the American people, and the

McCarthyism

Fear of communism became extreme after World War II. Although the Soviet Union was a U.S. ally during the war, mistrust of the communist superpower ran high among Americans. When people learned that the Soviets had obtained classified information during the war from American spies, including information that helped them develop nuclear weapons, many Americans became convinced that communism posed a serious threat.

Rooting out communists in government, the media, and many other industries became popular. The federal government began removing suspected communists from positions of power. In 1947 President Harry S Truman established a loyalty review program that would investigate all federal employees, firing those suspected of communist affiliations or sympathies. That same year, the House Un-American Activities Committee (HUAC), a group

in the U.S. House of Representatives, began an investigation into the movie industry in Hollywood. The committee looked into allegations that communist or other left-wing sympathies thrived in Hollywood.

The HUAC obtained testimony from several people in the film industry who were conservative and deeply opposed to communism. These witnesses named people in the industry who were suspected of having communist ties. Those called to testify before the HUAC were given a choice: either provide names of suspected communists or be blacklisted (have their names placed on a list of people who would not be hired by any movie studio). Some cooperated, others refused. Several people received prison sentences for refusing to cooperate. Hundreds of careers were destroyed and many lives ruined.

Anticommunist hysteria increased in 1949 when the Soviet Union successfully detonated an atomic bomb. That year also saw communist forces gain control of China. High-profile spy cases, including those of Alger Hiss and Ethel and Julius Rosenberg, gave Americans the illusion that communist spies were everywhere and would have to be aggressively rooted out. The Rosenbergs' case sparked considerable debate, with the alleged guilt of Ethel Rosenberg called into question. The Rosenbergs left behind two young children when they were executed by electric chair in 1953. They were the only Americans executed for treason during the Cold War.

In early 1950, U.S. Senator Joseph McCarthy (1908–1957) of Wisconsin gained fame after announcing he had a list of dozens of names of U.S. state department employees who were communists. Although his claims were shaky at best, McCarthy fed the fear of Americans. His hunt to root out communism became known as McCarthyism. He was allowed to conduct far-ranging investigations into the political views of government employees and other citizens. Witnesses were aggressively questioned about their ties to communism. McCarthy pushed those who testified to give up the names of other alleged communists. If they supplied names, witnesses could have their names cleared. If they refused, they faced disgrace, the loss of their jobs, and imprisonment. Just being accused by McCarthy could destroy reputations and careers. The Federal Bureau of Investigation (FBI), led by J. Edgar Hoover (1895–1972), supplied McCarthy with information about suspected communists.

Anyone who challenged McCarthy's tactics became the next person he investigated. McCarthyism silenced many social reformers, including antinuclear activists, who were called traitors because they sought to bring change to America. By 1952 McCarthy had gained numerous enemies in the government and elsewhere. When McCarthy launched an investigation into the U.S. Army, questioning the loyalty of senior military officials, many believed he had gone too far. The televised Army-McCarthy hearings in the summer of 1954 gave the nation a good look at his ruthless tactics and unpleasant manner. Later that year, his fellow senators voted to censure him. This public condemnation of his actions thus ended McCarthy's reign of terror.

Partial Test Ban Treaty was in large part the result of pressure applied by citizens to their government.

The Vietnam War (1954–75) begins

Vietnam, located in Southeast Asia near China and India, had been a French colony for many years. In the early 1950s Vietnam engaged in a war with France for its independence. At the conclusion of that war in 1954, the northern part of Vietnam was under the control of Ho Chi Minh (1890–1969), a communist leader. At a conference in Geneva, Switzerland, officials from the United States, Great Britain, France, the Soviet Union, and China met in an attempt to settle the conflicts in both Korea and Vietnam. As a temporary measure, until elections could be held, it was decided that Vietnam would be divided into two halves. North Vietnam would be ruled by Ho Chi Minh, while South Vietnam would have an independent, non-communist leadership. The Soviet Union and China supported North Vietnam, while the United States supported South Vietnam. Ho Chi Minh wished to unify Vietnam under his leadership, while Ngo Dinh Diem (1901–1963), the leader in the south, resisted. It wasn't long before fighting broke out between the two sides.

As with the Korean war, the United States began lending support to the anti-communist forces. America sent money and military equipment. It also sent a few thousand troops, which were referred to as "advisors," to train the South Vietnamese army. The Soviet Union and China supplied weapons to Ho Chi Minh in North Vietnam. The U.S. government told the American people that its troops in Vietnam were there to train, not to engage in combat. In truth, American soldiers were flying bombing missions and aiding South Vietnamese troops in ground combat.

U.S. military involvement in Vietnam went on for several years on a small scale before an incident in the summer of 1964 changed the nature of the conflict. In early August, a U.S. Navy ship in the Gulf of Tonkin, off the coast of North Vietnam, exchanged fire with some North Vietnamese torpedo boats. According to the U.S. government, the North Vietnamese initiated the attack, a report that continues to be disputed. A few days later, on August 10, 1964, the U.S. Congress passed the Gulf of Tonkin Resolution, giving President Lyndon B. Johnson (1908–1973; served 1963–69) the power to wage war against North Vietnam.

Initially, many Americans supported the nation's military involvement in Vietnam. The government painted a dire picture of the consequences of allowing a communist takeover in Vietnam. Officials explained this as the "domino theory" of communism. They stated that if Vietnam became a communist nation, the other countries around it would also succumb to communism, giving China and the Soviet Union a dangerous advantage. Some antiwar groups, particularly student groups on college campuses, staged protests during the early 1960s. But opposition to the war had not yet developed into a broad, national movement.

When the United States began heavily bombing North Vietnam in early 1965, the number of people voicing objections to the war increased. Many raised questions about the costs of the war, in terms of both money and human life. A number of people also expressed concern about the morality of the war, particularly the killing of innocent Vietnamese civilians through bombing raids and other means. A significant number of protests centered on the draft, known as the Selective Service. Young

Washington, D.C., was the site of many demonstrations during the Vietnam War. Here, a group of right-wing activists stages a pro-war rally in response to the many antiwar protests held throughout the United States. NATIONAL ARCHIVES AND RECORDS ADMINISTRATION (NARA).

men were legally required to register for the draft, after which each received a draft card with a number on it. When a cardholder's number was selected, that person was required to report for duty in the armed forces. College campuses remained a central part of the growing antiwar movement. Professors conducted teach-ins, sessions designed to inform students about the war in Vietnam.

Two significant developments in American society at that time had a strong impact on the Vietnam antiwar movement. The civil rights movement, which had begun in the mid-1950s, had grown in size and influence. The injustices committed against African Americans, particularly in the South, had motivated vast numbers of people, especially college students, to become social activists. As American involvement in Vietnam deepened, many of these reformers began speaking out against what they saw as an unjust war. They had seen from the civil rights movement that ordinary citizens, working together, could make a real difference. They wanted to use their influence to bring about an end to the Vietnam War. They applied the techniques and strategies they had learned in civil rights protests to antiwar demonstrations, staging nonviolent protests and acts of civil disobedience. Among the youth-oriented organizations that shifted their focus from civil rights to the Vietnam War were Students for a Democratic Society (SDS) and the Free Speech Movement (FSM).

A growing number of college students became increasingly radical, both politically and socially. They felt that they had little in common with older adults, differing in appearance, values, politics, and goals. The lack of understanding between young and old became known as the "generation gap." These young people, usually sporting long hair and colorful, casual clothes, became known as "hippies." This term was often used negatively by more conservative observers. In return, the hippies critically referred to mainstream society—the media, corporations, and government—as the "Establishment."

The youth movement, also described as the counterculture, opposed the war, consumerism, and big business. Many embraced rock and roll, free love, and mind-altering experiences through drugs, meditation, and other agents. Others expressed their rebellion politically, in a movement known as the New Left. Promoting the principles of peace and justice, members of the counterculture zeroed in on the Vietnam War as a symbol of everything that was wrong with the Establishment.

The war, and the antiwar movement, escalate

As the war continued, the U.S. government drafted more and more men to send to Vietnam. Opposition to the draft intensified, with thousands of men joining a national draft-evading organization called the Resistance. Many young men staged protests where they burned their draft cards. Others evaded military service by fleeing the country, with many finding sanctuary in Canada. Some simply refused to be drafted, facing imprisonment instead. Some of the controversy regarding the draft stemmed from the ability of the wealthy and powerful to keep their family members out of Vietnam. Parents with political connections obtained non-combat assignments for their sons, while working-class boys chose between serving in the military or breaking the law.

By 1967 the antiwar movement had spread far beyond college campuses. Religious associations, civil rights organizations, and community groups participated in marches and other protests. In April of that year, hundreds of thousands of antiwar demonstrators marched in New York City. Later that year, in October, some seventy thousand protesters marched in Washington, D.C., surrounding the Pentagon and other Washington-area landmarks. Numerous marchers were arrested during

In protest of the Vietnam War, peace activists burn their draft cards at the Pentagon, the headquarters of the U.S. Department of Defense in Washington, D.C. HULTON ARCHIVE/GETTY IMAGES.

what many historians consider to be a turning point for the administration of President Johnson. The formerly popular president was under siege, encountering antiwar protesters at every public appearance and facing dramatically lower approval ratings.

Johnson had attempted to improve morale at home by conveying positive news about progress in Vietnam. He enlisted the help of military experts to tell the public that the war was winding down. Evidence to the contrary came out in early 1968 when the communist forces in Vietnam staged a surprise attack. Known as the Tet Offensive, the action began in late January. Although the U.S.-led forces eventually repelled the attack and regained lost territory, many thousands died on both sides. The images broadcast on the television news showed chaos and devastation. The news coverage revealed that, far from coming to a close, the war was reaching its peak.

Two months later, Johnson announced that he would not seek re-election to the presidency. During the Democratic National Convention in Chicago in August 1968, thousands of demonstrators surrounded the convention hall, demanding that the delegates inside the hall make ending the war a priority. The police and Illinois National Guard came down hard on the demonstrators, spraying tear gas, beating protesters, and making arrests. A full-blown riot erupted, with dozens of injuries on both sides and a number of protesters sent to jail.

Johnson's successor, President Richard Nixon (1913–1994; served 1969–74), inherited a messy, unpopular war and a deeply divided nation. Reflecting the views of many in his generation, Nixon considered the antiwar movement to be a destructive force that was encouraging American enemies and extending the war. Nixon decided that the best way to change opinions about the war was to withhold information from the public, a plan that later backfired. In March 1969, Nixon ordered a secret bombing campaign of Cambodia, a neutral nation adjacent to Vietnam where communist forces had been hiding out. The bombing of Cambodia was hidden not only from the public, but also from many members of the U.S. Congress and even several military leaders. When news of the bombings in Cambodia reached the American public during the summer of 1969, citizens were angered by the deception. Many lawmakers charged that President Nixon had violated the U.S. Constitution.

Also in March 1969, a company of U.S. Marines entered a Vietnamese village called My Lai to find and destroy enemies. The attack turned into a massacre, with more than three hundred unarmed villagers,

For members of the Quaker faith, the promotion of peace is an important part of their religion. Quakers have voiced their antiwar beliefs for many years. Here, they read out the names of those who have died during the Vietnam War, c. 1970. © HULTON-DEUTSCH COLLECTION/CORBIS.

including women, the elderly, and children, killed by American soldiers. The incident was kept from the American people until a journalist published details of the massacre in November. Even supporters of the war reacted with shock and outrage. In response, several hundred thousand antiwar protesters marched in Washington, D.C., on November 15, staging the largest peace march to date in the United States.

During the spring of 1970, Nixon announced that U.S. forces had begun a land invasion of Cambodia. This decision sparked another wave of protests. On college campuses across the nation, students expressed their anger and frustration. Years of peace activism had made little difference in U.S. policy. By 1970, many activists had abandoned the principle of peaceful protest. They set fires, broke windows, and sometimes hurled rocks at the police. In early May, at one such demonstration on the campus of Kent State University in Ohio, some students set fire to the Reserve Officers Training Corps (ROTC) building. In response, the governor of Ohio called in the National Guard. On May 4, after four days of demonstrations, the National Guard threw tear gas at the demonstrators, who responded by throwing rocks and insults. Amid the haze and confusion, several dozen troops opened fire on the unarmed protesters, shooting into a crowd of students for thirteen seconds. Four students were killed, including two who just happened to be walking by on their way to class. Several more were injured.

News of the tragedy at Kent State spread rapidly. Students all over the country gathered on their campuses to protest the killings. Over the next several days, hundreds of campuses were shut down by student strikes or, in some cases, by college administrators fearing that further violence would erupt. A large demonstration was staged in Washington, D.C., five days after the deaths at Kent State. The nation, however, remained deeply divided. As millions mourned the deaths of the students, others voiced intense resentment toward antiwar protesters. Many saw the peace activists as traitors whose failure to support the U.S. government and troops was tearing the nation apart.

As veterans from the Vietnam War returned home, they were surprised to encounter hostility from some of their fellow citizens rather than support or gratitude. The conditions in Vietnam were grueling, and veterans came home bearing emotional and often physical scars. Many felt pained by the actions of antiwar protesters, but others agreed that the war was immoral and could not be won. Some believed that American troops should withdraw from Vietnam. A number of such veterans joined the organization Vietnam Veterans Against the War. One member of this group, John Kerry (1943-), later became a U.S. senator and the 2004 Democratic candidate for president.

In the months before the 1972 presidential election, President Nixon, aware that antiwar activists could help prevent him from being re-elected, announced that secret negotiations with North Vietnam had begun. In August, Nixon announced that American combat troops had left Vietnam, though the U.S. military maintained a strong presence in the air and the sea. Nixon was re-elected in November 1972. During the next month, after unfavorable developments in the peace talks, American planes bombed the

John Kerry (right) walks with another member of the Vietnam Veterans Against the War during a silent protest at Arlington National Cemetery in Washington, D.C. in 1972. The cemetery is the final resting place for many veterans. © STEVEN CLEVENGER/CORBIS.

Vietnamese cities of Hanoi and Haiphong for eleven solid days, killing numerous civilians. Antiwar activists stepped up their protests, with more and more citizens and organizations joining the movement in response to what was widely viewed as an immoral and unjust war.

Due in part to pressure applied by peace activists, American involvement in Vietnam finally ended in early 1973. A peace treaty was signed at the end of January, and the last American troops left by the end of March. Two years later, in violation of the peace treaty, North Vietnam invaded South Vietnam and the two nations soon became one. They became united under communist rule, the very outcome the war had been designed to prevent.

American Social Reform Movements: Almanac

COINTELPRO: Crushing Dissent

When social activists express dissent, or opposition to government policies, government officials take notice, wondering if the dissent of a particular group poses a threat to the nation's power structure or security. The First Amendment of the U.S. Constitution, however, protects all citizens, including dissenters, by guaranteeing freedom of speech, freedom of the press, and the freedom to assemble and petition. At certain points in American history, members of the government have violated those rights, justifying such transgressions as necessary actions to maintain national safety.

In 1956 the longtime director of the Federal Bureau of Investigation (FBI), J. Edgar Hoover, established a counterintelligence program known as COINTELPRO. It was designed to uncover information about dissenting organizations and to take steps to weaken them. COINTELPRO, initially aimed at the Communist Party, was expanded to include a number of other activist organizations. It set up secret and illegal surveillance, spying on American citizens who had expressed disagreement with government policies. Among others, COINTELPRO campaigns targeted the civil rights movement,

including Martin Luther King Jr., the antiwar movement, and the New Left, a movement of political activists seeking social change.

In addition to spying on activists, the FBI used numerous tactics to undermine targeted groups. FBI agents infiltrated organizations, pretending to be members in order to gather information. They also caused problems within organizations by asserting false claims that loyal members were in fact government spies. In addition, the FBI waged a propaganda campaign, planting false or exaggerated stories in the media to discredit activist groups and issuing fake pamphlets and other publications in the name of such groups. The FBI also harassed activists, in some cases physically intimidating them, and arrested others on fraudulent charges.

COINTELPRO continued in secret until 1971, when a radical citizens' group broke into an FBI field office and stole numerous documents recounting illegal counterintelligence activities. These documents were passed on to the news media. Once the information became public, it was only a matter of months before COINTELPRO was dismantled.

The antinuclear campaign

In 1980, just a few years after the end of the Vietnam War, Ronald Reagan (1911–2004; served 1981–89) was elected president of the United States. Early in Reagan's presidency, tensions between the United States and the Soviet Union intensified, ending a period of relative calm between the two nations. The threat of nuclear war and global devastation again loomed as both countries engaged in a massive buildup of nuclear weapons. In response to the nuclear arms race, a broad coalition of organizations and citizens united in what many believed to be a struggle to save all humankind. Antinuclear activists pointed out that nuclear war held the potential to destroy all human life. As such, it was vital for all citizens to pressure the government to end the arms race.

Peace groups from the 1960s, notably SANE, continued to exert influence. They were joined by many new organizations at the local, state, and national level. Numerous political organizations, religious groups, labor unions, and community associations joined the antinuclear movement. In a paper delivered in January 2006, Lawrence S. Wittner characterized it as "the greatest outburst of peace movement activism in world history."

The focus of the movement was exemplified by the goals of both SANE and another major national organization, the Nuclear Weapons Freeze Campaign (NWFC). The groups sought to bring a halt to all testing, production, and detonation of nuclear weapons in both the United States and the Soviet Union. Once this "freeze" had been achieved, activists intended to shift their focus to reducing the number of existing nuclear weapons. The nuclear freeze movement held rallies and staged protests while also working at the political level to elect pro-freeze candidates and pass pro-freeze legislation. Polls taken at the time reflected widespread support for the freeze movement, with as many as 70 percent of Americans opposing the nuclear arms buildup. In June 1982 activists gathered in New York City for what turned out to be a massive peace demonstration, the largest protest rally up to that point in American history. Estimates of the number in attendance at what was called the "No Nukes" rally ranged from 500,000 to 1 million demonstrators.

Initially, President Reagan gave little indication that the antinuclear movement had any impact on his policies. He spoke of a desire to avoid nuclear war. Yet he continued to believe that the best insurance against a Soviet nuclear attack was to possess the weapons necessary to destroy the Soviet Union. By the mid-1980s, however, with the rise to power in the Soviet Union of reform-minded Mikhail Gorbachev (1931–; served 1985–91), the United States and the Soviet Union began peace talks with the eventual goal of reducing or eliminating nuclear weapons. The Cold War officially ended in 1991 with the breakup of the Soviet Union into a number of separate nations. Although relations between the United States and Russia warmed considerably in the final years and the aftermath of the Cold War, both nations, and a number of additional countries, continue to maintain nuclear weapons.

Peace activism in the aftermath of September 11

When terrorists hijacked planes and flew them into the Twin Towers of the World Trade Center, the Pentagon, and a field in Pennsylvania on September 11, 2001, nearly three thousand people were killed. After investigating the crime, the U.S. government concluded that the attacks had been carried out by members of an Islamic fundamentalist group known as al-Qaeda. Not affiliated with any one nation, al-Qaeda proved to be a difficult target for retaliation. Afghanistan, ruled by the fundamentalist movement known as the Taliban, had close ties with al-Qaeda and was thought to have provided safe haven for al-Qaeda's leaders, including Osama bin Laden (1957–).

After a brief internal debate and attempts to persuade the Taliban to hand bin Laden and other al-Qaeda leaders over to the U.S. government, the United States invaded Afghanistan in October 2001. Peace activists opposed the invasion, pointing out that the Afghan people would be made to pay the price for the actions of the Taliban. However, the vast number of American citizens supported the invasion, hopeful that it would not only remove the repressive Taliban from power but also lead to the capture of bin Laden. As a result of the invasion, the Taliban were removed from power, but bin Laden managed to escape. Afghanistan remained politically unstable.

A few months after the invasion of Afghanistan, President George W. Bush (1946–; served 2001–) began making serious allegations about the leader of Iraq, Saddam Hussein (1937–). Hussein was widely considered to be a brutal and repressive dictator who harbored hostility toward Western nations, particularly the United States. Some ten years earlier, a short-lived war had occurred in that region. Led mainly by U.S. forces, Operation Desert Storm (1991), also known as the Persian Gulf War, had ended Iraq's occupation of neighboring Kuwait. However, the war failed to remove Saddam Hussein from power.

At the conclusion of the Persian Gulf War, United Nations weapons inspectors had searched throughout Iraq for evidence of weapons of mass destruction (WMD). These included nuclear, chemical, or biological weapons. The raw materials for such weapons were destroyed whenever possible. Weapons inspections continued for the next several years. Iraq's cooperation with the inspectors was inconsistent during that period. Hussein tried to use cooperation as a bargaining tool to end the harsh sanctions that were imposed on Iraq after the Persian Gulf War. Some believed his failure to cooperate was an attempt to slow inspections so weapons could be moved to another site. On December 16, 1998, the United Nations recalled its inspectors hours before air strikes were launched by the United States and Great Britain, thus putting a halt to weapons inspections for the next four years.

In the spring of 2002, President Bush began threatening a military attack if Hussein did not allow the UN inspectors back into Iraq. In September 2002, Hussein agreed to let the inspectors back in. Despite this concession, President Bush continued to warn the American people that, even if such weapons were not found during the inspections, Iraq still posed an imminent threat to the United States. Bush further claimed that Iraq had close ties to al-Qaeda and offered support to terrorists, a claim that was widely disputed.

The Bush administration repeatedly told the American public that the weapons inspections were not working and that the only way to eliminate the threat Hussein posed was to invade Iraq and remove the dictator from power. In October 2002, the U.S. Congress passed a resolution authorizing the use of force in Iraq. The Bush administration also sought a United Nations resolution authorizing a military strike, but the UN did not endorse the invasion.

The U.S. government attempted to build a coalition of nations to participate in an Iraq invasion—dubbed by President Bush as the "coalition of the willing." Several world leaders did pledge their support for the U.S.-led effort. Without the endorsement of the UN, however, most of the United States' major allies, with the exception of Great Britain, Italy, and a few others, refused to participate at all, or pledged a token number of troops to aid in the invasion. U.S. plans to invade Iraq continued, regardless of the lack of widespread international support.

President Bush continued his warnings that Saddam Hussein posed a great danger to Americans. This persuaded many citizens that a pre-emptive attack was justified. A pre-emptive attack is one that is designed to prevent a possible future attack rather than to defend against a current or clearly imminent one. A significant number of Americans, however, opposed the impending invasion of Iraq for several reasons. They pointed to a lack of evidence that Iraq possessed WMDs, noting that the UN weapons inspections had been an effective means of thwarting Iraq's destructive capabilities. In addition, critics questioned the claim that Hussein had an alliance with al-Qaeda. Opponents of the impending war also pointed out that a U.S.-led invasion would devastate Iraqi towns and cities, killing many civilians. They believed that invading Iraq without a UN resolution was a poor decision, not to mention illegal. Some suggested that the true reason for the invasion was to protect American business interests in the region, particularly those related to oil production.

In the months leading up to the March invasion, antiwar sentiment spread throughout the United States and in numerous other countries as well. In an unusual development in the history of antiwar expression, this movement developed prior to the start of the war. This showed that the activists hoped that a groundswell of opposition could prevent the invasion from occurring. On February 15, 2003, citizens in countries all over the world gathered for historic peace demonstrations. They assembled in dozens of American cities, large and small, and in several hundred cities throughout Europe and the world. According to the British Broadcasting Corporation (BBC), estimates of the total number of participants worldwide range from six to ten million, with some estimates much higher. Many of the larger cities hosted record-breaking crowds. The approximately three million demonstrators in Rome, Italy, constituted the

People continued to demonstrate against the war in Iraq in various ways. Activists in Los Angeles walked in a parade carrying coffins draped with American flags to represent the 1,900 U.S. soldiers who had died up until that time (September 2005) during the conflict. © J. EMILIO FLORES/CORBIS.

world's largest antiwar rally, according to the *Guinness World Records* Web site.

In spite of the unprecedented opposition, President Bush and the leaders of allied nations such as Great Britain and Australia did not stray from their course. Plans for the invasion continued. On March 17, 2003, Bush gave Saddam Hussein forty-eight hours to leave the country. Hussein refused, maintaining that he had complied with UN weapons inspectors. On March 20, 2003, U.S.-led forces invaded Iraq on land and by air. After less than three weeks, on April 9, 2003, Saddam Hussein's government had been toppled and President Bush announced that the Iraq war was officially over. Hussein himself was captured several months later, in December 2003.

The postwar policy of the Bush administration was that American troops would remain in Iraq to aid in the rebuilding of the country and the establishment of a new government. Once Iraq was stable, American troops would withdraw. In the months following the invasion, however, it became clear that stability in Iraq was a long way off. The task of unifying the Iraqi people under a democratically elected government appeared extremely difficult. Furthermore, while some Iraqis appreciated the removal of the brutal dictator, others intensely resented U.S. interference. Hostility toward the United States and its allies spread throughout many regions of Iraq. Insurgents, or rebels acting against the nation's established authority, staged numerous attacks, such as planting car bombs in crowded urban areas and ambushing military caravans. The insurgents also targeted members of the Iraqi police force and of the temporary government, asserting that any Iraqis who cooperated with the Western nations occupying their country were traitors.

As the hope for rapid troop withdrawal dwindled, objections of antiwar activists became more impassioned. Many felt the situation in Iraq echoed that of Vietnam, and they dreaded another lengthy, costly, and deadly involvement in a war that could not be won. The U.S. government referred to peace demonstrators as unpatriotic, and many citizens agreed. Bush earned enough support among voters to win election to a second term as president in 2004. As his second term went on, however, and the fighting in Iraq showed no signs of slowing down, opposition to the occupation increased.

No WMDs had been found in Iraq, and news reports revealed that some of the evidence of WMDs that had been used to justify the invasion was faulty. Some members of the Bush administration backed away from the claim that Saddam Hussein had ties to al-Qaeda and the attacks of

To counter antiwar protests during the war in Iraq, "Support Our Troops" rallies were held throughout the country. Many military families participated in rallies, such as this one held in Washington, D.C., in September 2005. AP IMAGES.

September 11, 2001. Many Americans, including a number of law-makers in Congress, expressed the opinion that they had been deceived into supporting the invasion. President Bush's approval ratings declined, and a number of lawmakers, Democrat and Republican, came out in favor of troop withdrawal.

Department of Peace

Many people believe that wars are inevitable and that combat between nations will never be eliminated, regardless of the size and strength of the antiwar movement. Antiwar activists, however, continue to hope for and work toward a more peaceful future. A campaign begun at the start of the twenty-first century aimed to establish a U.S. Department of Peace (DOP), a Cabinet-level federal agency dedicated to finding nonviolent ways to resolve conflict. The organization behind this initiative, the Peace Alliance, introduced legislation to the U.S. House of Representatives and the U.S. Senate to establish the DOP. The DOP would seek to address the causes of violence rather than reacting to the symptoms. Promoting peace on the international level, the DOP would advise government officials and military leaders on root causes of violence, share techniques for resolving conflict, and educate workers for deployment in overseas peacekeeping operations.

On the domestic level, the DOP would work with schoolchildren to develop strategies for avoiding violence and solving problems. The DOP would also offer prevention programs to address violence in the home, gang wars, and drug- and alcohol-related conflicts. In addition, the DOP would establish a U.S. Peace Academy, the counterpart of the U.S. Military Academy, designed to teach the most advanced techniques for minimizing violence at home and abroad.

The Department of Peace initiative is supported by a grassroots network of citizens groups in every state. A number of prominent individuals have lent their support as well. Popular spiritual author Marianne Williamson and actor Joaquin Phoenix have spoken out in favor of the DOP. Numerous organizations, including Amnesty International, the National Organization for Women (NOW), and Veterans for Peace, have all endorsed the DOP initiative. Ohio Congressman Dennis Kucinich (1946–), a vocal critic of the Iraq war, made the establishment of a Department of Peace a key issue in his election campaign. In an essay on his Web site, Kucinich displayed the optimism of peace activists everywhere: "We can conceive of peace as not simply the absence of violence but the presence of the capacity for a higher evolution of human awareness, of respect, trust, and integrity . . . . We can bring forth new understandings where peace, not war, becomes inevitable. We can move from wars to end all wars to peace to end all wars."

For More Information

BOOKS

American Decades. Detroit: Gale, 2003.

Feldman, Ruth Tenzer. *World War I: Chronicle of America's Wars.* Minneapolis: Lerner Publications, 2004.

Fincher, E. B. *The Vietnam War.* New York: Franklin Watts, 1980.

Grant, Reg. *The Korean War.* Milwaukee, WI: World Almanac Library, 2005.

Keim, Albert N. *The CPS Story: An Illustrated History of Civilian Public Service.* Intercourse, PA: Good Books, 1990.

Kent, Zachary. *World War I: "The War to End Wars."* Berkeley Heights, NJ: Enslow Publishers, 1994.

Nickelson, Harry. *Vietnam*. San Diego, CA: Lucent Books, 1989.

Scherer, Randy. *The Antiwar Movement*. San Diego, CA: Greenhaven Press/ Thomson Gale, 2004.

Thomas, William. *The Home Front in the Vietnam War*. Milwaukee, WI: World Almanac Library, 2005.

WEB SITES

"Antinuclear Movement in the 1980s." *DISCovering U.S. History*. Online Edition. Gale, 2003. Student Resource Center. http://galenet.galegroup.com/servlet/SRC (accessed on April 3, 2006).

"Department of Peace." *Dennis Kucinich*. http://www.kucinich.us/issues/departmentpeace.php (accessed on May 23, 2006).

"Largest Anti-war Rally." *Guinness World Records*. http://www.guinnessworldrecords.com/content_pages/record.asp?recordid=54365 (accessed on May 23, 2006).

"Millions Join Global Anti-war Protests" (February 17, 2003). *BBC News*. http://news.bbc.co.uk/1/hi/world/europe/2765215.stm (accessed on May 23, 2006).

"Our Campaign." *Department of Peace: The Peace Alliance*. http://www.thepeacealliance.org/ (accessed on May 23, 2006).

Wittner, Lawrence S. "Have Peace Activists Ever Stopped a War?" Paper delivered at the annual meeting of the American Historical Association, January 7, 2006. Available at *ZNet*. http://www.zmag.org/content/showarticle.cfm?ItemID=9543 (accessed on May 23, 2006).

3

The Civil Rights Movement

Social reform movements begin when a large group of people, feeling frustrated and unhappy with some aspects of society, join together to create change. A number of social reform movements greatly altered American society during the twentieth century. In particular, the civil rights movement achieved dramatic and significant gains. It not only changed the way African Americans live, but also affected the thoughts and beliefs of mainstream white America. It prompted many citizens to demand that the government live up to its principles, uphold standards of fairness, and provide equal protection to all.

The main civil rights movement in America took place throughout the 1950s and 1960s. It involved displays of extraordinary courage and determination on the part of the movement's leaders and millions of activists. For opponents of equal rights for African Americans, the civil rights movement brought on intense feelings of fear, resentment, and rage. This often led to acts of hostility and outright violence. On many occasions, civil rights activists placed themselves in the midst of heated confrontations. They risked their jobs, their homes, and their personal safety to fight for justice. The conflicts of that era were played out on the streets and in the schools, in courthouses, and in the halls of government, both state and federal. Victories were achieved with great difficulty, and the setbacks and obstacles were numerous.

However, progress was made slowly and a nation was changed. The civil rights movement helped improve African Americans' access to education and jobs. It also safeguarded voting rights and provided equal protection under the law. The struggle against racism (the belief that race determines traits and abilities, and the discrimination based on race) continues today. Yet the victories of the civil rights movement provided the framework for ongoing progress.

Civil rights are basic rights guaranteed by the U.S. Constitution (the laws and principles of the nation) to all citizens. These freedoms include

WORDS TO KNOW

civil disobedience: The purposeful and usually peaceful violation of laws or rules that are considered unfair or morally wrong.

civil rights: Personal rights guaranteed by law to all citizens.

desegregation: To eliminate laws or conditions that create or force segregation.

integration: The mixing together of racial, cultural, or religious groups that had been formerly separated.

Jim Crow: A set of laws, customs, and regulations in the American South that separated blacks from whites to ensure that blacks were kept on a lower social footing. "Jim Crow" also describes the time period during which such laws were common, from the Reconstruction Era (1865–77) until the mid-1960s.

nonviolence: The deliberate avoidance of violence during demonstrations or protests designed to change a law or custom.

racist: A person who discriminates or is prejudiced against a group due to the group's race. Racism is based on the notion that one race is naturally superior to another based on genetic makeup.

Reconstruction Era: A period from 1865 to 1877 of rebuilding after the American Civil War (1861–65) when the southern states were re-admitted to the Union and former slaves were briefly granted basic civil rights.

segregation: The separation of groups based on racial or cultural differences.

sit-in: A nonviolent form of protest popular during the civil rights movement that involved activists occupying seats in a segregated establishment, like a restaurant, and refusing to leave until they were served.

---

the right to have a fair trial, to vote, and to choose where to live and where to go to school. When historians discuss the civil rights movement, they note its origins in the Thirteenth, Fourteenth, and Fifteenth Amendments to the U.S. Constitution. The Thirteenth Amendment, which was ratified, or formally approved, in 1865, abolished slavery. The Fourteenth Amendment, ratified in 1868, states that any person born in the United States—or any person naturalized, or admitted to citizenship—is a citizen. All citizens, as written in the Fourteenth Amendment, are guaranteed "the equal protection of the laws."

In addition, no one can be deprived of "life, liberty, or property" without due process, which means a strict upholding of the rules of a legal proceeding, like a trial. Ratified in 1870, the Fifteenth Amendment states that all U.S. citizens have the right to vote, regardless of race. The Fifteenth Amendment granted voting rights to African Americans, but it applied only to men.

Many historians mark the beginning of the civil rights movement with the landmark 1954 Supreme Court case *Brown v. Board of Education of Topeka, Kansas.* This ruling outlawed segregation in schools. The end of the movement, although difficult to pinpoint exactly, is thought by many to be during the summer of 1965. During that summer, the last significant civil rights law of that era, the Voting Rights Act of 1965, was passed. Also, several of the major organizations behind the civil rights movement began to splinter, weakening the movement. The battle for equality and freedom did not suddenly end during the summer of 1965, and in fact it continues today. Similarly, the American civil rights movement did not suddenly begin with a single court case in 1954. It had been building momentum for decades.

Slavery and Reconstruction

In the early history of America, most Africans came to the country not by choice but rather in chains. They arrived on slave ships beginning in the 1600s. Slavery thrived in the United States for more than two hundred years. The practice of owning and selling slaves was gradually outlawed in northern states. However, it remained legal in the South until the Thirteenth Amendment banned the practice in 1865. Slavery, an explosive issue between the northern and southern states, was one of the major causes of the American Civil War (1861–65). At the end of the Civil War, President Abraham Lincoln (1809–1865; served 1861–65) began a program known as Reconstruction. This program was a plan to reunite a divided nation and help the South cope with its postwar status. But Lincoln never saw this plan take shape as he was assassinated just days after the war ended. His successor, Andrew Johnson (1808–1875; served 1865–69), continued with the Reconstruction.

During the post–Civil War period, the U.S. Congress was controlled by northern lawmakers. These politicians helped pass constitutional amendments and civil rights laws that outlined and protected the rights of the newly freed slaves. The Fourteenth Amendment, which gave blacks the rights of citizenship and legal protection, and the Fifteenth Amendment, which gave all citizens the right to vote, became the basis for Civil Rights Acts in 1866, 1871, and 1875. These laws attempted to protect African Americans from racially motivated discrimination and violence. Many black men voted for the first time during this period. However, women of all races were prevented from voting nationally until

1920. As a result of the new voting power, a number of black politicians were elected to local, state, and even some national offices.

Despite the legal protections offered to blacks, their daily lives continued to be marked by brutality and restrictions. After the slaves were freed, many southerners were afraid the free blacks would rise up in a violent rebellion against their former masters. In addition, southern landowners were concerned that they would no longer have laborers to work their fields. In response to these fears, many southern states passed Black Codes. These rules placed severe limitations on the liberty of black citizens and imposed harsh penalties for criminal acts committed by blacks. The Black Codes were designed to keep blacks fearful of whites and constantly aware of their status as second-class citizens.

Blacks' fears were further heightened by random and brutal attacks by gangs of white southern men. These groups, including the Ku Klux Klan (KKK) and several others, terrorized black citizens. African Americans were subjected to kidnappings, beatings, fires being set to destroy their homes, and in some cases murder. Such murders, also known as lynchings, often involved hanging the victim from a tree and leaving his/her body in a public place to serve as a warning to other blacks.

The few freedoms granted to blacks following the Civil War faded away with the end of Reconstruction. The conclusion of the Reconstruction Era occurred after an 1877 political compromise between northern and southern lawmakers. Following Reconstruction, the federal government's role as protector of African American civil rights ended for many decades.

Supreme Court reversals and Jim Crow laws

The legal protections offered by the civil rights laws and constitutional amendments crafted after the Civil War were weakened in the South. Widespread opposition had formed on the part of ordinary citizens, state and local lawmakers, and even the U.S. Supreme Court. Although the Civil Rights Act of 1875 was supposed to guarantee black citizens equal access to public places like hotels, theaters, and trains, many whites simply refused to comply. Blacks were routinely turned away from inns or forced to sit in black-only train compartments. In 1883 the U.S. Supreme Court allowed such refusals to be legal when it overturned part of the 1875 law, ruling that it was unconstitutional.

The Civil Rights Act of 1875 had been based on the rights guaranteed by the recently drafted Fourteenth Amendment. This amendment offered citizenship and equal protection under the law to all citizens, regardless of race. The U.S. Supreme Court argued that the Fourteenth Amendment prohibited discrimination by the government and its officials. The court decided, however, that private companies or citizens who owned businesses used by the public could do as they wished.

A few years later, with the landmark *Plessy v. Ferguson* case, the U.S. Supreme Court issued another ruling supporting racial discrimination. This 1896 decision supported a Louisiana law that mandated separate railway cars for black and white passengers. The court ruled that the law was not discriminatory. The judges stated that the law allowed all passengers access to the railway cars, but in separate facilities. The *Plessy v. Ferguson* case gave rise to the expression "separate but equal." It became the basis for widespread legal discrimination throughout the South for many decades to come. The separate but equal ruling offered a way out for governments wishing to adhere to the Constitution but wanting to continue segregation, or separation of the races. In reality, facilities for blacks, whether in railway cars, schools, or hospitals, were far from equal to those for whites.

Decisions like that of *Plessy v. Ferguson* allowed state and local governments in the South to make numerous laws that restricted or denied blacks access to places like beaches and parks. Known as Jim Crow laws, these regulations provided for strict separation of the races. Blacks had to use separate bathrooms and water fountains. They were sent to separate schools. Many restaurants and hotels barred African Americans completely, while hospitals treated black patients in segregated areas. Even in death, the races could not mix. Blacks could only be buried in all-black cemeteries. Everywhere they turned, African Americans received the message that they were not just separate, but somehow lower class. The Jim Crow laws remained in place for decades, until they were overturned by civil rights laws in the 1960s.

Voting restrictions One of the most significant ways southern states prevented black citizens from achieving equality was to reduce their political power. Technically, the Fifteenth Amendment guaranteed all citizens the right to vote. However, the governments of southern states became skilled at drafting laws that lessened that right for African Americans. One such law, the poll tax, effectively denied many black voters the ability to cast their ballots. The poll tax required voters to pay a fee to vote. Most black southerners, barred from finding quality jobs, were extremely poor and could not afford to pay a poll tax. Some states started residency requirements, demanding that voters live in one place

The Origins of "Jim Crow"

The phrase "Jim Crow" was commonly used to describe the system of racial discrimination and segregation in the American South during the nineteenth and twentieth centuries. It had its origins in an 1820s minstrel show. Minstrel shows were popular song-and-dance routines featuring white performers dressed up as exaggerated stereotypes of black people. The shows, considered extremely racist and insulting today, serve as an indication of just how widespread racial prejudice was toward African Americans during that era. Minstrel performers blackened their faces, a practice known as blackface. They also dressed in sloppy, clownish clothes. They performed silly dances, told jokes, and sang songs designed to comically illustrate the unfair stereotype of blacks as lazy, ignorant, and foolish.

In the 1820s, a white actor named Thomas Dartmouth Rice wrote a minstrel routine featuring a song called "Jump Jim Crow." The popularity of the song led to the common usage of the term "Jim Crow" to refer to a black person in a negative way. Over time, the phrase evolved to refer specifically to the separation of the white and black races, or segregation. By the early 1900s, Jim Crow systems, in the form of

Thomas Dartmouth Rice appeared in "Jump Jim Crow."
THE LIBRARY OF CONGRESS.

laws and social customs, were established throughout the South. Blacks were separated from whites in their housing, jobs, schools, and hospitals. The Jim Crow laws were designed to keep black citizens "in their place," humiliated and defeated.

for two years prior to an election in order to vote. African Americans generally did not own homes and moved around frequently, preventing them from meeting residency requirements.

Most southern blacks were illiterate, or unable to read. Some states in the South required voters to pass a literacy test, an impossibility for many blacks. Literacy tests often required voters to read and explain the meaning of a complicated document, such as the state constitution. Many southern whites would have had difficulty with the literacy test as well, but most were able to get around that requirement through a "grandfather clause." This clause stated that a voter did not have to pass the literacy test if he was the descendant of someone who had been able to vote prior to the passage of the Fifteenth Amendment. All such descendants were white, since blacks could not vote prior to that amendment's passage.

In some southern states, black votes were made meaningless by a policy known as the white primary. A primary is an election that determines the candidate of a political party who will later run in the general election. The Democrats had overwhelming power in the South. This meant that the winner of the Democratic primary was virtually guaranteed to win the general election. By 1915 every southern state had instituted the white primary, excluding blacks from voting in the primary elections. Once the white voters had chosen their Democratic candidate in the primary, it wouldn't matter which person black citizens voted for in the general election because whites outnumbered blacks. The Democrat was sure to win.

In addition to poll taxes, literacy tests, and white primaries, many southern whites relied on violence and intimidation to prevent black voters from having a voice in politics. Black citizens who tried to register to vote faced the threat of being fired from their jobs, being beaten by angry mobs, or having their homes set on fire. Some were even threatened with the prospect of being lynched.

In his book *The Civil Rights Movement,* John M. Dunn points out that the combined impact of these tactics effectively erased black political power. In Louisiana alone, the number of black voters went from 130,334 to just 1,342 between 1896 and 1904. With most blacks prevented from voting, it didn't take long for the few African Americans who had been elected to local or national office to be voted out. The modest gains of the Reconstruction Era had been completely reversed.

The beginnings of a movement

The decades following the end of Reconstruction in the South were marked by poverty, humiliation, and violence for African Americans. Many former slaves continued working as farm laborers in a system known as sharecropping. White landowners allowed black laborers to farm a portion of their land and share in the profits made from selling the crop. The sharecroppers borrowed money from the landowners for seed and living expenses. This system, often corrupt, kept many black workers in constant debt to the landowners. The sharecroppers could never repay their debts after receiving their portion of the crop's profits. Thus, they began each new planting season in debt to the landowners and were

In the highly segregated South, a young girl takes a sip of water from a drinking fountain designated for "Colored" people only. Separate facilities were common in the South and included schools, modes of transportation, public places like parks and beaches, restaurants, theaters, restrooms, and even water fountains. THE LIBRARY OF CONGRESS.

continually unable to pay off that debt. The law said that they had been freed from slavery, but their daily lives had changed little since the Civil War ended.

Southern blacks also lived with constant reminders that the larger society considered them inferior and even unclean. Blacks could not drink from the same water fountains as whites, nor could they sit near whites on trains or boats. In addition to these daily assaults on their self-esteem, African Americans in the South also faced the threat of physical violence. Black people, particularly men, were expected to behave in a certain way around white people. They were to address whites as "sir" or "ma'am," keep their eyes lowered, and generally act in a submissive, or obedient, way. Any violations of this unwritten code of conduct could result in a scolding at best, a beating, or even murder at worst.

Angry white mobs terrorized black communities. They usually attacked at night, under the cover of darkness. They took victims from their homes and then beat and tortured them. Many such victims were hung from tree branches, a crime known as lynching. A common excuse given for a lynching was that the black man had raped or otherwise assaulted a white woman. However, few of these supposed offenses were ever officially reported to the police. Other excuses for lynchings included lesser "crimes," such as speaking to a white woman or showing disrespect to a white person. Regardless of the imagined or real offenses committed by the victims of lynchings, the white gangs that conducted these murders were acting outside of the law. They were rarely, however, brought to trial. Lynchings usually went completely unpunished. Between 1889 and 1918, more than three thousand people, most of them black, were killed by lynching.

The Emancipation Proclamation, President Abraham Lincoln's declaration on January 1, 1863, that all slaves shall be free, had held great promise for African Americans. But the reality of post-Civil War life in America was very disappointing. The hope of someday achieving equality among the races still burned brightly for many, however. Significant civil rights organizations took shape in the late nineteenth and early twentieth centuries. The Afro-American Council (AAC) is considered the first civil rights organization in the United States. Founded by black journalist T. Thomas Fortune (1856–1928) in 1898 in New York City, the AAC focused primarily on the issue of racially motivated violence. The organization lasted only a few years, but it gained attention and historical importance, in part, for its Anti-Lynching Bureau. The head of this bureau, a black journalist named Ida B. Wells-Barnett (1862–1931), investigated and reported on the problem of lynchings at great personal risk.

Booker T. Washington Early civil rights activists differed in their goals and in their means of accomplishing them. One of the most influential and controversial civil rights leaders of that era was Booker T. Washington (1856–1915). Washington suggested that acceptance and cooperation on the part of blacks would be the most effective path to improving their condition. Washington was a former slave and the founder of the Tuskegee Normal and Industrial Institute (also known simply as the Tuskegee Institute) in Alabama. The institute trained black students to be teachers and schooled them in farming methods or in a trade such as carpentry or plumbing. Washington believed that the first goal for African Americans should be receiving a moral and practical education that would help them become part of the American economy. Only then, he felt, would they have any hope of achieving social equality.

In 1895 Washington gave a famous speech, known as the Atlanta Compromise. Speaking at the white-organized Cotton States and International Exposition in Atlanta, Georgia, Washington urged white people to offer blacks economic opportunities. He suggested they donate money to black schools and make jobs available to trained black workers. He also suggested that black people give up their hopes for social and political equality, for the time being. Washington's recommendations met with approval by most whites. They agreed with the suggestion that black people accept their second-class status. Some blacks agreed with Washington's views, believing that any progress, even if it just meant better education and job training, would improve their lives. Washington did earn the financial support of a number of wealthy northerners, enabling many poor students to attend the institute. And he quietly worked behind the scenes to make changes to the laws that so restricted African Americans' lives.

W. E. B. Du Bois and the Niagara Movement Many prominent black citizens felt strongly that Washington did great harm to the cause of black equality by publicly urging blacks to give in to the wishes of the white majority and to passively accept their situation. John Hope (1868–1936), an African American and later the president of Atlanta University, responded angrily. As quoted in Sanford Wexler's *The Civil Rights Movement:* "If we are not striving for equality, in heaven's name for what are we living?"

One of the best-known critics of Washington's policies was William Edward Burghardt Du Bois (pronounced due-BOYZ; 1868–1963), better known as W. E. B. Du Bois. A professor and writer, Du Bois was the first black person to earn a Ph.D. from Harvard University in Cambridge, Massachusetts. He objected to Washington's suggestion that black people accept their fate.

In his landmark 1903 collection of essays, *The Souls of Black Folk,* Du Bois argued that "Negroes must insist continually, in season and out of season, that voting is necessary to modern manhood, that color discrimination is barbarism [backwards and primitive], and that black boys need education as well as white boys." (Du Bois left it to later activists to defend the importance of girls having the right to vote and

W. E. B. Du Bois is shown seated with other members of the Niagara Movement, which marked the beginnings of the civil rights movement in the early 1900s.

be educated.) He also pointed out a flaw in Washington's reasoning. He contended that even the smallest goals of Washington's compromise, simply economic progress, could not be met without political equality and access to higher education.

During the summer of 1905, Du Bois arranged a meeting with twenty-eight other black leaders at Niagara Falls, in Ontario, Canada. The purpose of this secret meeting was to forge a plan for working toward complete civil rights and the end of racial discrimination. Known as the Niagara Movement, this organization marked the beginning of the modern civil rights movement. The Niagara Movement soon began recruiting members, setting up chapters throughout the United States. The organization struggled financially, however, and only lasted about five years.

However, several key members of the Niagara Movement, including Du Bois and Wells-Barnett, joined together with black ministers and a group of whites sympathetic to the African American cause to form the National Negro Committee in 1909. The following year, that organization changed its name to the National Association for the Advancement of Colored People, or NAACP. This institution continues to have a prominent role in the ongoing struggle for civil rights today.

The civil rights movement grows

In the early decades of the twentieth century, the NAACP and other civil-rights organizations worked to achieve gains for African Americans primarily through legal challenges. One of the first goals of the NAACP was to lobby Congress for the passage of federal antilynching laws. This legislation to make lynching a federal crime was supported by many in Congress. However, a number of southern lawmakers prevented the bills from passing.

A number of court cases from that period met with greater success. In 1915 the U.S. Supreme Court struck down the grandfather clause that allowed many southern states to limit the voting rights of African Americans. The grandfather clause forced black citizens to pass a difficult literacy test in order to vote, while white voters could register as their grandfathers had done—without passing any such test. Two years later, in 1917, the U.S. Supreme Court declared unconstitutional any city ordinances that dictated where blacks could live. In 1923 the court overturned a murder conviction against a black man, saying his trial had been unfair because none of the jurors were black. One aspect of a fair trial involves being tried by a jury of one's peers, meaning people of similar social standing. The U.S. Supreme Court decided that a black man facing an all-white jury would be less likely to meet with justice than if some of the jurors had been black.

World War I and its aftermath When the United States entered World War I (1914–18) in 1917, many African Americans enlisted in the military. Despite the fact that they were placed in segregated units and assigned menial, or low-skill tasks that no one else wanted, more than 360,000 black American soldiers served during the war. They risked their lives fighting to ensure freedom and democracy abroad, only to return home to a nation that continued to deny them opportunities.

Returning black soldiers expected fellow citizens to be grateful to them for their service. Instead, these veterans were treated the same way they had been before the war: as inferior, and even dangerous, citizens.

Some whites feared that black soldiers, having experienced the importance and power associated with being a soldier during wartime, would rebel against their low social status at home. White citizens' fear, along with the raised expectations of the black soldiers, increased tensions between the two races.

One source of conflict between blacks and whites involved job opportunities. During the pre–World War I military buildup, jobs in northern defense industries had been plentiful, and many southern blacks moved north in search of work. After the war, when American soldiers returned home and the defense industries were no longer flourishing, competition for jobs increased. Many blacks were forced out of their jobs, a situation that only worsened the problems of poverty and overcrowding in northern cities. In many U.S. cities, north and south, hostility between the races continued to grow in the years following World War I. Lynchings and other violent crimes against African Americans rose. In 1919, in some twenty-five cities all across the country, blacks responded to violence with violence. Riots erupted in cities like Chicago, Illinois; Washington, D.C.; and Tulsa, Oklahoma.

During the 1920s, black citizens, particularly in the North, did find some reasons to celebrate. Blacks in the North were free to vote. They exercised that right, resulting in increasing political power. In 1928 Oscar De Priest became the first black U.S. congressman of the twentieth century. He represented a district in Chicago and served three terms. The 1920s also brought a period of extraordinary accomplishment among African American artists and writers. It was a time known as the Harlem Renaissance. African Americans were encouraged to celebrate their heritage, a welcome change from past pressures to accept second-class status in white society.

The Great Depression and the New Deal The end of the 1920s marked the beginning of a period of terrible hardship for many Americans as well as much of the industrialized world. With the stock market crash of October 29, 1929, the Great Depression began. Many Americans were plunged into poverty, losing their jobs and sometimes their homes. Unemployment rates were high, with as many as 25 percent of Americans out of work. For blacks, the consequences of the Depression were even more severe. As many as 50 percent of black laborers could not find work.

With the election of President Franklin Delano Roosevelt (1882–1945; served 1933–45) in 1932 came some promise of aid. Roosevelt

First lady Eleanor Roosevelt (left) earned the respect of many African Americans after she resigned from the Daughters of the American Revolution (DAR) organization, which had canceled the performance of singer Marian Anderson (right) at Constitution Hall because she was black. THE LIBRARY OF CONGRESS.

spearheaded an aggressive plan of economic recovery and relief for the poor. He called his program the New Deal. The Roosevelt administration launched dozens of programs in an attempt to stabilize the U.S. economy, get as many people as possible back to work, and provide some government support for those hit hardest by the Depression. With his New Deal programs and strong leadership at a time of crisis, Roosevelt earned widespread admiration.

Roosevelt was popular with African Americans in part because he organized an unofficial advisory committee known as the Black Cabinet. Unlike his official Cabinet, a group of presidential advisers including the Secretary of State and Secretary of Defense, the members of the Black Cabinet were not actually part of the executive branch of the government. Many were community leaders and some held important roles in various

New Deal agencies. Roosevelt consulted with the Black Cabinet periodically on issues significant to the African American community.

Eleanor Roosevelt (1884–1962), the president's wife, also earned the respect of African Americans for her dedication to civil rights. In 1939 opera singer Marian Anderson was invited by the Daughters of the American Revolution (DAR), a patriotic women's organization, to perform at Constitution Hall in Washington, D.C. When the DAR realized that Anderson was black, they canceled the performance. Furious with this act of racial discrimination, Eleanor Roosevelt ended her membership in the DAR. She later staged a free outdoor concert on the steps of the Lincoln Memorial at which Anderson performed for an audience of seventy-five thousand people. Their admiration for the Roosevelts prompted many black voters to change their political loyalty from the Republican Party, the party of Abraham Lincoln, the president who had freed the slaves, to the Democratic Party.

Court victories chip away at school segregation In the mid-1930s, just as it had done twenty years earlier, the NAACP achieved some measure of racial justice through the nation's court system. Led by the organization's chief legal counsel, Charles Houston (1895–1950), the NAACP launched a campaign to end school segregation. Houston's ultimate goal was to end segregation for black students of all ages. He chose to begin this effort by addressing inequalities at the graduate-school level. He felt that the integration of graduate schools would be less threatening to whites than the integration of elementary schools. In addition, he believed that the inequality was far more obvious at the graduate-school level.

For school-age black children in the South, all-black schools, though inferior to the all-white schools, were always provided. Many black students wishing to pursue graduate studies, however, had no options. They were not admitted to the all-white programs, and in many states there were no black graduate schools. Houston felt this circumstance obviously violated the "separate but equal" principle established by *Plessy v. Ferguson.*

Houston enlisted the help of a talented young lawyer named Thurgood Marshall (1908–1993), a man who later became the first African American U.S. Supreme Court justice. In 1935 Houston and Marshall took on the case of Donald Gaines Murray, a black man who had been denied admission to the all-white law school at the University of Maryland. The lawyers argued that the university must admit Murray to the white law school because the state offered no black law school as an alternative. The Baltimore city court agreed, ordering the University of Maryland to admit Murray to its law school.

A few years later, in 1938, Houston and Marshall took a similar case all the way to the U.S. Supreme Court. A black student named Lloyd Lionel Gaines had been denied admission to the all-white law school at the University of Missouri. After more than two years of court battles, the case was heard by the U.S. Supreme Court, which ordered the University of Missouri law school to admit Gaines. These legal victories weakened the *Plessy v. Ferguson* decision, the basis for all segregationist laws. The next step for the NAACP was to address segregation in public elementary and secondary schools and to try to bring down *Plessy v. Ferguson* completely.

Charles Houston Leads the Charge

Other civil rights activists may be better known than Charles Houston. Yet his years of behind-the-scenes work to end school desegregation laid the groundwork for the landmark U.S. Supreme Court ruling *Brown v. Board of Education,* which declared school segregation unconstitutional.

Charles Hamilton Houston was born on September 3, 1895, the only child of William and Mary Houston. He grew up in Washington, D.C. William Houston earned a law degree from Howard University, a black school, by attending night classes. He established a successful law practice and later became an instructor at Howard. Mary Houston, trained as a schoolteacher, opted to work as a hairdresser because she could earn more money that way and help provide for her child.

Unlike many black schoolchildren, Charles Houston attended a high-quality all-black school that focused on preparing students for college, rather than training them for a trade. He excelled in school, graduating as class valedictorian, an honor usually reserved for the student with the highest grades. Graduating early from high school, Houston moved to Massachusetts to attend Amherst College at age sixteen. The sole

black student in his class, Houston performed well academically, graduating with honors in 1915.

As the United States began planning to enter World War I (1914–18; U.S. involvement, 1917–18), Houston knew that he would probably be drafted. If so, he would likely end up performing unpleasant duties that white soldiers never wanted to do. He and several Howard faculty members persuaded the government that black troops should have black officers. Thus, he served during the war as an officer. While in the army, Houston became involved in legal cases and was dismayed at the unfair treatment black soldiers received as compared to whites. He decided at that time to become a lawyer and work to help those who were powerless in the legal system.

Houston attended Harvard University Law School, where he became the first black student to join the editorial board of the *Harvard Law Review.* After graduating, Houston worked at his father's law firm and taught part-time at Howard University's School of Law. In 1929 Houston became vice dean of the law school and set about making dramatic changes. He ended the program's popular part-time night school, hired established black scholars as professors, and quickly raised the school's reputation to that of an institution that turned out high-quality black lawyers. With all of his students, Houston emphasized the importance of using legal knowledge to improve society and to help those who needed it most.

In 1935 Houston began work as the chief legal counsel for the NAACP and began his mission of using the courts to attack school segregation. After winning high-profile cases to integrate graduate schools, Houston left the NAACP work to Thurgood Marshall and other young lawyers he had helped train. He then returned to Washington,

D.C. Over the next several years, he took on numerous cases that challenged segregation and discrimination. In 1948 he began work on another school segregation case. He devoted more than two years to the case, but in early 1950 had to hand it off to a colleague following a severe heart attack. He died on April 20, 1950.

The school segregation case that Houston had worked on was *Bolling v. Sharpe,* one of the five cases that were argued together in front of the U.S. Supreme Court as *Brown v. Board of Education of Topeka, Kansas.* The *Brown* case, decided in 1954, marked the end of legal segregation in U.S. public schools.

World War II As the lawyers of the NAACP fought for school desegregation, other civil rights activists tackled inequalities elsewhere. When it became clear that the United States might be drawn into another large-scale war, jobs in defense-related industries became abundant. Still, such jobs were primarily reserved for white workers. African American labor leader A. Philip Randolph (1889–1979) approached the U.S. government with a demand. He called for an end to discrimination against black workers in the defense plants. In 1925, Randolph had founded the first black union in the United States. He had organized railroad porters into the Brotherhood of Sleeping Car Porters.

In 1941, on the eve of U.S. entry into World War II (1939–45), Randolph announced that if his demand for defense jobs for blacks was not met, he would organize a massive march on Washington, D.C. He promised that tens of thousands of protesters would gather in the nation's capital to demand equality in the workplace. President Roosevelt was concerned that such a protest would be too disruptive at a time when the nation was preparing for war. So, he agreed to Randolph's demand. The march was canceled, and Roosevelt issued Executive Order 8802 on June 25, 1941. The order desegregated defense-related industries with government contracts.

During World War II, about one million African Americans served in the military. Randolph had tried to achieve desegregation of the military, but he had not succeeded. As they had done during World

Among the African Americans who served in World War II were the Tuskegee Airmen. Here, Col. Benjamin O. Davis Jr. (left) and 1st Lt. Lee Rayford (right) discuss strategies. THE LIBRARY OF CONGRESS.

War I, black soldiers served in segregated units and were often stuck with the jobs no white soldiers wanted. They were prevented from combat positions, except in cases where the need for additional soldiers was particularly high. Black soldiers risked their lives and performed heroic acts, but they received few medals for their service.

As with World War I, African Americans played a significant role in the fight for democracy overseas, but they returned home to the dreary realities of racial discrimination. It wasn't until three years after the end of World War II that the military was desegregated. In 1948 President Harry S Truman (1884–1972; served 1945–53) issued Executive Order 9981, calling for the desegregation of armed forces and government agencies.

Asian American Civil Rights

Asian Americans have experienced racially motivated discrimination and violence for many years. For example, during the 1800s, many Asian immigrants could only find work in low-wage jobs. Some worked as cooks and servants; others built railroads. Many Chinese immigrants worked on the Transcontinental Railroad. Paid lower wages than whites, they were often given the most dangerous tasks, such as setting dynamite to clear rocky cliffs. Lowered on ropes, the men placed and lighted explosives. Some died in the blasts or fell to their deaths. Many were treated as if they were expendable.

Anti-Asian sentiment surged during World War II, particularly toward Japanese Americans. This occurred after the Japanese military bombed the U.S. naval base at Pearl Harbor, Hawaii, bringing the United States into the war in December 1941. Many citizens became fearful of all Japanese Americans, regardless of how long such families had lived and worked in the country. Some worried that Japanese Americans would help Japan's war effort by spying on or sabotaging U.S. military facilities. This culture of fear made life difficult for Japanese Americans, who were surprised by such accusations.

In February of 1942, President Roosevelt issued Executive Order 9066 requiring Japanese Americans and Japanese immigrants living on the West Coast to be relocated to internment camps. Allowed to bring only what they could carry, they were forced to sell their remaining property quickly, often receiving far less than fair market value. The camps were set up in remote, desert areas where

farming was difficult. The men, women, and children interned were surrounded by fences and guards. Some 120,000 people lived in the camps in long, wooden barracks. The camps were often overcrowded and offered poor living conditions. In 1945 the executive order was repealed.

Many Americans came to view the internment as a major civil rights violation. In 1976 President Gerald R. Ford issued a presidential proclamation noting that the internment was a national mistake. In 1989 a federal law awarded $20,000 to each surviving victim. Four years later, the courts ruled that the internment of Japanese Americans had violated their constitutional rights.

In the late 1960s Asian Americans joined together to fight for civil rights. For the first time, Asians from various countries—Japan, China, Korea, the Philippines, and others—joined forces to make their voices heard. The Asian American movement did not receive the same level of attention as the other civil rights movement of the era, but it did make significant gains. Asian American organizations set up community centers in urban areas to provide food for the poor as well as legal aid and other types of assistance.

During 1968 and 1969 Asian American students joined with other students of color, including Hispanic Americans, Native Americans, and African Americans, to demonstrate at two California universities for equal rights. The students conducted these "third world strikes" to persuade universities to admit more students of color and to establish special departments devoted to the study of various ethnic groups. Not every demand was met to their satisfaction, but their protests led to the creation of ethnic studies departments at the universities. Since then, universities across the nation have created similar departments.

In 1982 the murder of Vincent Chin, a Chinese American, brought renewed interest to the Asian American civil rights movement. The incident shows how during troubled economic times, many white Americans have blamed high unemployment rates on competition from Japan and other Asian countries. Chin was beaten to death by two autoworkers in Detroit with a baseball bat. The two men had assumed Chin was Japanese and vented their anger at Japanese carmakers on Chin. They were convicted of manslaughter, sentenced to probation, and fined a few thousand dollars. Asian Americans throughout the United States were angered that Chin's killers received no prison time. The two men were later tried for violating Chin's civil rights. One was acquitted and the other's guilty verdict was overturned.

Brown case marks beginning of new era

The NAACP's modest victories in the 1930s that led to the integration of some all-white graduate schools had little impact on the lives of black schoolchildren in the South. Many southern states had increased spending on black schools to head off any lawsuits stating that their school systems were separate and unequal. But the segregation of elementary and secondary schools was still the law in many states. The situation seemed nearly impossible to change. The NAACP, however, became determined to prove that school segregation was unconstitutional.

In the early 1950s the NAACP filed lawsuits in several states attacking segregation. Unsuccessful in the lower courts, five such cases earned the right in 1952 to be heard by the nation's highest court, the U.S. Supreme Court. The court combined these cases under the name of one case that had originated in Kansas, one of four western states that permitted school segregation. *Brown v. Board of Education of Topeka, Kansas* had originated from the frustration of an African American named Oliver Brown. He was unhappy that his seven-year-old daughter Linda had to take a bus across town to attend a black school when they lived just a few blocks from a white school. So, Brown filed a lawsuit against the Topeka Board of Education.

Arguments in the *Brown* case, as well as the four other related cases, were presented to the Supreme Court in December 1952. The attorneys in each case argued that the separate school facilities for black and white children were grossly unequal. They contended that the situation violated the Fourteenth Amendment, which guaranteed equal protection under the law for all citizens. In addition, the lawyers said racial segregation of schools was psychologically damaging to the black children. They noted that black students clearly understood society's message that they were considered inferior to white children.

More than a year later, on May 17, 1954, the court issued its decision. It declared that school segregation was unconstitutional. As quoted in *Eyes on the Prize,* Chief Justice Earl Warren wrote: "We conclude, unanimously, that in the field of public education the doctrine of 'separate but equal' has no place. Separate educational facilities are inherently unequal." The *Brown* decision came to be considered one of the most important U.S. Supreme Court cases of the twentieth century. Although it took many years before southern schools were truly integrated, the *Brown* case set in motion a movement that altered nearly every aspect of life for African Americans in the South.

Fear and fury in the South

It soon became clear that the *Brown* decision would not bring a swift end to school segregation. The southern states that bordered northern states generally held moderate views. However, many in the so-called Deep South (states like Mississippi, Alabama, and Georgia) clung to Civil War–era beliefs. They felt that individual states should make their own rules, and the federal government should have little power over their lives.

The growing civil rights movement and court rulings like the *Brown* decision struck fear into the hearts of many southerners. Supporters of segregation became increasingly nervous that their way of life was being threatened. They feared any change to the balance of power between whites and blacks. They worried that the black population would rise up in revolt and try to dominate southern society. Large numbers of southern citizens and lawmakers reacted to the *Brown* decision with a furious determination to ignore the ruling.

Many white southerners responded to the potential changes in their lifestyle with a sense of angry rebellion and determination to preserve the old ways. Citizens' Councils, made up of middle class and professional whites, arose throughout the South with the purpose of economically intimidating any black citizens who supported desegregation. The councils threatened to take away the jobs and homes of African Americans who defied their will. And if such tactics failed to intimidate, then the KKK would be called into service to terrorize blacks through physical violence. The number of lynchings and other violent acts toward blacks rose during the mid-1950s. One case in particular represented the powerlessness of blacks in the Jim Crow South, and the lengths some people would go to prevent change.

Emmett Till was a fourteen-year-old African American visiting relatives in a small Mississippi town in August of 1955. He came from Chicago, where he lived in a black neighborhood and attended an all-black public school. But while Till understood the realities of a segregated community, he was unfamiliar with the social customs in the South. Visiting a country market with his cousin and some friends one evening, Till whistled at the white woman behind the counter. He said "Bye, baby" on his way out the door. That small act of teenage rebellion in a region where blacks were expected to keep their distance from whites, especially white women, would cost Emmett Till his life.

Three days after the incident, the woman's husband, Roy Bryant, and another man, J. W. Milam, showed up at the house where Till was staying and abducted the boy. They beat him severely, shot him in the head, and dumped his body in the Tallahatchie River. The two men were arrested and tried for murder, but an all-white jury acquitted them after deliberating for just about one hour. The men later admitted their guilt to a journalist who paid them $4,000 for their story. They claimed that the boy needed to be taught a lesson for his bold behavior.

Millions of people, particularly in the North, reacted with outrage and disgust that such a crime had occurred and that the perpetrators had gone unpunished. Emmett Till's mother, Mamie Bradley, insisted on an open casket at her son's funeral. She wanted all to see the horrifying evidence of her son's brutal murder. Thousands lined up to view the body over a four-day period. The tragedy of the Emmett Till case awakened many in the North, both black and white, of the need for change.

In *Eyes on the Prize,* Juan Williams reflected on the incident's impact. "It is difficult to measure just how profound an effect the public viewing of Till's body created. But without question it moved black America in a way the Supreme Court ruling on school desegregation could not match." Bradley, as quoted in *Eyes on the Prize,* explained how her son's murder changed her own perspective: "When something happened to the Negroes in the South [before the murder] I said, 'That's their business, not mine.' Now I know how wrong I was. The murder of my son has shown me that what happens to any of us, anywhere in the world, had better be the business of us all."

The Montgomery bus boycott

After the *Brown* case delivered its blow to school segregation, more and more African Americans began to feel it was possible to get rid of segregation in other aspects of their lives. In Montgomery, Alabama, a highly segregated city, the treatment blacks received on the city bus lines became a focus of their frustration. African American passengers were forced to sit in "colored" sections at the back of the bus. If a bus became too crowded, black passengers were required to give up seats in the colored section for white riders. In addition, black passengers had to pay at the front of the bus, then exit and re-enter through the rear door. Those who dared break these rules faced arrest and, in some cases, severe beatings from angry white passengers.

Black citizens of Montgomery became increasingly fed up with the system. Some began to speak of a boycott. Three-quarters of the city's bus riders were black. Thus, if they banded together and refused to ride the buses, the bus company would suffer a significant loss of income. Jo Ann Robinson, the president of a black women's organization called the Women's Political Council, began to plan for a citywide boycott. She and other black community leaders waited for an incident to take place that would inspire enough anger and frustration on the part of black citizens to unite them behind the boycott. On December 1, 1955, that incident occurred.

On that day, a forty-three-year-old black seamstress named Rosa Parks (1913–2005) boarded a bus after work. Parks had been active in the NAACP for many years, working at one time as secretary of the Montgomery chapter. She had run into trouble on a city bus twelve years earlier, in 1943, getting kicked off for refusing to enter through the rear door. On this Thursday in December 1955, Parks took a seat in the colored section. Later, as the bus became more crowded, the driver ordered Parks and three others to give up their seats for white riders. The others complied, but Parks refused to get up. The bus driver called the police, and Parks was arrested. Immediately, black community activists like Robinson began to spread the word that a one-day bus boycott would be held the following Monday to protest bus segregation in general and Parks's arrest in particular.

The one-day boycott was a huge success, with most black bus riders finding other ways to reach their destinations that day. Many walked, some carpooled, others took taxis or rode bicycles. The Montgomery Improvement Association (MIA), a group of religious and community

When she refused to give up her seat on a Montgomery, Alabama, bus to a white passenger, Rosa Parks was arrested and fingerprinted. Her arrest sparked a bus boycott, which gave fuel to the civil rights movement. AP IMAGES.

leaders, formed to plan the next steps. They elected as their leader a young, educated, charismatic minister who had recently moved to Montgomery and who would become the civil rights movement's most visible leader: Martin Luther King Jr. (1929–1968). Ralph Abernathy (1926–1990), another major force in the movement, was also an instrumental figure in the MIA. With the support of the black community, the MIA voted to extend the boycott.

The bus company, as well as many downtown businesses, quickly began to lose money. The city's white leaders tried various measures to force the boycott to end, including arresting King and dozens of others. Montgomery's black citizens faced tremendous pressure, including harassment, beatings, and the threat of losing their jobs. Yet they continued to stay off the city's buses. King's home and that of another black leader, E. D. Nixon (1899–1987), were bombed by mobs of angry white citizens. But in spite of the risks, the boycott continued. What had begun as a one-day demonstration stretched into a year-long movement.

In addition to the boycott, the MIA and NAACP attempted to end segregation of the city bus lines through the court system. After months of legal battles, the Montgomery City Lines bus company was forced to end its policy of racial segregation on December 20, 1956. Black passengers could enter through whichever door they wished and sit wherever they wanted. The Montgomery bus boycott ended the next day.

Martin Luther King Jr. and the SCLC

Through his role in the Montgomery bus boycott, Martin Luther King Jr. became known as a gifted and inspiring civil rights leader. He had the ability to persuade reluctant citizens to become dedicated activists, passing along his considerable passion for justice to all who heard him speak. Soon after the bus boycott ended, Ella Jo Baker (1903–1986), a dedicated civil rights activist, approached King about forming a new organization that would coordinate civil rights activities throughout the South. In early January 1957, King and a group of more than sixty black ministers gathered at Ebenezer Baptist Church in Atlanta, Georgia, the church led by King's father. The ministers created the Southern Christian Leadership Conference (SCLC) and elected King as its president. Ella Jo Baker spent more than two years as the SCLC's master organizer and strategist, lending her years of experience as an activist to the new organization and its young leader.

The SCLC played a significant role in the early years of the civil rights movement. Its basic mission involved ending segregation and pursuing social justice through nonviolent means. King and other SCLC leaders preached repeatedly about the importance of fighting hate with love. The SCLC worked with local organizations all over the South, staging demonstrations, marches, and voter registration drives. By coordinating the activities of numerous other groups, the SCLC helped to build a massive grassroots, or locally based, movement throughout the southern states.

Conflict in Little Rock

The 1954 *Brown v. Board of Education* Supreme Court ruling declared that school segregation had to end. But the Supreme Court and other branches of the federal government gave no guidance as to how, or how quickly, to achieve integration. President Dwight D. Eisenhower (1890–1969; served 1953–61) disagreed with the ruling. Although he did not make his views known to the public, he never voiced any support for the ruling either. His silence on the subject was interpreted by southern segregationists as an opposition to school integration, leading them to feel more comfortable defying the ruling.

In addition, the Supreme Court issued a 1955 ruling known as *Brown v. Board of Education II* that further confused the situation. Stating that schools should desegregate with "all deliberate speed," the decision allowed for school boards to come up with plans for gradual integration. While "speed" suggests quickness, "deliberate" means to come to a decision carefully and even slowly. In states where integration was strongly opposed, *Brown II* was interpreted as a victory. The Supreme Court seemed to approve of long delays for school desegregation.

The school board of Little Rock, Arkansas, became one of the first in the nation to come up with a plan to gradually integrate the public schools. The plan initially called for the voluntary integration of one all-white high school, meaning that any black student brave enough to attend the white school could choose to do so. Only nine black students agreed to step forward. The integration of Little Rock's Central High School was supposed to begin in early September 1957, but in the weeks leading up to the first day of school, politicians and citizens scrambled to block the black students from entering the school.

Arkansas Governor Orval Faubus had not expressed strong views about segregation. However, in 1957 he became a staunch supporter of separate facilities for blacks and whites. His political opponents were gaining followers with their segregationist views, and Faubus worried that he would lose the re-election if he didn't express the same views. Two days before the first day of school, Governor Faubus announced on television that he had called in 250 National Guard troops to keep the black students out of Central High. Claiming to be concerned about violence and rioting, Faubus declared that if the troops were not there to block the black students, blood would "run in the streets" of Little Rock.

The first day of school was September 4. The school board had cautioned the parents of the nine black students not to take their children to school that day out of concern that their presence might spark a riot. The parents complied. Daisy Bates, the president of the Arkansas NAACP chapter, agreed to accompany the students in place of their

White students watch as a group of black students is escorted by a soldier to Central High School in Little Rock, Arkansas, in 1957.
© BETTMANN/CORBIS.

parents. Unable to reach one of the students, Elizabeth Eckford, the night before, Bates met the other eight at an intersection in Little Rock, where two police cars waited to drive the children to school.

Eckford approached the school alone, enduring threats and racist jeers shouted at her from the white crowd. She made her way toward the line of guards, thinking they would protect her. Instead, the guards raised their weapons and closed ranks, preventing her from entering the school. She made her way back through the crowd, away from the school. With the help of some sympathetic whites, she boarded a city bus and rode away. The other black students met with similar resistance from the crowd and the guards, and they, too, were turned away from the school.

A federal judge and the U.S. Justice Department intervened and forced Governor Faubus to call off the National Guard troops. On September 23, the Little Rock Nine, as the students came to be called, entered Central High with a police escort. The victory was short-lived, however. The threat of violence from students inside the school and angry white mobs outside convinced the authorities that the students were not safe and should be taken home. The following day, after President Eisenhower got involved, the students returned to the school accompanied by one thousand U.S. Army paratroopers. Eisenhower had also put the Arkansas National Guard under federal control, enlisting them to keep the peace in Little Rock. For the remainder of the school year, armed National Guardsmen patrolled the hallways of Central High.

Much of the conflict in Little Rock was captured by television news cameras. Many people around the world were shocked by the level of racial hatred shown there. But even some who supported integration in theory wondered if the results were worth all the trouble.

The rise of the student movement

In the years following the Little Rock crisis, school integration continued to proceed very slowly. Even in Little Rock, the gains made in 1957 were reversed in 1958, when Governor Faubus closed down the public schools altogether. A number of southern states took similar actions to avoid complying with the *Brown* decision. By 1960, six years after *Brown,* very few schools had desegregated. African Americans who had been school-children in 1954, the year of *Brown,* were now young adults. As each year passed and they realized they would not personally reap the benefits of the momentous Supreme Court decision, many of these young people decided to become activists and attempt to bring about change on their own. Although victories in courts and legislatures were significant, this growing group of activists realized there were other ways to achieve social justice.

Sit-ins Civil rights organizations like the Congress of Racial Equality (CORE), founded in 1942, and the SCLC and NAACP held training sessions to teach young activists about the principles of nonviolence. They explained the application of those principles to civil disobedience, or the peaceful violation of a law that many consider unjust or immoral. In early 1960, a new organization formed that embodied the restless, activist spirit of many young African Americans. The Student Nonviolent Coordinating Committee, or SNCC (pronounced "snick"), adhered to the principles of nonviolence supported by the more established civil rights groups. But SNCC took a more aggressive approach to civil rights than the older groups had, expressing the energy and idealism of the student members.

After the Greensboro sit-in, students staged similar protests in other cities in the South. Here, activists sit at a Woolworth's lunch counter in Atlanta, Georgia, waiting to be served. AP IMAGES.

SNCC was formed in the midst of a successful series of demonstrations held throughout the South. Activists were attempting to make lunch counters in department stores and drugstores open to people of all races. Many such businesses would sell clothing or other items to black customers but denied them service at the lunch counters within the stores. During the late 1950s, a few incidents were staged to challenge lunch-counter segregation. Activists undertook sit-ins at white-only counters. A sit-in involved black customers sitting at a lunch counter, asking to be served, and remaining in their seats after being denied service. On occasion, sympathetic whites joined the sit-in.

In February 1960, a group of four black students from North Carolina A&T (Agricultural and Technical) College, an all-black school in Greensboro, took action. They decided to stage a sit-in at the lunch counter of Woolworth's drugstore. They were refused service but stayed in their seats until the store closed. The following day, the Greensboro Four, as they came to be known, returned with nineteen black students to stage another sit-in. By the end of the week, several hundred students, including many white supporters, were taking turns occupying the seats of Woolworth's lunch counter.

Word spread quickly of the actions of the Greensboro Four, thanks in part to television coverage of the sit-ins. In the following weeks, student demonstrators staged sit-ins in cities throughout the South. Over the next year and a half, tens of thousands of black and white students participated in sit-ins at lunch counters, movie theaters, public swimming pools, hotels, and other places that served the public. Often conducted in conjunction with a boycott of those businesses and large demonstrations in the streets, the sit-ins proved extremely effective. They forced the integration of businesses in more than one hundred communities throughout the South.

Freedom Rides In the wake of the *Brown* decision and many other court rulings that banned segregation, civil rights activists learned that legal victories did not always bring real change. The U.S. Supreme Court could declare that a certain kind of segregation was illegal, but without the support of law enforcement officials, such rulings were ineffective. In much of the South, particularly the states known as the Deep South, there was strong opposition to integration. Most state officials refused to honor the authority of the nation's courts. Many black southerners kept quiet about instances of illegal segregation, fearing physical assault and other forms of intimidation.

A 1947 U.S. Supreme Court ruling had banned segregation on interstate buses and trains. At that time, the civil rights group CORE had sent black and white volunteers on bus rides in the South to determine if that ruling was being enforced. The riders found that segregation remained the custom, if not the law, and they were harassed and ultimately arrested. In 1961 the U.S. Supreme Court expanded on the 1947 ruling. The court specified that the waiting areas for interstate buses and trains could not be segregated either. Once again, CORE, under the leadership of James Farmer (1920–1999), set out to test the South's compliance with this ruling.

In May 1961, white and black CORE volunteers began a journey from Washington, D.C., to New Orleans, Louisiana. The plan involved black riders sitting in the front of the bus and refusing to move if ordered to do so. At rest stops, the black volunteers would enter the all-white waiting rooms. These volunteers, who came to be known as Freedom Riders, knew that their actions would provoke outcry and possibly violence from white southerners. In fact, the activists intended to spark a reaction. They figured that assaults on the Freedom Riders would force the U.S. government to acknowledge that federal laws were being ignored in the South. In turn, the government would have to step in to remedy the situation.

The Freedom Riders met with minor resistance in Virginia and North Carolina. They suffered a beating from a group of white men in Rock Hill, South Carolina. Dedicated to the principles of nonviolence, they refused to fight back. On May 14 the Freedom Riders split into two groups in Atlanta, Georgia, with some riding on a Trailways bus and others on a Greyhound bus. They then began the most dangerous leg of their journey as they approached Alabama and Mississippi, two of the states most hostile to civil rights efforts.

When the Greyhound bus pulled into the station in Anniston, Mississippi, an angry crowd threw stones at the bus and slashed its tires. The driver hastily pulled away, driving a few miles outside town until the flat tires forced him to stop. Many of those in the mob at the bus station followed in cars. When the bus stopped, one of them threw a firebomb through a window of the bus. As smoke filled the vehicle, the passengers were forced to leave through an emergency exit. The bus became consumed with flames, and the fleeing passengers were beaten by the waiting mobs. The beatings stopped due to the actions of an undercover Alabama patrolman, who had boarded the bus in Atlanta. Feeling duty-bound to prevent murder, he fired his gun into the air and threatened to shoot anyone who continued.

The Trailways bus also encountered attacks in Anniston and met with similar violence in Birmingham, Alabama. There, the riders were assaulted by a large crowd of people, many of whom beat the riders with metal pipes. In both Anniston and Birmingham, in spite of advance warnings that violence might take place, the local police departments were absent. Although they endured beatings, the Freedom Riders were determined to continue, prepared to give their lives to the cause. After the incidents in Anniston and Birmingham, however, no bus driver would agree to transport them.

Inspired by the bravery of the Freedom Riders, hundreds of volunteers traveled to the South to try to continue the journey. When Alabama Governor John Patterson promised to protect the riders, the Freedom Rides resumed. On May 20, in Montgomery, Alabama, it became clear that the governor had not kept his promise. Hundreds of angry whites surrounded the buses of the Freedom Riders, rioting in the streets and brutally attacking the civil rights workers. The state of Alabama seemed to have come unhinged. The situation improved when President John F. Kennedy (1917–1963; served 1961–63) ordered hundreds of federal marshals to the state to restore order.

A Freedom Rider bus burns after someone from an angry mob of segregationists tossed a firebomb through one of its windows. Members of that mob beat the civil rights activists who were onboard as they evacuated the bus through an emergency exit.
AP IMAGES.

Volunteers continued to show up for duty as the Freedom Riders prepared to enter Mississippi. Fearful for the riders' safety and concerned about alienating southern Democrats, the Kennedy administration chose the president's brother, Robert F. Kennedy (1925–1968), to negotiate an agreement with Mississippi officials. The state would guarantee that the Freedom Riders would not be attacked in Mississippi. And the U.S. government would allow Mississippi to enforce its segregation laws and arrest the black passengers who attempted to integrate waiting areas. Although the federal government controlled interstate travel, individual states retained control of bus stations within their state lines. The state laws permitting segregation conflicted with federal anti-segregation laws. Kennedy allowed Mississippi's state laws to prevail in the case of the Freedom Riders. Hundreds of Freedom Riders were subsequently arrested.

James Meredith and Ole Miss

Many of the conflicts during the civil rights era came down to tension between the southern states' desire to preserve their rights, including their longstanding tradition of racial discrimination, and the federal government's assertion of its power. One of several explosive civil rights battles took place in Mississippi, which was considered by many to be the South's most strongly segregated state. Governor Ross Barnett (1898–1987) pledged to prevent the integration of any Mississippi school as long as he was in office. His pledge came in the fall of 1962, when federal courts ordered the University of Mississippi to admit James Meredith. A black Air Force veteran, Meredith was a sophomore at the all-black Jackson State University. The University of Mississippi, nicknamed "Ole Miss," was a symbol of traditional white southern values. It had never admitted a black student, and Meredith set out to change that.

With the backing of the U.S. court system, Meredith attempted to register for classes in September, but he was blocked from doing so. In one instance, Governor Barnett personally prevented Meredith from registering. Barnett had appointed himself as the university registrar on the day the young student was to sign up for classes. The following day, Meredith was stopped by state troopers as he tried to register at the campus in Oxford, Mississippi. On Sunday, September 30, President Kennedy ordered federal marshals and state troopers to accompany Meredith to the university. The appearance of federal troops in Mississippi angered the governor and many white citizens in the state. Thousands of whites gathered on campus to engage in battle with the marshals. The outraged white mobs attacked the marshals with bats, bricks, bombs, and guns. Outnumbered, the marshals fought back. More than 150 people were wounded, many by gunshot. By early morning, Kennedy sent army troops to Oxford, and the rioting ended.

Later that morning, Meredith registered without incident and began attending classes. He graduated from the University of Mississippi in the summer of 1963. He had been accompanied by armed guards during his entire time at the school. Although Meredith's victory came at a great price, his battle against segregation at Ole Miss gave hope to blacks throughout the state that change was indeed possible.

The Freedom Rides did not achieve the dramatic changes to the enforcement of desegregation laws like the riders had hoped would occur. However, by autumn of 1961 the Interstate Commerce Commission (ICC) had issued new rules forcing bus and train companies to integrate waiting rooms. In communities throughout the South, Freedom Rides and other methods of confronting segregation laws continued. The original Freedom Riders, revered for their courage in the face of certain danger, were viewed as heroes by blacks throughout the South for many years to come.

The Albany Movement

In late November 1961, civil rights workers from SNCC, the SCLC, and the NAACP, among others, converged on Albany, Georgia. They were attempting to reverse segregation laws in that city. They faced an uphill battle, in part because the various civil rights groups working in Albany could not always agree about what goals or methods to use. In spite of their differences, numerous organizations banded together to form the Albany Movement, an umbrella organization to oversee civil rights activities in that city.

For the next several months, the Albany Movement coordinated a flurry of protest actions. These included sit-ins at transportation terminals, libraries, and restaurants, as well as protest marches and prayer vigils. The hope in Albany, as with civil rights actions in other cities, was to provoke a violent and angry reaction from the white community and Albany police, drawing the attention of the press and the sympathy of supporters from around the country. The Albany police, however, under the guidance of police chief Laurie Pritchett, undermined that effort. They treated the protesters courteously and protected them from angry white crowds.

Many demonstrators were arrested by the Albany police, but the clashes remained largely nonviolent. Albany officials stated publicly that the arrests were for such violations as parading without a permit, trespassing, or loitering. They carefully avoided using inflammatory language about the racial issues behind the protests. The Albany police kept tabs on the Albany Movement through informers. Once they learned of the tension within the movement, they exploited that weakness.

In July 1962 the Albany Movement was dealt a blow when a federal judge issued a restraining order prohibiting further demonstrations in Albany. A few days later, an appeals court judge reversed the order. Protesters responded by staging a huge march through the streets of Albany. The march eventually broke into violence on the part of protesters, some of whom threw rocks and bricks at police. That event was a great disappointment to the civil rights leaders who had long argued for nonviolent resistance.

Although the Albany Movement continued until 1965, it became clear by the end of the summer of 1962 that the movement had lost much of its steam. Civil rights organizations turned their efforts elsewhere. Some observers suggested that the Albany Movement had been a failure, but many of those involved disagreed. The demonstrations in Albany had involved numerous African Americans who had never stood up for their rights before, and the experience profoundly changed them. In addition, the civil rights groups in Albany learned many valuable lessons about waging a successful campaign, lessons they applied to future efforts.

Conflict erupts in Birmingham

Like many other cities in the Deep South, Birmingham, Alabama, was thoroughly segregated and extremely hostile to African Americans working for change. The city's public safety commissioner, Theophilus Eugene "Bull" Connor (1897–1973), had repeatedly expressed his contempt for civil rights activists and made no secret of his racist views. Between 1957 and 1963, eighteen bombs had exploded in Birmingham's black neighborhoods. None of the bombing cases had been solved, primarily because the Birmingham police had no interest in investigating the incidents. The city had thus earned the nickname "Bombingham."

Many of the city's leaders were involved in the KKK, which attracted broad support from Birmingham's white citizens. Segregation in Birmingham was the law and the custom. When a federal desegregation order came through in 1962, the city closed down its parks, playgrounds, public pools, and golf courses rather than comply with the order. Alabama Governor George Wallace (1919–1998) was one of segregation's most vocal supporters. He brought cheers from the crowds at his inauguration speech. As quoted in *The Washington Post,* Wallace said: "I draw the line in the dust and toss the gauntlet before the feet of tyranny, and I say, segregation now, segregation tomorrow, segregation forever."

In early 1963, the SCLC, along with the Alabama Christian Movement for Human Rights, began planning its strategy for desegregating Birmingham. Their plan was dubbed "Project C," with the "C" standing for "confrontation." It involved a variety of protest tactics, including sit-ins, boycotts, marches, and other types of demonstrations. The civil rights groups focused on downtown department stores. Such businesses allowed black customers to enter but refused to serve them at lunch counters and discouraged them from trying on clothes before buying. Black customers had to use separate bathrooms and fitting rooms. And, black employees served in menial positions, never allowed to advance to higher jobs.

On April 3 the protests began. The police responded by arresting hundreds of demonstrators at a time. On Palm Sunday (the Sunday before Easter), April 6, Martin Luther King Jr.'s brother, A. D. King,

In Birmingham, Alabama, police used attack dogs to break up protests. Here, an African American man tries to pass by police only to be grabbed by the officer and attacked by his dog.
AP IMAGES.

led a march through the streets. The protesters were attacked by the police with batons and dogs. A few days later, a circuit court judge issued an order banning King and more than one hundred other leaders from participating in any demonstrations. Martin Luther King Jr. chose to violate the order, knowing it would result in his arrest. He led a march on April 12, which was Good Friday, the Friday before Easter. King and others were immediately arrested, and King was put in solitary confinement.

A number of moderate white religious leaders criticized King's actions in a full-page advertisement in one of Birmingham's newspapers.

Disappointed by their lack of support, King quickly wrote a lengthy response, scribbling on toilet paper scraps and in the margins of the newspaper. His essay, titled "Letter from Birmingham Jail," was soon published as a pamphlet and distributed widely. King's "Letter" became one of the best-known writings of the civil rights movement. In it, he wrote, "We know from painful experience that freedom is never voluntarily given by the oppressor; it must be demanded by the oppressed."

After weeks of demonstrations and mass arrests, the campaign in Birmingham had lost many supporters, some of whom feared getting arrested and losing their jobs. In a controversial move, the leaders of the campaign decided to stage a children's march, noting that an aggressive police response to young protesters would be unacceptable to the American public. On May 2, hundreds of young people age six to eighteen marched through the streets. The Birmingham police arrested more than 950 of them, carting them off in school buses. The following day, more than one thousand children showed up to march. Bull Connor, desperate to halt the march, ordered firefighters to turn their hoses on the marchers. Children crouched in the street and were sent tumbling into curbs and parked cars by streams of water powerful enough to take bark off trees.

The nation was outraged by footage of the young marchers being attacked by the police. African Americans in Birmingham turned out in full force to continue the demonstrations, many of which then turned violent. As the protests threatened to become out of control, the civil rights leaders and white business owners, who had suffered economic setbacks during the weeks of protests, forged a secret deal. On May 10, the deal was announced. The protests would end, and the downtown stores would desegregate, with black store employees promised better positions.

The fragile truce began to unravel when angry members of the KKK bombed the hotel where King was staying as well as the home of his brother, A. D. King. Riots erupted, and the chaos was only brought under control when President Kennedy threatened to send in federal troops. The events in Birmingham brought civil rights to the forefront of the Kennedy administration's agenda. In June 1963 Kennedy announced that he would send a bill to Congress ending segregation in places that served the public. This included restaurants, hotels, libraries, and stores, as well as buses and trains.

The March on Washington

Leaders of the civil rights movement rejoiced at the possibility of a sweeping law to protect the rights of African Americans. They had been planning a large-scale, peaceful march in Washington, D.C., the seat of the federal government, to demand their rights. When President Kennedy sent the civil rights bill to Congress, the goals of the march expanded to include a show of support for the legislation. A number of organizations came together to plan the March on Washington for Jobs and Freedom, scheduled for August 28, 1963. Black civil rights groups, as well as white activists and representatives of the Catholic, Protestant, and Jewish faiths, joined forces to coordinate the massive demonstration. The principal planners were A. Philip Randolph and Bayard Rustin (c. 1910–1987), both of whom had been involved in many significant civil rights actions.

Initially, President Kennedy opposed the march. He was concerned that it might turn violent and would be seen as threatening to the white lawmakers. Faced with the insistence of civil rights leaders that the march take place, Kennedy agreed to offer his support.

The planners expected, and hoped for, about 100,000 attendees. On the morning of August 28, more than 250,000 people showed up in the nation's capital, including some 60,000 white people. The marchers had come from all over the country, traveling to Washington by train, bus, car, and even on foot. They marched from the Washington Monument to the Lincoln Memorial, where they gathered for an afternoon of stirring music and rousing speeches. Folksingers and gospel singers including Joan Baez, Bob Dylan, Odetta, and Mahalia Jackson performed.

The leaders of the movement, including Randolph, John Lewis (1940–) of SNCC, and Martin Luther King Jr., spoke of their views of the future—a future that held unparalleled opportunities for African Americans. King delivered his "I Have a Dream" speech, one of his most moving and famous orations. The audience at the Lincoln Memorial and those watching the events on television listened intently as King spoke of his dream of a day "when little black boys and black girls will be able to join hands with little white boys and white girls as sisters and brothers." In his passionate and emotional delivery, King asked the entire nation to "let freedom ring."

The largest demonstration for human rights in American history to that point, the March on Washington showed the world that African Americans would not accept second-class citizenship any longer. It also

During the March on Washington for Jobs and Freedom in August 1963, civil rights leader Martin Luther King Jr. (center) is joined by (l-r) Rabbi Joachim Prinz, Eugene Carson Blake, Floyd McKissick, and Matthew Ahmann, among others. ROBERT W. KELLEY/TIME & LIFE PICTURES/GETTY IMAGES.

demonstrated that harmony between the races was possible, with whites and blacks marching, singing, and praying side by side.

Victories mingled with tragedies

While the March on Washington stood out as a high point of the civil rights era, the movement also endured many dark days at that time. Two months before the march, Medgar Evers (1925–1963), the field secretary of the NAACP in Mississippi, had been murdered in his own driveway. Evers's murder, in addition to the troubles in Birmingham, sparked hundreds of protests and riots in towns throughout the South during the summer of 1963. Less than three weeks after the March on Washington, on September 15, a bomb exploded inside Birmingham's Sixteenth Street Baptist Church, a black church. Four black girls, at the church for Sunday school, were killed. Later that day, a black teenage boy was shot and killed by the police, and another teenage boy was murdered by white teenagers who had earlier attended a segregationist rally.

On November 22, 1963, President Kennedy was shot and killed by an assassin. The nation mourned the loss of the young president, and civil rights activists worried about the future. Kennedy had been the first president of the modern era to actively promote civil rights. His successor, Lyndon Baines Johnson (1908–1973; served 1963–69), was a southerner. Black leaders feared that he would be less likely to support the civil rights bill. However, Johnson quieted their fears a few days later when he announced his support for the bill during an address to a joint session of Congress.

Several months later, after intense lobbying from supporters and detractors of the bill and a lively debate in Congress, the bill became law. The Civil Rights Act of 1964 was passed on July 2. It marked the end of Jim Crow segregationist laws, prohibiting racial discrimination in places serving the public, in schools, and in the workplace. The law also banned discrimination based on gender. It established the Equal Employment Opportunity Commission (EEOC), which enforces the law as it relates to employment. The Civil Rights Act of 1964 was the most significant civil rights legislation since the Reconstruction Era after the Civil War.

Freedom Summer

Although the passage of the Civil Rights Act was celebrated by activists, the law failed to guarantee African Americans the right to vote, a freedom that had become the primary focus of the civil rights movement. SNCC and other organizations zeroed in on Mississippi, a state that had rigidly resisted any attempts at desegregation. They sought to raise the number of black voters there. Blacks made up 45 percent of the population in that state, but only 5 percent of the black population was registered to vote in 1960. The state officials were hard-line segregationists, and the state had the highest number of lynchings, beatings, and unexplained disappearances of blacks in the South. Mississippi was the poorest state in the nation, and black residents were the poorest of the poor.

Black and white SNCC workers, many of whom dropped out of college to devote themselves full-time to the movement, had been risking their lives to increase voter registration in Mississippi since 1960. In 1962 SNCC, CORE, SCLC, the NAACP, and several local civil rights groups joined forces to create the Council of Federated Organizations, or

The Life and Death of Medgar Evers

Medgar Evers was born in 1925 in Decatur, Mississippi. As a young child, he quickly became acquainted with the racism and violence that marked the daily lives of blacks in Mississippi. He was taunted by whites on his way to school. He witnessed blacks being harassed by whites on a regular basis. On occasion, Evers even faced the horror of a black person in his community being lynched by white gangs.

After fighting for democracy and freedom abroad as a soldier during World War II, Evers became determined to improve the lives of blacks in the South, particularly in Mississippi. He attended Alcorn A & M (Agricultural and Mechanical) College from 1948 to 1952, becoming increasingly involved at that time with the NAACP. During his senior year, he married Myrlie Beasley.

After graduating from college, Evers began selling insurance. His work took him through many small towns in Mississippi. He became more and more disturbed by the desperate poverty of his fellow black citizens. He quit the insurance business and began working full-time for the NAACP. He was soon promoted to field secretary, coordinating voter registration efforts and following up on reports of anti-black intimidation and violence.

Evers was regarded as a dangerous man by many white Mississippians. The activist and his family received death threats regularly.

Even after his home was bombed, Evers remained dedicated to the cause of civil rights. He was determined to make a better life for his children and all future generations. On June 11, 1963, he returned home late at night from NAACP functions. Evers was shot in the back after getting out of his car. The thirty-seven-year-old civil rights leader died less than an hour later.

Much of the evidence, including fingerprints on the murder weapon, pointed to a white supremacist, someone who believes in the absolute superiority of the white race. The suspect, Byron De La Beckwith (1920–2001), was tried for Evers's murder twice in the months following the crime. Each time, an all-white jury failed to deliver a guilty verdict. At the time, Beckwith was treated with respect and admiration by many white Mississippians, who regarded him as a hero for his actions. Many years later, in 1994, Beckwith was tried a third time for the murder. He was convicted by a racially mixed jury in Mississippi. He went to prison for the remainder of his life, dying in 2001 at the age of eighty.

COFO. The civil rights activists working to register black voters in Mississippi were threatened, beaten, and arrested. At that time, they had very little to show for their efforts. Black voter registration increased by less than 2 percent between 1960 and the summer of 1963.

Although the number of registered voters did not change dramatically, the civil rights workers felt they achieved a great deal in terms of education. Many poor blacks had been denied an education and did not even know they had the right to vote. The civil rights activists spoke to workers in the fields and in the factories, informing them of their rights. They spread the notion that black voters could potentially elect black officials, who could then effect real change in Mississippi.

Activists planned to renew their efforts during the summer of 1964, which came to be known as Freedom Summer. They called for volunteers to travel to Mississippi that summer. Hundreds responded. They knew that their activism came with great personal risk. Many of the volunteers were white, and many came from northeastern upper-middle-class families. Their average age was twenty-one. A primary goal for the summer was to register black voters and prepare them for the upcoming presidential election.

On June 20, the first group of volunteers traveled to Mississippi. The following day, one of the volunteers, a white man named Andrew Goodman, disappeared, along with two CORE workers: Michael Schwerner, a white man, and James Chaney, a black Mississippi native. After driving to the town of Lawndale to investigate the burning of a black church, the three men had been arrested and then later released. Soon after they were let go, they disappeared. When they failed to check in at Freedom Summer headquarters, fellow activists became greatly concerned.

The bodies of Goodman, Schwerner, and Chaney were found later that summer. All three men had been shot, and Chaney had also been brutally beaten. The families wanted the three men to be buried together, but Mississippi officials denied the request. They would only allow Chaney's body to be buried in an all-black cemetery.

The nation was outraged over the murder of the three young men, a detail that many southern blacks attributed to the fact that two of the victims were white. Time and again black people had disappeared and were later found murdered. However, those crimes failed to attract attention or sympathy from the rest of the country. Twenty-one men were eventually arrested in connection with the murder of the three civil rights workers, though the murder charges were later dropped. Twelve of the suspects later faced federal charges of civil rights violation, and seven were convicted.

But the quest to bring the killers to justice did not end. In June 2005 a jury convicted Edgar Ray Killen of manslaughter in the slayings. An ordained minister and a member of the KKK, Killen was in his late thirties when the murders occurred. He had been tried in 1967, but the jury became deadlocked because one juror could not bring herself to convict a minister. At his retrial in 2005, Killen was eighty and suffering from ill health. His conviction occurred forty-one years after the murders of Chaney, Goodman, and Schwerner.

MISSING CALL FBI

THE FBI IS SEEKING INFORMATION CONCERNING THE DISAPPEARANCE AT PHILADELPHIA, MISSISSIPPI, OF THESE THREE INDIVIDUALS ON JUNE 21, 1964. EXTENSIVE INVESTIGATION IS BEING CONDUCTED TO LOCATE GOODMAN, CHANEY, AND SCHWERNER, WHO ARE DESCRIBED AS FOLLOWS:

ANDREW GOODMAN   **JAMES EARL CHANEY**   **MICHAEL HENRY SCHWERNER**

RACE:	White	Negro	White
SEX:	Male	Male	Male
DOB:	November 23, 1943	May 30, 1943	November 6, 1939
POB:	New York City	Meridian, Mississippi	New York City
AGE:	20 years	21 years	24 years
HEIGHT:	5'10"	5'7"	5'9" to 5'10"
WEIGHT:	150 pounds	135 to 140 pounds	170 to 180 pounds
HAIR:	Dark brown; wavy	Black	Brown
EYES:	Brown	Brown	Light blue
TEETH:		Good; none missing	
SCARS AND MARKS:		1 inch cut scar 2 inches above left ear.	Pock mark center of forehead, slight scar on bridge of nose, appendectomy scar, broken leg scar.

SHOULD YOU HAVE OR IN THE FUTURE RECEIVE ANY INFORMATION CONCERNING THE WHEREABOUTS OF THESE INDIVIDUALS, YOU ARE REQUESTED TO NOTIFY ME OR THE NEAREST OFFICE OF THE FBI. TELEPHONE NUMBER IS LISTED BELOW.

DIRECTOR
FEDERAL BUREAU OF INVESTIGATION
UNITED STATES DEPARTMENT OF JUSTICE
WASHINGTON, D. C. 20535
TELEPHONE, NATIONAL 8-7117

June 29, 1964

Following the disappearance of three civil rights workers, the FBI created a missing persons poster in an attempt to learn the whereabouts of Andrew Goodman, James Earl Chaney, and Michael Henry Schwerner in 1964. MPI/GETTY IMAGES.

The Mississippi Freedom Democratic Party In addition to educating African Americans about voter registration, the Freedom Summer volunteers also set up "freedom schools" to educate black children, health clinics to provide free medical advice and care, and legal clinics to help protect the rights of blacks. Volunteers also worked to sign people up as

Native American Civil Rights

Native Americans, a group also known as American Indians, have endured racial prejudice from white Americans for hundreds of years, since the first white settlers arrived in the New World from Europe. Many of these settlers viewed Native American tribes as savage and violent because the Indian way of life was so different from their lifestyle. Settlers used such characterizations to justify waging war with the Indians and taking their land. Native Americans lost many people to wars as well as diseases that were brought to America by the Europeans. They lost their land to settlers who overpowered them with military might.

In many cases, Native American also lost land and power after agreeing to treaties with the U.S. government that were subsequently broken. By the twentieth century, Native Americans were primarily living on reservations, land that had been set aside for them by the government. Poverty, segregation, and discrimination in jobs and housing have been major problems for the various Native American nations throughout the twentieth and into the twenty-first century.

Throughout the 1960s and 1970s, spurred on by the gains of the African American civil rights movement, Native American activists began filing lawsuits. They attempted to retrieve Indian lands that had been taken as a result of treaty violations in previous decades. The American Indian Movement (AIM) formed in 1968 to help protect the rights of Native Americans. That same year, the U.S. Congress passed the American Indian Civil Rights Act, guaranteeing for Native Americans the same rights that all other Americans were entitled to under the Constitution. This law also, however, limited the authority of tribal governments, each of which is considered a sovereign, or self-governing, nation.

Native American civil rights groups, with AIM being the best known and most visible, led a number of militant protest actions throughout the 1970s. These groups often clashed with police just as African American activists had done. A number of AIM members were killed during confrontations with police, and many allege that others were killed under mysterious circumstances.

One of the most notorious actions took place in early 1973. Members of the Oglala Sioux nation (also known as the Lakota) occupied the area known as Wounded Knee with the help of AIM activists. Located on the Pine Ridge Reservation in South Dakota, Wounded Knee was the site of a tragic massacre of Indians by U.S. troops in 1890. In 1973 the Native American occupiers demanded that the government investigate broken treaties and ill treatment of the Oglala Sioux. The government responded by surrounding the area with massive military firepower.

The standoff ended after seventy-one days with the government making promises but ultimately failing to meet the Oglala Sioux's demands. The years following the standoff proved highly volatile, with the U.S. government and Indian tribes intensely distrustful of each other. A firefight between Federal Bureau of Investigation (FBI) agents and residents of the Pine Ridge Reservation led to the controversial arrest of AIM activist Leonard Peltier (1944–) and others for the murder of two agents. The case was hotly debated. Claims were made that those prosecuting Peltier had committed improprieties. The American Indian activist was convicted of the agents' murders and sent to prison for two life sentences. Supporters from around the world have continued to protest his imprisonment.

Although individual protest actions of the Native American civil rights movement were not always successful, taken together these protests raised awareness among Native Americans, Americans of other races and ethnicities, and the U.S. government. Crime, alcoholism, and poverty continue to be significant problems for many Native American nations. However, a number of gains have been made through civil rights laws, victories in court, and the schooling of many Americans on the value and richness of Native American history and culture.

members of the Mississippi Freedom Democratic Party (MFDP). An official, legal political party, it was set up as an alternative to the all-white Democratic party in Mississippi. By the end of the summer, 80,000 African Americans had signed up for the MFDP.

One of MFDP's most visible and inspiring activists was a black woman named Fannie Lou Hamer (1917–1977). The youngest of twenty children, Hamer had worked in the fields alongside her parents from the age of six. She had endured terrible poverty and never received much education. At the age of forty-four, Hamer attended a voter registration meeting held by the SNCC and soon became a full-time activist. She worked tirelessly to register African Americans to vote.

Activists had been campaigning to have delegates from the MFDP replace the white delegates from the Democratic party at the Democratic National Convention in Atlantic City, New Jersey, in August of 1964. Each state would be sending delegates to the party's national convention to determine the Democrats' nominee for president. MFDP members argued that they more accurately represented the people of Mississippi and that their political views were more in line with the national party than the white Mississippi Democrats.

Although the MFDP gained considerable support from Democrats in many states, President Johnson and many other Democrats opposed the idea of MFDP delegates replacing the traditional Democrats at the convention. Eventually the MFDP was offered a compromise: the white Democratic delegates from Mississippi would be seated and have a vote at the convention, while just two MFDP delegates would be allowed to attend but would not be associated with Mississippi. The compromise also stated that in the future, the Mississippi delegation would have to be integrated.

Some in the MFDP urged acceptance of the compromise, but others felt it was an all-or-nothing situation. The differences among members of the party pointed to a growing rift between the civil rights movement's "old guard," represented by Martin Luther King Jr. and the SCLC, and the more aggressive members of SNCC. SCLC members preached patience, insisting that change could only happen slowly. However, SNCC members were tired of waiting and felt ready to demand their rights rather than politely requesting them.

The MFDP lost its bid to gain political strength at the convention, but it did lay the groundwork for the integration of Mississippi's Democratic party. In addition, the many other projects of Freedom Summer continued on. President Johnson provided federal funding for health clinics, schools, nutrition programs, and legal clinics in rural Mississippi. And Johnson's Head Start, the national preschool program for low-income families, evolved from activities begun during Freedom Summer. Perhaps most important, numerous poor blacks developed a sense of empowerment and dignity through their participation in the political process.

A power struggle in Selma

In early 1965 King and the SCLC joined SNCC for a campaign for voting rights in Selma, Alabama. The two groups set out to increase pressure on the federal government to pass a law protecting voting rights for all. They hoped to stage demonstrations, provoke a hostile response from law enforcement, and compel the federal government to step in and make changes. Like many other cities in the Deep South, Selma had a large black population, about 15,000, which was half of the city's total population. Nevertheless, it had very few registered voters. Only 156 blacks were registered to vote in Selma as of 1963. Also like many other southern cities, the law enforcement and political officials were deeply opposed to integration in any form and readily used violence to crush signs of activism.

The Johnson administration had already begun writing legislation that would eliminate obstacles to voting imposed by southern states. However, civil rights activists felt that Johnson was acting too slowly and that voting rights needed to be a higher priority for the president. On January 18, King and the SCLC began conducting marches to the courthouse in an attempt to register voters. The marchers were prevented from registering. A series of marches followed over the next several days, with hundreds of protesters being arrested. King himself was arrested on February 1, an act that guaranteed the national spotlight would remain on Selma. A few days later, the controversial civil rights leader Malcolm X (1925–1965) traveled to Selma to make a speech in support of King. He suggested that white people should be grateful to King for preaching peaceful protest, suggesting that not all civil rights leaders urged their followers to refrain from violence.

In early March, civil rights leaders announced an upcoming march from Selma to Montgomery, the capital of Alabama, to present a list of complaints to the governor. Alabama Governor George Wallace had no intention of receiving this list and tried to prevent the march from taking place. Determined, hundreds of marchers set out for Montgomery on March 7. They marched without being harassed at first. But when they reached the Edmund Pettus Bridge leading out of Selma, they saw the Selma police as well as one hundred state troopers, all decked out in riot gear. The marchers were ordered to disperse. But before they could react, the police were upon them. The activists were attacked with batons, chains, electric cattle prods, and tear gas. Dozens of marchers were injured, some seriously. The entire incident was captured on film by television news reporters. Once again, the nation reacted with shock to the scenes of police brutality directed toward civil rights activists. That day became known as "Bloody Sunday."

On March 9, fifteen hundred marchers again attempted to reach Montgomery. When they arrived at the bridge, a crowd of state troopers awaited them and ordered them to turn around. The marchers sang "We Shall Overcome," the song that had become the anthem of the civil rights movement. King and other leaders knelt in prayer. Then, to the surprise of many, King turned the crowd around and headed back. He wished to avoid further beatings. He felt they had made their point, revealing again that peaceful demonstration was being met with the threat of violence. Many of his followers felt betrayed, however, wondering why King had refused to confront the police. That night, a group of three white ministers who supported the civil rights movement were attacked by white thugs in Selma. One of them, James Reeb, was beaten with a club and later died of his injuries.

A few days later, President Johnson announced at a press conference that he would send a voting rights bill to Congress that would prevent states from restricting a person's right to vote. The following day, a federal judge ruled that the march from Selma to Montgomery could legally take place. Governor Wallace refused to provide the marchers with police protection from angry white mobs. President Johnson stepped in and placed the Alabama National Guard under federal control, ordering the troops to protect the marchers. Johnson also called in two thousand soldiers

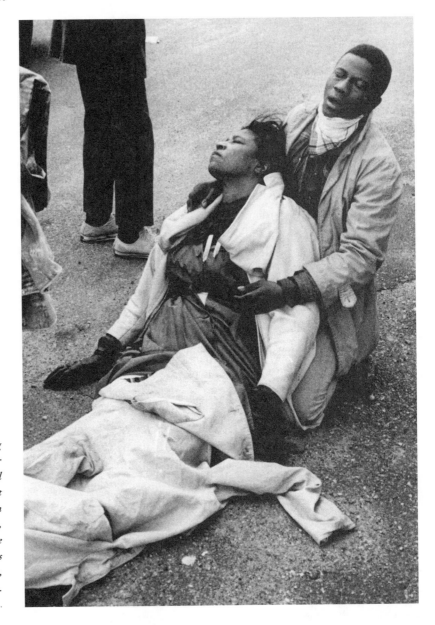

A young man is shown holding an unconscious woman after police broke up a peaceful march for voting rights that began in Selma, Alabama, in March 1965. Police used clubs, whips, and tear gas to stop the marchers. The police actions, as photographed by the media, shocked the nation.
© BETTMANN/CORBIS.

from the U.S. Army as well as hundreds of other federal agents. Some four thousand marchers left Selma on March 25, 1965. Five days and fifty-four miles later, twenty-five thousand people reached Montgomery. A few months later, on August 6, President Johnson signed into law the Voting Rights Act of 1965, outlawing such voting restrictions as poll taxes and literacy tests.

Hispanic American Civil Rights

Hispanic Americans are a large and fast-growing population with roots in one of a number of Spanish-speaking countries, including Spain, Mexico, and many nations in Central and South America and in the Caribbean. The term "Latino," which refers to people from Latin America, is often used instead of "Hispanic." Hispanic America immigrants to the United States, as well as later generations, have endured a great deal of discrimination.

Like African Americans, Hispanics have often been segregated in schools, housing, and other aspects of their lives. They have been denied employment or offered nothing but the most menial, unpleasant jobs. They have suffered higher rates of poverty, joblessness, and imprisonment than the white population.

The Hispanic American civil rights movement was most active during the 1960s and 1970s. An important action in the movement involved the formation of a union of farm laborers in 1962 known as the National Farm Workers Association. The organization later became the United Farm Workers (UFW) in 1966. Led by a charismatic community organizer named César Chávez (1927–1993), the group consisted primarily of Hispanics. In September 1965, the organization began a strike against grape growers. They fought for years for the right to organize as a union and to bargain with growers. The growers fought back, using the court system and violence to limit the strikers' effectiveness.

As the strike continued for months on end with little sign of success, Chávez initiated a boycott of grapes. He persuaded many consumers around the country to boycott grapes grown by targeted companies. Activist groups in many states pressured supermarket chains not to carry grapes that weren't approved by the UFW. The boycott was eventually expanded to cover all table grapes (the type usually bought by consumers) grown in California. After five years of striking and close to three years of the boycott, the grape growers finally gave in. They agreed to the demands of the farm workers. Soon, other growers followed suit, giving farm laborers the same types of workplace rights that other laborers have.

Hispanic American civil rights gained attention during spring 2006, as the U.S. Congress debated a controversial immigration bill. Activists for immigrants' rights, represented in large numbers by Hispanic immigrants from Central and South America, organized national protests. During April, students staged walk-outs while thousands attended marches throughout the country. On May 1, a day to celebrate the achievements of working people, thousands of immigrants, including a significant number of illegal, or undocumented, immigrants in the United States, participated in a one-day boycott to emphasize their importance to the national economy. In many cities, students stayed out of school and others refrained from going to work or spending any money in stores or restaurants. Although the economic impact of the one-day boycott was minimal, the events received tremendous media notice, focusing the nation's attention on the difficulties encountered by immigrants living and working in the country illegally.

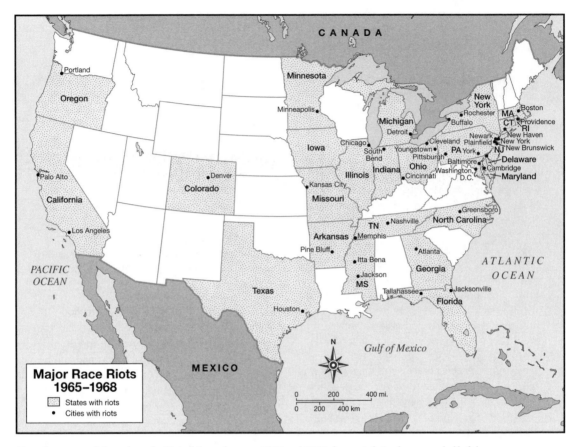

Race riots occurred throughout the United States between 1965 and 1968, but mainly in the eastern half of the country.
THOMSON GALE.

A divided movement

The passage of the Voting Rights Act was a meaningful victory for the civil rights movement. Within months, black voter registration had increased significantly throughout the South. Black voters soon began electing black officials, primarily for local offices. And more and more blacks occupied positions of importance in the federal government. Thurgood Marshall, for example, was appointed the first black justice of the U.S. Supreme Court in 1967.

Legislative victories, however, were not enough to satisfy restless, frustrated urban blacks. While many of the legal methods of discrimination had been prohibited, overwhelming numbers of blacks still suffered from crushing poverty and faced considerable obstacles to jobs, housing, and education. A massive race riot in the Los Angeles neighborhood of

Watts in August 1965 left dozens dead and hundreds injured. Over the next three years, 150 race riots tore apart cities all over the nation.

The leaders of the civil rights movement seemed unsure of how to address the needs of a diverse population of African Americans. The movement became weakened by strong differences of opinion among its leaders. Some continued to advocate nonviolent resistance, while others, like Stokely Carmichael (1941–1998), leader of SNCC from 1966 to 1967, took a more militant stance. He roused crowds with chants of "Black Power." Leaders like King had always worked toward integration. However, a number of younger black community leaders, including Malcolm X and Carmichael, supported separatism, a rejection of white culture and the embrace of African American heritage.

Another development that weakened the civil rights movement was the assassination of some of its most powerful leaders. Malcolm X was gunned down on February 21, 1965, and Martin Luther King Jr. was murdered on April 4, 1968. Without the leadership of these charismatic men, many of their followers drifted away from the cause. In addition, growing opposition to the Vietnam War (1954–75), especially among the nation's youth, drew attention and energy away from African American issues.

A mixed legacy

The civil rights movement unquestionably brought about vast and important changes, particularly in the American South. Over time, the Jim Crow laws were overturned and racially discriminating voting restrictions were prohibited. The lives of many southern blacks changed significantly in the span of a few decades. A major blow was dealt to institutional racism—racism that is woven into the fabric of a government or organization.

Legislation cannot overcome personal racism, however, and outlawing discrimination does not make it disappear. Millions of blacks, particularly in urban areas, remain in ghettoes, poor neighborhoods where residents struggle with inadequate housing and dead-end jobs. Black inmates far outnumber white inmates in the nation's prisons. The United States has yet to achieve the equality and justice envisioned by participants in the civil rights movement. However, the gains of the movement continue to demonstrate the power ordinary people possess in achieving social reform.

For More Information

BOOKS

Andryszewski, Tricia. *The March on Washington 1963: Gathering to Be Heard.* Brookfield, CT: Millbrook Press, 1996.

Dunn, John M. *The Civil Rights Movement.* San Diego, CA: Lucent Books, 1998.

King, Martin Luther, Jr. *Letter from the Birmingham Jail.* San Francisco: Harper San Francisco, 1994.

McKissack, Patricia and Fredrick. *The Civil Rights Movement in America from 1865 to the Present.* Chicago: Children's Press, 1987.

Meltzer, Milton. *There Comes a Time: The Struggle for Civil Rights.* New York: Landmark Books, 2001.

Powledge, Fred. *Free at Last? The Civil Rights Movement and the People Who Made It.* Boston: Little, Brown, 1991.

Stein, R. Conrad. *The Assassination of Martin Luther King Jr.* New York: Children's Press, 1996.

Turck, Mary C. *The Civil Rights Movement for Kids: A History with 21 Activities.* Chicago: Chicago Review Press, 2000.

Wexler, Sanford. *The Civil Rights Movement.* New York: Facts on File, 1999.

Williams, Juan. *Eyes on the Prize: America's Civil Rights Years, 1954–1965.* New York: Viking, 1987.

Winters, Paul A., ed. *The Civil Rights Movement.* San Diego, CA: Greenhaven Press, 2000.

WEB SITES

Birmingham Civil Rights Institute. http://www.bcri.org/index.html (accessed on May 21, 2006).

The History of Jim Crow. http://www.jimcrowhistory.org/home.htm (accessed on May 21, 2006).

"The Martin Luther King Jr. Papers Project." *Stanford University.* http://www.stanford.edu/group/King/mlkpapers/ (accessed on May 21, 2006).

Pearson, Richard. "Former Ala. Gov. George C. Wallace Dies" (September 14, 1998). *Washingtonpost.com.* http://www.washingtonpost.com/wp-srv/politics/daily/sept98/wallace.htm (accessed on May 21, 2006).

We Shall Overcome: Historic Places of the Civil Rights Movement. http://www.cr.nps.gov/nr/travel/civilrights/ (accessed on May 21, 2006).

OTHER SOURCES

Eyes on the Prize. 14 vols. VHS. Turner Home Entertainment, 1995.

The Education Reform Movement

The public school system is a significant part of the American land-scape, an institution that many people take for granted. It's difficult to imagine a time in history when education was a privilege, not a right, a time when only the children of the wealthy received an education. But in the United States as recently as the mid-1800s, the idea of free, publicly funded education for all children was considered extremely radical. Due to the efforts of nineteenth-century reformers such as Horace Mann (1796–1859), the public school system became a reality. Although the American public school system is far from perfect, and undergoes nearly continuous reform, it remains one of the great democratic institutions of the nation. It holds the promise of equal educational opportunity for all children.

The colonial era

During the early years of the American colonial era, the opportunity for education depended primarily on a family's income level and place of residence. Colonial governments did not require any sort of education, and schools existed only in communities where the residents or the local church established them. Some communities valued education more highly than others, offering even poor children the opportunity for some learning.

A thorough education, however, was the privilege of upper-class children, primarily boys, who were sent to private schools in preparation for a university education. Children in private schools were likely to focus on studying the Bible, Latin, English, and Greek. Although some schools only allowed boys to attend, others allowed girls as well. In some communities, boys attended school during the winter, leaving them free to work on family farms during the summer; girls attended school during the summer, allowing them to focus on indoor chores during the winter months.

In many communities, young children whose families could afford to pay modest sums attended "dame schools," which were run by women

WORDS TO KNOW

common school: A public school, free and available to all children; term used during the nineteenth century.

dame school: Schools conducted by women in their homes during the colonial era; also known as "petty schools."

integration: The mixing together of racial or ethnic groups that had formerly been separated.

parochial school: A privately funded religious school.

private school: A school controlled by private agencies and funded through private means,

including student tuition and donations, rather than by the government.

public school: A school supported by taxes that is free and available to all students and run by an elected school board.

secondary school: A school attended between elementary and college.

secular: Not religious.

segregation: The separation of groups based on racial or cultural differences.

in their homes. The students in dame schools memorized Bible passages and learned basic reading, writing, and math skills. In areas that were sparsely populated, including much of the South, families that could afford to educate their children hired tutors to come to their homes. Some sent their children to one-room schoolhouses, where students of all ages learned together. On occasion, privileged children were sent away from home to live at boarding schools and receive a broad education.

Religious groups were instrumental in creating schools in the American colonies. For some children, Sunday school was the only type of education they received. Religion was a prominent subject in the teaching program of nearly every school. Puritan (English Protestant) leaders in colonial America advocated literacy so that all children could read the Bible and keep the devil at bay. Education was highly valued by the Quakers, a Protestant sect that promoted equality and tolerance. The Dutch Reformed Church, along with the Dutch West India Company, opened schools in Dutch communities such as New Amsterdam, which was later renamed New York. Even among the very poor, many children learned to read, tutored by their parents at home, so that they could study the Bible.

Educational opportunities for African American and Native American children were extremely limited. Most schools did not allow white children to be taught together with American Indian and black

Students who attended school in colonial America often were educated in one-room schoolhouses. © BETTMANN/CORBIS.

children. In some communities, however, Quakers and other groups established schools open to all children, or schools specifically for non-white pupils. Many educators who sought to teach Native American and African American children did so because they wanted to convert them to Christianity.

In 1642 Massachusetts passed the first law requiring schooling for every child. The law dictated that every town establish a school. The type of school depended on the town's population and would be funded by the families in that community. In many towns, the citizens believed it was not the government's place to make such laws, and they opted to pay a fine rather than establish a school. The residents of the town of Dedham, Massachusetts, however, took their duty seriously. They set up a school in 1645 that was available for free to all children, making it one of the first public schools in the nation. The following year, in 1646, lawmakers in Virginia voted to set aside public money to establish schools. Such schools, however, were only available to white children.

Young students in the colonial years had minimal school supplies. They were often given hornbooks, which were paddle-shaped pieces of wood with a piece of paper attached. Printed on the paper was usually the alphabet and a religious verse, such as the Lord's Prayer. The paper was covered by a plastic-like transparent sheet made from an animal's horn. Students also learned with the aid of primers, or introductory reading books.

From the late 1600s through the 1700s, many colonial schoolchildren used *The New England Primer* in addition to the Bible. The primer contained lessons on spelling, reading, and religious verses. Students learned primarily by rote, memorizing the verses in their primer and reciting them back for the teacher. The teacher maintained strict discipline in the classroom, using physical punishments, like a rap on the wrist with a ruler, to keep students in line.

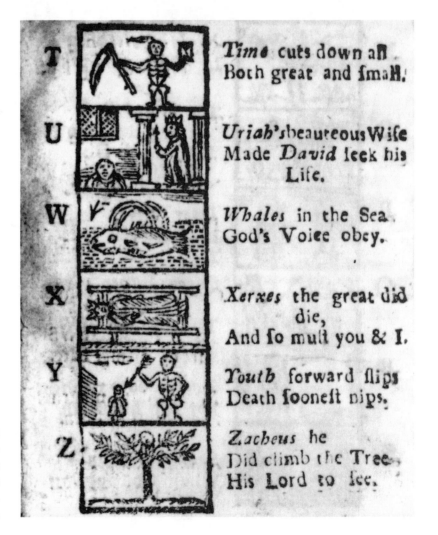

A page from The New England Primer, *a school book used by colonial students, shows pictures and text of an illustrated alphabet, c. 1721.*
THE LIBRARY OF CONGRESS.

A new nation

As the borders of America expanded throughout the 1700s, the needs of its citizens also grew. More and more people felt that a child's education should go beyond religious instruction, reading, and writing. They thought school should include science, mathematics, and other practical subjects. Some citizens went so far as to suggest that Bible study and secular, or non-religious, education should be completely separate. They believed that churches' roles in education should be limited to Sunday school.

During the 1700s, a number of important universities and colleges were founded, including Yale, Princeton, and Columbia. American scholar and statesman Benjamin Franklin (1706–1790) was instrumental in forming the University of Pennsylvania, which became the first American university that was established without a church affiliation and for the express purpose of secular higher education.

Many colonial communities also began to resist British influence on their schools, wishing to forge a unique American identity. Renowned man of letters Noah Webster (1758–1843) played a significant role in that arena, publishing a textbook in 1783 known as *The Blue-back Speller*. This book, widely used and hugely influential for more than a century, helped establish American English as distinct from British English. The *Speller* outlined different spellings and pronunciations for English words. For example, it suggested that "theatre" should be spelled "theater" and "plough" should be spelled "plow." Many years later, Webster published his *American Dictionary of the English Language*. A groundbreaking work, it served as the model for American dictionaries for many generations.

In the aftermath of the American Revolution (1775–83), leaders of the newly established United States promoted the idea of broad education for the nation's citizens, or at least for the white males. During this era, education for African Americans was regarded as unnecessary and, where slaves were concerned, dangerous. Most slave owners believed an education would only make slaves more inclined to rebel or escape. Thus, teaching slaves to read and write was outlawed in many southern states. Many felt the same way about educating girls, though some disagreed, noting that teaching girls was critical in building a strong democracy. Most girls would grow up to be mothers, and mothers were regarded as a great moral and intellectual influence on their children. If mothers were educated and enlightened, they would likely raise educated and democratically inclined children. This would help to strengthen the principles of the new republic.

Using the same argument, America's founding fathers, particularly President Thomas Jefferson (1743–1826; served 1801–09), contended that publicly funded education was a critical part of building and sustaining a democracy. Jefferson pointed out that it was a government's obligation, and in the government's best interest, to produce future generations of educated, enlightened potential leaders and voters. If the people could not read and write, then they could not vote. As a result, the democracy would collapse. Jefferson also explained that a public school system in which local communities maintained control was an excellent way for citizens to practice self-rule.

In 1778 Jefferson proposed to the Virginia Assembly a program offering three years of public school to all children (with the exception of black children). The outstanding male students would then have the opportunity to continue their schooling, eventually earning scholarships to universities. Citizens strongly resisted the idea of publicly funded education, objecting to the increased government involvement and the higher taxes necessary to pay for public schooling. Jefferson's proposal was rejected by the assembly. Jefferson submitted his proposal two more times during the next few decades and each time it failed to pass. Although his efforts did lead to the creation of the University of Virginia and laid the groundwork for future public school systems, Jefferson died several years before public education became a reality.

Growing pains in the early 1800s

The transition to independent nationhood and a new century did not immediately result in changes to the existing methods of educating children. Sophisticated schooling continued to be available only to children of the wealthy at private academies. In some communities, churches sponsored schools, paying part of students' tuition. Charity schools were funded by private donations, offering inexpensive or free education to lower-income families. Conditions in schools other than private academies were usually poor. Class sizes were very large and included students of all ages. Schools struggled to heat the building in winter and to keep the facilities clean. As in earlier generations, Sunday school was the only source of learning for many children. For others, education came in the form of an apprenticeship, a period of learning a particular trade, such as carpentry, from a master of that trade.

During the early decades of the 1800s, dramatic change was brewing in the United States due to the Industrial Revolution, which had started in England in the mid-1700s and had begun trickling into the United States by the late 1700s. The Industrial Revolution was characterized by numerous inventions and innovations that transformed American society from a loosely connected group of agrarian, or farming, states to an economically powerful nation based in urban manufacturing. Abundant factory jobs drew people to cities in the American Northeast, many from nearby family farms and others from European countries. As the cities grew, so did social ills such as poverty, crime, overcrowding, and disease. Searching for solutions to these problems, more and more citizens began calling for a public school system.

Among the most determined supporters of public schools were those most likely to benefit from them: members of the working class. In the absence of free education, the working classes saw a future where they were unable to improve their lives, stuck in low-income jobs and tenement housing while the wealthy few became richer and more powerful. As stated by Leonard Everett Fisher in his *The Schools,* "The result would be a virtual economic slavery that would undermine the course of political freedom envisioned by the Founding Fathers and in the end destroy the very meaning of a free America." For this reason, publicly funded education became one of the major issues of the early labor unions. Workers understood that a just society requires all children to be educated, not just those of the wealthy. As quoted on the *Digital History* Web site, a union organization known as the Philadelphia Workingmen's Committee declared in an 1830 document: "The original element of a despotism [a government possessing absolute power] is a monopoly of talent, which consigns [relegates] the multitude to comparative ignorance, and secures the balance of knowledge on the side of the rich and the rulers."

Working people understood that even free schools might not be accessible to the poorest working families, who needed their children's wages in order to survive. As a solution, some proposed manual labor schools that would combine wage-earning with study, allowing even children from desperately poor families to be educated. For families with children too young to work, a free school system would relieve them of the need to pay someone to care for their children while the parents worked.

Workers, and other citizens as well, argued that public education was an essential tool for competing in an increasingly industrialized world. A

During the Industrial Revolution in the United States, American workers and immigrants flocked to cities in search of factory jobs. Many lived in poverty in tenements and had no opportunities for schooling. Such conditions led reformers to call for a public school system. THE LIBRARY OF CONGRESS.

sophisticated and broad-based school system would produce a more highly skilled workforce. Better schooling would also lead to more inventions and innovations, critical to the continued growth of American manufacturing.

In addition to those in the working class, a number of middle-class citizens also supported the notion of public education. Some advocated universal schooling, or free education for all children, out of a moral obligation to improve others' lives. Many considered it a necessity for imposing control on a rapidly changing nation. With the explosive

Massachusetts: Educational Pioneer

Massachusetts played a critical role in early American history and in many respects led the way in the development of a public school system.

During the early colonial era, Massachusetts was the center of cultural and intellectual activity in the New World. The city of Boston was home to the nation's first secondary school, a private academy known as Boston Latin, which was established by Puritans in 1635. The following year, Harvard College was founded, the first institute of higher education in the colonies. The first class consisted of nine students. In its earliest years, Harvard's mission was to educate graduates of Boston Latin for the ministry. In 1639 the Mather School was founded in Dorchester, becoming the first free American school. In 1642 Massachusetts passed the first law in the colonies mandating that all children be educated. The government gave no indication of how such a task would be accomplished. It only indicated that it was the duty of each town to establish some type of school to be paid for by the families in that community.

Just as it had been during the colonial era, Massachusetts was an education pioneer of the nineteenth century. In 1821 the city of Boston opened the English Classical School (later known as the English School), the nation's first public high school. Unlike the public schools of the modern era, the English School charged tuition. What made it

different from the private academies of that era was that some of its funding came from the government. A few years later, in 1827, Massachusetts passed a law stating that all towns with five hundred or more families had to establish at least two high schools, one for girls and one for boys. In 1837 Mary Lyon (1797–1849) founded Mount Holyoke Seminary, which was not actually a seminary but in fact the first non-religious institute of higher learning created just for women. Forty years later, Helen Magill White (1853–1944), having studied at Boston University, became the first woman in American history to earn a Ph.D.

Much of Massachusetts' prominence as a leader in school reform is due to Horace Mann, the champion of the common, or public, school in the mid-1800s. Mann was a Massachusetts state legislator before becoming the secretary of the state's first board of education in 1837. As part of his campaign to establish quality education for all children, Mann played a key role in the founding of the nation's first teacher training institute, which opened in Lexington in 1839. More than a decade later, in 1852, thanks to Mann's tireless lobbying, Massachusetts became the first state to require every child to get an education. In 1855, the state again became a leader for the nation as the first state to admit all students to public schools, regardless of religion, race, or ethnicity.

population growth in cities, ever-increasing numbers of young people spent their days wandering the streets, looking for ways to fill their time. Public schools would get children off the streets, instilling obedience and discipline. In addition, schools were seen as a valuable tool for dealing with the numerous immigrants moving to

American cities. Enrollment in public school would help immigrants assimilate, or blend into American culture, by teaching them American values and practices.

Some Americans, particularly business owners and other elite members of the upper classes, strongly opposed the idea of a public school system. One reason for this opposition was fear that they would bear an undue burden in the tax-based funding of schools. In addition, they worried that educating the working classes would, in the future, deprive owners of their needed workers. They felt that once all citizens had the opportunity of education, few would choose to perform manual labor. If large numbers from the working classes could rise to the middle class, the social structure on which the wealthy elites had built their fortunes would collapse. Many religious leaders also objected to the establishment of a public school system. They were concerned that such schools would not teach religious doctrine and would reduce the importance of religion in citizens' lives.

Horace Mann and the common-school era

Beginning in the late 1830s, Massachusetts reformer Horace Mann led the charge for the nation's first statewide public-school system. As a member of the Massachusetts state legislature, Mann fought for the separation of church and state. He also worked to make many changes to his state's criminal justice system. He fought for the separation of the mentally ill from general prison populations, abolished the practice of public hangings, and established more appropriate punishments for petty crimes, many of which had formerly been punished by hanging. Mann also addressed the issue of public education, embarking on a lifelong quest to establish free, mandatory schooling for American children. He convinced the Massachusetts legislature to establish a board of education for the purpose of building a statewide school system, the nation's first. In 1837 Mann became the first secretary of Massachusetts' newly formed board of education.

As the head of the board of education, Mann traveled throughout Massachusetts, inspecting schools and persuading the citizens to support public education. Over the course of six years, Mann inspected hundreds of schools. However, his findings troubled him. Many of the schools were in terrible condition, with inadequate lighting and heating, structural problems, and minimal textbooks and other supplies for the students. During his travels, Mann held town meetings to discuss the terrible state

Horace Mann suggested the creation of teacher training schools. Called normal schools, such facilities taught many women how to instruct students. Many of these schools still exist, although their names have changed over the years since they were founded.
THE LIBRARY OF CONGRESS.

of the existing schools and to propose the establishment of a statewide network of free public schools, which he referred to as common schools.

Mann's vision for common schools involved high-quality education with professionally trained teachers. School would be mandatory and free for all children, funded completely by tax dollars. The state board of education would impose standards that all schools in the state would follow, including the use of standardized textbooks. Mann went so far as to outline details of school life such as the use of bells and blackboards, the practice of dividing children by age and ability, and the tradition of midmorning recess for younger students.

Mann encountered strong opposition wherever he went. People resented the idea of the government getting involved in local matters, and they objected intensely to paying higher taxes. Particularly offensive was the notion that even the people who did not have children would have to pay taxes to educate the children of others. Factory owners also protested the loss of child workers, the cheapest segment of their workforce. Parents worried about meeting expenses without their older children's income. Mann ultimately persuaded people that quality education was necessary not only for the welfare of the children but for the survival of democracy in the United States.

Having won the support of the people, Mann went on to victory in the legislature, which dedicated a large sum of money to building a statewide school system. By the early 1850s, the Massachusetts legislature passed a law requiring all children to attend school and also mandated that the school year be at least six months long, the first such laws in the nation. A significant part of Mann's proposal involved teacher training. He obtained funding from the Massachusetts legislature to create the country's first teacher training college, built in Lexington in 1839. Mann's influence extended far beyond Massachusetts. His reports on school reform were widely read in the United States and in other nations as well. He traveled throughout the Northeast to lobby for common schools in those states. His efforts led directly to statewide school systems throughout the region, and his tireless efforts laid the groundwork for the entire nation's public school systems.

Discrimination in common schools Although common schools were to provide a quality education to all children, the reality was that many children were excluded. In the northeastern United States, the number of European immigrants continued to grow. Many from Ireland were Catholic, and they encountered resentment and discrimination from the largely Protestant populations of American cities. Such discrimination was readily apparent in schools and became a particular source of tension in the New York City schools. Education reformers spoke of common schools as nonsectarian, or not favoring one religion or denomination over another. But in practice, New York public schools used the Protestant version of the Bible and Protestant hymn books. In addition, many textbooks contained anti-Irish and anti-Catholic references. In *School: The Story of American Public Education*, historian Carl Kaestle recalled one such offensive reference. It read: "The Irish immigration has emptied out the common sewers of Ireland into our waters." Many teachers encouraged anti-Catholic stereotypes, suggesting that Catholicism was in opposition to democratic values.

In response to such teachings, many Catholic parents in New York prevented their children from attending public schools. Catholic religious and community leaders voiced objections to paying taxes for schools where their children faced discrimination. They demanded that the government designate tax dollars for the construction of Catholic schools. Opponents feared that this demand would soon be echoed by Jewish leaders and by other Christian denominations, resulting in a greatly diminished school fund.

Thus began a debate in New York City about government funding of religious schools that has continued throughout the nation into the twenty-first century. Rather than award each religion its own share of public funding, New York officials made an effort to eliminate anti-Catholic bias in public schools. As a result, more Catholics did enroll in public schools. At the same time, however, the Catholic Church began establishing an extensive system of parochial schools, which are privately funded religious schools. An 1841 New York law officially prohibited all religious teaching in public schools, but the law was widely ignored in classrooms.

In addition to discrimination against Irish immigrants, many non-English-speaking immigrants were treated unfairly or excluded from public schools. Girls also faced discrimination. Many people considered it unnecessary to educate girls. The children most routinely and systematically denied educational opportunities, however, were African Americans. In the South, most black children were slaves, and very few were allowed to learn basic skills like reading and writing. Attending school was not an option. In the free states, black children were either prevented from attending public schools or, in cities like Boston and New York, were sent to all-black schools that were highly inferior to the white schools.

Some black citizens felt that their best option was to improve the quality of black schools. However, most believed that segregation (the separation of the races) was wrong, and that they had to fight for their children to be allowed to enroll in the all-white public schools. In the mid-1840s, one African American parent began a fight with the Boston school district. He wanted his daughter to be able to attend an all-white school near their home rather than travel a great distance to an all-black school. Benjamin Roberts sued the City of Boston and lost, then pleaded his case to the Massachusetts legislature. In 1855 Massachusetts became the first state in the nation to pass a law prohibiting segregation in schools.

Reconstruction and westward expansion

Problems faced by the growing network of public schools soon faded into the background as the nation split in two over the issues of slavery and states' rights. Tensions between the North and South escalated throughout the mid-1800s, culminating in the American Civil War (1861–65). After the war, the federal government began a program known as Reconstruction, designed to rebuild the South and unify the war-torn nation. With the passage of the Thirteenth Amendment to the U.S. Constitution in 1865, slavery was abolished throughout the United States. Constitutional amendments and civil rights acts followed which further expanded the legal rights of African Americans. They were granted citizenship, equal protection under the law, and the right to vote, among other rights.

For a brief period, until the Reconstruction Era (1865–77) ended, African Americans were able to exercise some rights in American society. Finally being able to receive an education was among their most treasured

Slaves in the South were not allowed to attend school or to learn how to read and write. When slaves were freed, schools were established to help African Americans, as shown in this photograph by famed Civil War photographer Mathew Brady. NATIONAL ARCHIVES AND RECORDS ADMINISTRATION (NARA).

goals. For most southern blacks, the post–Civil War period was their first opportunity to attend any kind of school. The Freedman's Bureau, an agency designed to help former slaves find jobs and homes after emancipation, or freedom from slavery, built numerous schools for African American children during Reconstruction. Once Reconstruction had ended, and the federal government no longer had any control in the South, most southern states dramatically cut their education budgets, with black schools hit the hardest. For the next several generations, southern schools were the poorest in the nation, with black schools being deprived the most.

Elsewhere in the nation, public schools experienced tremendous growth in the last decades of the 1800s. While many citizens continued to oppose the practice of taxing all citizens' property to pay for some citizens' children to go to school, more and more cities successfully established public school systems. For many newly established states in the West, education was seen as a critical way to build communities and attract settlers. Government officials saw public schools as an effective way to tame the Wild West, teaching pioneer children proper American values and behavior.

A series of books known as the McGuffey readers played a significant role in that campaign. Used by millions of schoolchildren during the 1800s, the McGuffey readers served as standardized textbooks teaching children how to read, write, and spell. Those textbooks intended for older students also contained instruction in history, science, and philosophy. Equally important to parents and teachers, the McGuffey readers, named for their authors, William Holmes McGuffey (1800–1873) and his brother Alexander (1816–1896), taught religious, patriotic, and moral values. The McGuffey readers, through their teachings about the importance of hard work and the divine blessings of the United States, are credited with spreading the American value system to the entire nation.

To meet the rapidly growing demand, schools in the western states were established quickly, in whatever space was available. Numerous women, trained as teachers in the Northeast, made the long journey west to teach pioneer children. Thanks to the efforts of women's rights advocate Catharine Beecher (1800–1878), teaching had become a respected and popular profession for women. As such, many women felt it was their duty to travel far from home to bring enlightenment to the frontier. The conditions of most of the pioneer schools were shocking to the newly arrived teachers, with some schools little more

Catharine Beecher

Catharine Beecher, a member of a prominent family in nineteenth-century New England, devoted her life to expanding women's rights. She particularly promoted the right of girls to receive a broad education and the right of women to deliver that education as teachers. Beecher's outlook was not radical. She advocated an education for women so that they could excel in their traditional role as wives and mothers, not so they could break free of the barriers that society placed on them. She believed women would be excellent teachers because of their nurturing skills and their ability to serve as moral guides.

Beecher was born in New York in 1800, the eldest of nine children born to Lyman and Roxana Beecher. Lyman Beecher was a well-known and influential minister. Catharine's sister Harriet, writing as Harriet Beecher Stowe, later became famous as the author of Uncle Tom's Cabin, a novel depicting the horrors and humiliation of slavery. The Beecher family moved to Litchfield, Connecticut, in 1809. Catharine Beecher entered a private school for girls, learning about manners and morals as well as painting and music. At the age of sixteen, Beecher had to leave the school when her mother died. She spent the next few years helping to care for her siblings and run the family home.

At the age of eighteen Beecher took a job as a teacher at a private girls' school in New London, Connecticut. In 1824 she opened her own school in Hartford called the Hartford Female Seminary. She rapidly gained a reputation for providing young women with a quality education, a rare experience in that era. Her students studied the usual female topics of morals and religion, but Beecher also featured courses in algebra, chemistry, physics, history, Latin, and other subjects. When her father moved to Cincinnati in 1832, Beecher went with him, opening another school there, the Western Female Institute.

Around that time Beecher had begun a quest to educate women for the teaching profession. She believed it was an appropriate job for respectable women. She also felt women could play an important role in the nation's growth by educating children in the expanding western territories. At her Western Female Institute, Beecher trained women to become teachers, hoping to inspire the founding of numerous teacher training schools.

Beecher's mission to civilize the Wild West and protect the nation from ignorance began to gain widespread support. Her Central Committee for Promoting National Education trained hundreds of women as teachers and sent them west to educate pioneer children. Beecher became a well-known figure, and her fame increased dramatically with the 1841 publication of her book A Treatise on Domestic Economy for the Use of Young Ladies at Home and at School. In this work, Beecher gave practical advice on running a household while also praising the importance of so-called women's work. Her book was extremely popular and only served to increase her influence on American society. Many historians credit Beecher with opening the profession of teaching to women. During her lifetime she brought about a shift in the nation's perceptions, making teaching a respectable option for women.

than shacks hastily built on the prairie. Western society was rougher and less civilized than that of the Northeast, and many of the adults were barely able to read and write. The emergence of women teachers during that era, in the West and elsewhere, changed the tone in American classrooms. As historian Kathryn Kish Sklar stated in *School,* women teachers "created a new ethic in schools . . . in which the teacher cared for the students."

Reforms of the Progressive Era

The Progressive Era, which roughly covers the first three decades of the 1900s, was a period of widespread social activism. The United States had been growing at a rapid rate, both in terms of population increases due to massive numbers of immigrants and in terms of industrial expansion. Reformers, also known as progressives, tackled numerous aspects of society, hoping to improve living and working conditions for all Americans. Some addressed women's rights, others fought against government corruption. Still others sought to improve working conditions in plants and factories. Many progressives devoted their time to helping the poor, while others dedicated themselves to outlawing alcohol. A significant number of reformers addressed the educational system. They used varying approaches and applied different methods, but all sought alternatives to traditional schooling.

One of the goals of reformers was to make sure every child could go to school. A significant number of children in the early twentieth century went to the factory to work each day rather than going to school. Progressives sought to end the practice of child labor and make attendance at school mandatory. Reformers also placed high importance on dealing with the massive influx of immigrants. In the forty years between 1890 and 1930, more than twenty million immigrants from dozens of different countries came to the United States. Most were poor and many could not speak English. The public school system faced a tremendous challenge in trying to educate such a diverse population. In spite of such challenges, the goal for the American school system was a lofty one. Schools were seen as the most effective way to help immigrant children assimilate, learning not just the English language but the American way of life.

During the 1870s, American educator Francis W. Parker (1837–1902), having spent three years in Europe studying educational theory, introduced a radical new method of teaching to the school system in

Quincy, Illinois. Most classrooms at that time were run in a strict, authoritarian fashion, with students learning all subjects by memorizing passages of books and reciting them back. Parker brought an alternative approach that led directly to the progressive education movement of the early 1900s and permanently altered the state of American education. Basing his theories on those he learned in Europe, Parker introduced a style of teaching that relied less on discipline and more on creativity, free expression, and learning through experience.

Known as the Quincy Movement, these methods promoted child-centered education, theorizing that children would learn better if lessons incorporated their experience and interests. Parker's approach met with immediate success. The students thrived and Parker was asked to take the Quincy Movement to the public schools of Boston. Parker also played a significant role in training teachers in his methods. He opened a teacher training school in Chicago that, in 1901, became the School of Education at the University of Chicago.

While Parker laid the foundation for progressive education, renowned educator John Dewey (1859–1952) expanded on Parker's theories and spread them throughout the country. Dewey established the Laboratory School at the University of Chicago in 1896 as a way to implement his theories, many of which echoed those of Parker. Dewey emphasized the notion of school as a means to teach children to be good democratic citizens. He noted that lessons should be tailored to best meet the needs and appeal to the curiosity and interests of each individual. Promoting a hands-on, interactive approach over conventional teaching methods, Dewey believed that going to school should involve far more than sitting at a desk and reciting memorized lessons.

In addition to teaching children the educational basics, Dewey advocated physical exercise and field trips outside the classroom. Many people misinterpreted Dewey's program, believing that he was suggesting a lax, undisciplined environment. But while Dewey rejected the strict control and physical punishments of earlier generations of teachers, he did not support the idea of an uncontrolled classroom. Rather, he believed teachers should closely supervise students, giving them guidance and encouragement.

Another facet of Progressive Era education reforms had less to do with child-centered teaching and more to do with school administration. This group of reformers sought to make school systems more efficient. They centralized school administration and brought in experts to run

Developed to help the military identify potential officer candidates as shown above, IQ tests were later used in schools to measure a child's natural intelligence. © LAKE COUNTY MUSEUM/CORBIS.

schools. A new generation of administrators had been trained to take a scientific approach to managing schools. A commonly held belief among such administrators was that children should be evaluated early on and placed on an educational path appropriate to their intellectual abilities. Those children who performed well in school early on were placed on a scholarly track, headed for high school and college. Those who performed poorly in academics were given what was called vocational education. Such students were placed on an industrial track, taking courses that would teach them a trade or vocation.

To help them determine which track each student should take, administrators turned to a new type of analysis known as "intelligence quotient (IQ)" tests. These tests were developed during World War I (1914–18) to determine which soldiers qualified as officers. After the war, psychologists specializing in education convinced school administrators that the IQ tests would effectively determine the path each child should take in school. Rather than measuring what the children had learned, experts claimed IQ tests measured a child's natural intelligence.

These tests were promoted as the most accurate, efficient, scientific way to determine children's needs and set their course for the future.

Critics warned against relying on IQ tests. They suggested that such tests were slanted in favor of children who had received more opportunities in life. For example, a child whose parents spoke English, were well educated, and had been actively involved in their children's education would score far better than a child whose parents did not speak English and had to work long hours at their jobs. For such reasons, children from low-income minority families generally scored lower on IQ tests. A low IQ score could restrict a child's opportunities for the rest of his or her life. Many educators believed that such tests were another way for society to discriminate against ethnic and racial minorities.

Protests about intelligence testing, however, were largely ignored. Soon, the tests became a regular part of the American education system. IQ tests served as the model for another widely administered exam: the Scholastic Aptitude Test, or SAT. Later known as the Scholastic Assessment Test, the SAT was developed in the 1940s as a screening device for college admissions. The test is still in widespread use today.

Mid-century changes

During the middle of the twentieth century, American schools underwent dramatic changes, many of which stemmed from new laws offering unprecedented educational opportunities. One of the most significant of such laws was the Servicemen's Readjustment Act of 1944, better known as the GI Bill of Rights or, simply, the GI Bill. "GI," which means "government issue," is a term commonly used to refer to any member of the American armed forces. The GI Bill offered all military personnel who had served during World War II (1939–45) federal funds to pay for college tuition, books, and even some living expenses during college.

Numerous veterans took advantage of the GI Bill. Many came from poor families and would not have been able to receive a higher education otherwise. The nation saw these veterans succeed in college, graduate, and secure high-paying jobs. At that point, the notion of college as something reserved for the elite members of society changed. More and more people began to see a college education not only as an attainable goal, but as the necessary path to career success. The GI Bill was eventually expanded to cover all members of the military, whether or not they had served during wartime.

After World War II, the United States became deeply involved in the Cold War (1945–91) with the Soviet Union. It was a conflict marked not by physical battles but by intense political tension and a fierce nuclear arms race. Fear of nuclear warfare and domination by the Communist Soviet Union guided American culture and policy during this era. The education system did not escape this influence. Many people began to feel that U.S. schools needed to improve their academic program in order to compete with Soviet-educated children.

In addition, some educators and citizens had come to believe that progressive education had gone too far, and that American schools had strayed from an emphasis on core subjects. Such critics felt that students needed to spend more time studying math and science and developing critical thinking skills and less time on art, home economics, and hygiene. A 1958 law designated $100 million of federal funds to be spent to improve schools, with a focus on developing more advanced math and science classes to better prepare students for global competition.

Over the course of a few decades, high school attendance had increased dramatically. By mid-century, vast numbers of American students were graduating from high school. According to the *Digest of Education Statistics, 2004,* only 6.4 percent of seventeen-year-olds in the 1899–1900 school year had graduated from high school. That number jumped to 59 percent by 1949–1950. The number would rise even higher, reaching 77.1 percent in 1968–1969.

But while many American children enjoyed expanded educational opportunities, others were being held back by systematic, institutional racism. In the southern states, segregation laws prevented African American children from attending school with white children. Black students were forced to attend all-black schools, most of which were far inferior to white schools in terms of the conditions of the facilities, the available supplies, and the courses offered. With the landmark U.S. Supreme Court decision *Brown v. Board of Education of Topeka, Kansas* in 1954, school segregation was declared illegal. Although the *Brown* decision marked a giant step forward, the battle for truly equal opportunity continued for many decades and had yet to be won at the start of the twenty-first century.

Much of the progress made toward the goal of educational opportunity during the 1960s and beyond was the result of laws passed during the presidency of Lyndon B. Johnson (1908–1973; served 1963–69). Becoming president following the assassination of John F. Kennedy

(1917–1963; served 1961–63), Johnson brought about the passage of a wide-ranging civil rights law initiated by Kennedy. Called the Civil Rights Act of 1964, it allowed for legal fights to be waged against schools that failed to integrate. It also denied federal funds to any institution that practiced racial discrimination. This law forced reluctant school administrators to end discriminatory practices and to offer educational opportunity to all Americans.

Johnson also began a far-reaching program to aid the poor, known as the War on Poverty. He worked to gain passage of several economic bills that had a major impact on education. The Economic Opportunity Act of 1964 created several programs to bring educational opportunities to the disadvantaged. One of the best known and most successful of these programs was Head Start, a federally funded program to offer poor children the advantage of a preschool education. Studies showed that underprivileged children who did not attend preschool before kindergarten lagged behind their more advantaged classmates. Such students did not catch up even with tutoring and other assistance. Experts believed that early intellectual stimulation—such as being read to, playing games, singing songs, and taking field trips—was a critical factor in a child's development. The Head Start program was hugely successful from the beginning and continues to enroll millions of children.

Two 1965 laws further aided the disadvantaged in the quest for an education. The Elementary and Secondary Education Act set aside federal funds for school districts in poverty-stricken areas. The Higher Education Act created a program that offered grants and low-interest loans to help low-income students pay for college tuition. The law also took several steps to improve the quality of teaching, including establishing the National Teacher Corps to train educators working in low-income districts. The Higher Education Act made it possible for millions of low-income young people to attend college. It also benefited colleges by increasing enrollment. In addition, any school that accepted students who had received federal grants or loans was forced to comply with federal anti-discrimination laws. Eager for a larger student body, many colleges accepted federal loan recipients and ended admission policies that discriminated against racial and ethnic minorities and women.

Expanding students' rights

The gains made for African Americans during the civil rights movement of the 1950s and 1960s inspired other minority groups to organize and

Lady Bird Johnson (right) and President Lyndon B. Johnson (center) shake hands with Frank Mansera, a Mexican American boy who participated in the Head Start program in the 1960s. Mansera's mother (third from left) looks on.
© BETTMANN/CORBIS.

protest unfair treatment in areas like the workplace and the schools. Hispanic American students, particularly newcomers to the country who spoke primarily Spanish, experienced widespread discrimination. In many schools, Hispanic students were forbidden to speak Spanish. Even in communities where the vast majority of students were Hispanic, the curriculum offered no information about Hispanic culture and history. Many teachers in such schools sent clear messages to the Hispanic students that little was expected of them academically and that they should give up any hope of going to college.

During the late 1960s, Hispanic American students began to rebel, fed up with being discriminated against by white teachers and white school boards. In numerous schools, the Hispanic students presented a list of demands, including the hiring of some Hispanic teachers, the addition of courses and textbooks that included Hispanic history, and an overall improvement in the selection of courses and the treatment of Hispanic students. In many districts, Hispanic students went on strike, refusing to go to school and conducting protest marches. Such activism helped reshape a number of school districts, opening up opportunities for Hispanic students.

One of the more controversial changes from that period arose from the Bilingual Education Act, part of President Johnson's War on Poverty. Bilingual education meant that some schools would offer courses taught in a language other than English, gradually teaching enough English so that students could take all their classes in that language. The program has been controversial since its beginning, with some critics suggesting that it hurts non-English-speaking students by allowing them to spend years in American public schools without learning English. Advocates of the program say it is invaluable for new immigrants to be able to learn in their native language. They contend that it helps them academically and it shows respect for their culture and ethnicity.

Title IX From the beginning of the nation's history, girls had been discriminated against in schools. As late as the 1970s, institutional discrimination against girls was extremely common and extended from elementary school through the university level and beyond. Textbooks for young children routinely showed starkly different images of boys and girls, as pointed out by Leslie Wolfe in *School:* "Boys were strong, boys were masters, boys were active. Girls were sweet, girls were passive, girls watched, girls helped." In the older grades, girls were discouraged from pursuing advanced classes in math or science and from participating in sports. Girls' athletics programs at junior high and high schools were minimal or nonexistent. Colleges and professional schools, such as law or medical school, could legally reject applicants based on gender. According to *School,* in 1970 less than 1 percent of medical and law degrees were awarded to women, and only 1 percent of high school athletes were girls.

In 1972 the U.S. Congress passed a law that made such discrimination illegal. In that year, a series of amendments to the Elementary and Secondary Education Act of 1965 included one known as Title IX. With the passage of Title IX, schools at all levels that received funding from the federal government were forbidden from excluding or otherwise discriminating against any student based on his or her sex. Athletic programs at all schools, including colleges and universities, must provide equal opportunities to female athletes and equal access to sports facilities. Colleges and professional schools receiving federal funding cannot bar students because of gender, a policy that protects men as well as women. Textbooks that used gender stereotypes or showed gender bias had to be removed from classrooms.

It has taken numerous lawsuits and many years to achieve enforcement of Title IX, and the battle continues today. But such efforts have yielded dramatic changes in educational opportunities for girls. According to the *Title IX* Web site, the number of girls participating in high school athletics jumped from just under 300,000 in 1971 to 1972 to nearly three million in 2000 to 2001. The gains in college athletics have been more modest but are still significant. By the end of the twentieth century the number of women earning undergraduate degrees had risen to become roughly equal to that of men. Women still lagged behind men in earning professional degrees, though far more women received such degrees at the century's end than they had thirty years earlier.

Disabled students

Students with disabilities also derived enormous benefit from civil rights legislation in the 1970s. A 1975 law known as the Education for All Handicapped Children Act, which has since been renamed the Individuals with Disabilities Education Act (IDEA), ordered schools to provide opportunities to mentally and physically disabled students. Prior to the passage of that law, most disabled students either received no education or were sent to residential facilities, many of which were in poor condition. The 1975 law gave disabled children the right to attend public schools and receive special education, a process known as "mainstreaming." The government began providing schools with funding to pay for this program, which included transportation to and from school and structural changes to make schools accessible to those with physical disabilities.

The practice of mainstreaming has been controversial. Critics object to the inclusion of severely disabled students, citing high costs and the inability of teachers to give sufficient attention to nondisabled students. Overall, however, the 1975 law formed the basis for significant improvements in the treatment of the disabled in the United States.

Due to the Individuals with Disabilities Education Act (IDEA), more students with disabilities are able to attend public schools along with their peers. © GABE PALMER/ CORBIS.

A late-century wave of reform

When the U.S. economy took a downward turn during the 1970s, many government officials and business leaders blamed the nation's schools. They believed that standards were too low and that too many students graduated from high school ill-equipped to contribute to the nation's economic growth. In 1983 a panel of experts convened by the U.S. Department of Education delivered a report called "A Nation at Risk." The report, with its strongly worded condemnation of the American public school system, came as a shock to many people. It stated that the educational system was in the midst of a crisis and that the welfare of the nation would be in jeopardy if dramatic reforms were not implemented.

According to the report: "It is important, of course, to recognize that *the average citizen* today is better educated and more knowledgeable than the average citizen of a generation ago—more literate, and exposed to more mathematics, literature, and science. The positive impact of this fact on the well-being of our country and the lives of our people cannot be overstated. Nevertheless, *the average graduate* of our schools and colleges today is not as well-educated as the average graduate of 25 or 35 years ago, when a much smaller proportion of our population completed high school and college. The negative impact of this fact likewise cannot be overstated." The report writers added that "education should be at the top of the Nation's agenda."

Many educational experts, while acknowledging that public schools needed some reform, claimed that "A Nation at Risk" grossly overstated the problem. Such experts noted that, rather than experiencing a sharp decline, American schools had been steadily improving. Nonetheless, the report caught the attention of the American public and had the vigorous support of President Ronald Reagan (1911–2004; served 1981–89). A wave of new school reforms began.

Reformers suggested such changes as lengthening the school day and the school year, raising the standards that students had to meet in order to graduate, assigning more homework, and improving and increasing standardized tests. Ten years after these reforms had been implemented, educators found that academic achievement had improved only minimally. Some said the reforms were ineffective, while others suggested that the reforms were working but other factors combined to bring down the overall level of achievement. Such factors included a rise in the number of poor students during that same ten-year period and the underfunding and overcrowding of schools in poor, usually urban, districts.

School choice During the 1980s, a new approach to fixing the problems of inner-city schools took shape. Many reformers believed that the principles behind a free-market economy could be applied to public school systems: consumers would have the ability to choose the school their children attended, and schools would have to compete with each other to win new students. Supporters of this practice, known as school choice, asserted that poorly performing schools would suffer a drop in enrollment, forcing them to either improve or shut down.

School choice, implemented in many school districts across the nation, has sparked heated debate. Supporters believe that competition is healthy for schools and will ultimately benefit all students. Critics state that school choice can be exercised primarily by white, middle-class families. Disadvantaged families are less able to take advantage of school choice. Therefore the poorest students stay at underperforming schools that have been abandoned by more privileged students. Drops in enrollment mean decreases in government funding. Thus, with a loss of funding, inner-city schools cannot afford to make the necessary improvements.

Some school-choice programs have resulted in noticeable improvements in educational quality. An experiment begun in East Harlem in 1974 resulted in numerous smaller, alternative high schools that achieved significant academic success. The more traditional schools in the district began to improve in order to compete, and the standards of the entire district were lifted. One reason for the success in East Harlem, however, was extra federal funding designed to encourage innovation. Where such funding was unavailable, school choice programs proved less successful. For example, in Minnesota, the first state to offer statewide school choice, the program resulted in little or no improvement in the quality of education and the performance of the students.

The most controversial aspect of school choice has been the movement to offer vouchers for use at private schools. The government gives a fixed dollar amount to a public school for each student attending that school in a given academic year. Many parents have argued that they should be able to use that money to pay for private-school tuition. In 1990, Milwaukee, Wisconsin, became the first city to offer school vouchers. Those who wished to participate in the program received funds that could be applied to the tuition of a nonreligious private school. Opponents expressed concern that a voucher program would drain much-needed funds from public schools, but advocates argued that such a program would, like other school choice programs, force public schools to improve in order to remain competitive. Another criticism of voucher programs concerns the difficulty in determining the quality of education received at private schools, which are not subject to the same oversight as public schools.

In some areas of the country, voucher proponents have pushed to include private religious schools in voucher programs. This proposal has aroused vigorous opposition, with critics asserting that it amounts to the government and taxpayers financially supporting religious institutions, which is a violation of the U.S. Constitution's requirement to keep church and state separate. In spite of strong opposition, some school districts, notably in Cleveland, Ohio, and in Milwaukee, have gone forward with voucher programs for all types of private schools.

Charter schools Another controversial school reform that arose during the 1990s was the establishment of a new type of public school known as the charter school. Charter schools are free and open to all students. They receive per-pupil government funding comparable to a conventional public school. However, charter schools are run not by school boards but by groups of parents or teachers, by organizations, or, in some cases, by private companies. Any group that secures the approval of local or state school officials can open a charter school. That school must then demonstrate within a certain period of time that it has met its goals for academic achievement.

Often, charter schools focus on a particular program or a specific group of students. For example, some charter schools focus on the performing arts, science, or mathematics. Others serve at-risk students who have not functioned well in regular public schools. The first charter school was opened in Minnesota in 1991. In 1997 the U.S. Congress allocated $80 million for the construction of new charter schools. Within seven years, there were more than 3,000 charter schools throughout the nation.

The hope of charter-school supporters, as with other types of school-choice programs, is that offering more options to students will foster healthy competition and improve all public schools, charter and otherwise. Critics raise concerns about the level of quality at some charter schools, which are not subject to the same rigorous oversight as traditional public schools. In addition, as with aspects of school choice, many people fear that charter schools will drain much-needed funds from regular public schools, which still serve the vast majority of American students.

Corporations and schools Beginning in the early 1990s, some troubled school districts have turned to outside help, hiring private companies to

At the Nixyaawii Community School, a charter school on the Umatilla Indian Reservation in Oregon, a Native American language teacher instructs students in 2004. American Indian officials hope that charter schools will keep students in class who have dropped out or lost interest in learning at traditional public schools. AP IMAGES.

manage public schools. Most school districts are operated by school boards, which are composed of elected officials. In a few cases, corporations have taken over administrative duties, accepting as their fee the exact amount the school or district would receive from the government. Such companies assert that they can reduce expenses and streamline procedures so effectively that they can improve academic performance and upgrade school facilities while still making a profit. In 1992 the first of these companies, the Minnesota-based Education Alternatives Inc., or EAI, began operating an elementary school in Dade County, Florida. Soon after, EAI took over the administration of twelve public schools in Baltimore, Maryland, and then the entire district of Hartford, Connecticut.

EAI claimed that it saved money by eliminating waste and requiring contractors, from building maintenance companies to computer manufacturers, to compete for business. EAI also stated that it raised test scores and overall academic performance, though such claims were disputed by local school boards. Critics of EAI pointed out that the company had made cuts in special education and art and music programs. In *School,* Irene Dandridge, former president of the Baltimore Teachers Union, pointed out the basic problem with trying to run public schools for a profit: "There is just not enough money in public school education, particularly in urban centers, to have a profit and a good education, too." The school boards in Dade County, Baltimore, and Hartford all decided to terminate their relationship with EAI.

Aside from experiments with school management companies, many districts have initiated relationships with corporations as a way to boost school funding. As increasing emphasis is placed on standardized test scores, many schools have hired for-profit companies to assist in test preparation by tutoring students. A significant number of schools have accepted equipment from corporations in exchange for distributing certain materials to students. For example, a number of schools beginning in the early 1990s received free televisions, satellite dishes, and other media equipment from a company called Whittle Communications. In exchange, the schools had to broadcast twelve minutes per day of Channel One, a program consisting of ten minutes of news and two minutes of commercials. Numerous parents and educators objected to tax-supported public schools exposing students daily to commercials, many of which advertised products like gum, candy, and unhealthy snacks. Others suggested that such arrangements with corporations allow financially burdened school districts to acquire needed equipment that they otherwise could not afford.

Standardized testing A fundamental part of the education reforms implemented in the late twentieth and early twenty-first centuries was a renewed emphasis on standardized testing as a way of measuring academic achievement. With standardized testing, all students in a given state, or, in some cases, the entire country, are given the exact same test, administered according to strict guidelines. Students had been taking standardized tests for many years, but such exams assumed a position of increasing importance during the 1990s.

In 2002 the No Child Left Behind (NCLB) Act, promoted and signed into law by President George W. Bush (1946–; served 2001–), took standardized testing to a new level. Among other provisions, NCLB

Some education reformers believe the No Child Left Behind Act is geared toward white, middle-class students, putting lower-income minority students, like those pictured here, at a distinct disadvantage when taking the required standardized tests. This includes many immigrant students for whom English is a second language. AP IMAGES.

mandated that each state had to immediately develop grade-appropriate standards for math and reading, with science standards to be developed soon after. To measure the extent to which students meet expectations in reading, math, and science, standardized tests developed by each state must be given to students every year from third grade through eighth grade. The results of the tests are made public, allowing parents to judge the effectiveness of each school in meeting its goals. Schools that fail, over a period of years, to make progress toward the state standards, are in jeopardy of losing funding from the federal government.

From its inception, NCLB has been a controversial law. Supporters describe it as sweeping legislation that finally makes schools responsible for helping every student reach academic goals. They also assert that NCLB gives states and local school districts more freedom to determine how federal funding is spent and gives parents more choices about where to send their children. A growing opposition movement, however, criticizes the increased focus on standardized tests. Proponents assert that such exams are not an accurate reflection of students' academic and intellectual development.

For the affected students, critics note, preparation for the annual standardized tests consumes a significant part of each school year. This means that teachers spend a great deal of time readying students for taking a test rather than exploring the most innovative, effective ways to help each individual learn. Many reformers have also expressed concern that standardized tests reflect a social and cultural bias toward white, middle-class students. In addition, the fact that each state can devise its own standards has raised the question of whether some states might deliberately make standardized tests easier to avoid the risk of losing funding.

Educational experts often disagree on the best methods of reforming the nation's school system, though most do agree that the system is in need of reform. For all of its flaws, however, the American public school system performs an extraordinary function. At the start of the twenty-first century, nearly 90 percent of the nation's children attended public schools. One hundred years earlier, that figure was closer to 50 percent, and most children only stayed in school for an average of five years. And yet, at that time, the public school system was viewed as one of the nation's greatest treasures, offering every child the chance to achieve the American dream.

The present-day American public school system may have disappointed millions of underprivileged and at-risk children. However, it still holds the potential for being an instrument of universal equality and excellence.

For More Information

BOOKS

Fisher, Leonard Everett. *The Schools.* New York: Holiday House, 1983.

Mondale, Sarah, and Sarah B. Patton, eds. *School: The Story of American Public Education.* Boston: Beacon Press, 2001.

Unger, Harlow G. *Encyclopedia of American Education,* 3 vols. New York: Facts on File, 1996.

WEB SITES

"Guided Readings: The Struggle for Public Schools." *Digital History.* http://www.digitalhistory.uh.edu/database/subtitles.cfm?TitleID=23 (accessed on May 23, 2006).

"A Nation at Risk" (April 1983). *U.S. Department of Education.* http://www.ed.gov/pubs/NatAtRisk/risk.html (accessed on May 23, 2006).

National Center for Education Statistics. "High School Graduates Compared with Population 17 Years of Age, by Sex and Control of School: Selected Years, 1869–70 and 2004–05." *Digest of Education Statistics, 2004.* http://nces.ed.gov/programs/digest/d04/tables/dt04_102.asp (accessed on May 23, 2006).

"Overview of No Child Left Behind." *Pennsylvania Department of Education.* http://www.pde.state.pa.us/nclb/cwp/view.asp?a=3&Q=77815&nclbNav=%7C5483%7C (accessed on May 23, 2006).

Title IX. http://www.titleix.info/index.jsp (accessed on May 23, 2006).

The Environmental Movement

Asocial reform movement involves large numbers of ordinary citizens from all walks of life banding together to achieve change and fight injustice. Many reform movements throughout U.S. history have been designed to improve society by aiding one segment of the population. The civil rights movement of the 1950s and 1960s, for example, brought about many legal protections for African Americans. The women's suffrage movement of the late nineteenth and early twentieth centuries secured voting rights for women. The environmental movement, however, has sought to benefit all of humanity by improving and preserving the natural world.

The term "environment" refers to the surroundings of a living being that affect that being's health and survival. Environment includes air, land, water, plants, and animals. The environmental movement has sought to protect the natural world through a number of initiatives, including reducing pollution, conserving natural resources, preventing endangered species from becoming extinct, and shielding natural areas from destruction or overdevelopment.

Like many social reform movements, the environmental movement in the United States does not have a specific start or end date. Debates about environmental concerns like the best methods of farming and the most efficient use of natural resources, among other issues, began early in the country's history and will continue far into the future. Many historians mark the beginning of the environmental movement as a social and political force with the first Earth Day, on April 22, 1970. From the beginning, Earth Day had multiple purposes: a protest against harm done to the environment, a teaching tool, and a celebration of nature, among others. These efforts represent the goals of the entire environmental movement. The movement flourished throughout the 1970s and continued to be an influential force into the twenty-first century. Working to enact changes through laws and court decisions, environmental activists work to change the way people think and behave.

WORDS TO KNOW

biodiversity: The diversity of plant and animal species within an ecosystem. The term also refers to diversity within a species or diversity among a number of different species.

conservation: The protection and managed use of natural resources and wilderness areas.

ecology: The study of the relationship between an organism and the entirety of its surroundings.

ecosystem: A community of plants and animals that live in balance with one another.

environment: The surroundings of a living being that affect that being's health and survival.

extinction: The state of a species that has died out.

food chain: Sequence in which one organism is the food source for the next organism, which is the food source for the next organism in the chain. (Example: grass-rabbit-fox.)

fossil fuels: Energy sources that were formed hundreds of millions of years ago from the fossilized remains of plants and animals.

global warming: Theory that an increase of greenhouse gases in the atmosphere, resulting from pollution, has begun to cause a warming of Earth's climate.

habitat: The natural environment of an animal or plant.

naturalist: A person who studies nature or natural history.

ozone: A form of oxygen; forms a layer in the stratosphere that filters out harmful ultraviolet rays of the sun.

preservation: Safeguarding an area of the natural world from undue human interference.

species: Related organisms that are capable of breeding with one another.

Environmental issues in early America

The earliest debates about the environment in the United States began with the nation's first settlers. When Europeans first arrived on the shores of the New World, they viewed the wilderness of North America as something to be tamed. They had come from older, long-established countries and were a bit overwhelmed by the vastness and the wildness of America. They initially considered the region's natural resources and wildlife to be abundant, even limitless. If they needed wood to build a new town, they cut down an entire forest, confident that their supply of lumber would never run out. If an animal pelt would bring a good price, hunters would kill the animal.

An example of how white settlers viewed the animal population as limitless can be seen in the story of the American buffalo. Mighty herds of the animals once roamed the plains in the West. Many groups of Indians hunted buffalo, using the meat for food and the hides for clothing and shelter. They understood that the buffalo helped them to survive, and

During the 1800s, hunters decimated the buffalo population in the American West, killing the huge animals for their hides. Hunters sold hides for money in places like this in Dodge City, Kansas, where some 40,000 hides are piled high. NATIONAL ARCHIVES AND RECORDS ADMINISTRATION (NARA).

they hunted sparingly. Then white settlers began heading west. Soon, the settlers came to realize that buffalo hides could be turned into quality leather. Thus, a great demand was created for the hides.

According to Alvin M. Josephy Jr. in *500 Nations: An Illustrated History of North American Indians*: "The price of buffalo hides had shot up, and almost overnight the southern plains had filled with hide hunters, killing buffalo by the hundreds of thousands. It was an obscene period. Between 1872 and 1874, the hunters ... slaughtered almost four million of the great beasts." When the hunters killed the buffalo, however, they just skinned the hides, leaving the carcasses to rot in the sun. The slaughter continued into the 1880s, reducing the population from thirty million to about one thousand. The loss of the buffalo had a devastating effect on Native Americans.

Native Americans viewed the land and its resources much differently than the white settlers did. To the Native Americans, the land was their temporary home. It was not something to be conquered or owned. Many tribes used resources wisely, understanding that their survival depended on the survival of the other creatures around them. Laurence Pringle summed up this fundamental difference in *The Environmental Movement: From Its Roots to the Challenges of a New Century.* Native Americans "saw themselves as part of the natural world—nature's partners. Europeans saw themselves as separate and above the natural world—nature's masters."

The notion of taming the wilderness has persisted in the United States. However, some people began to notice early in the nation's history that resources like timber can be depleted if not used wisely. They also recognized that allowing cattle to graze excessively in one area can destroy a grassland. As many early Americans continued to push westward, developing and shaping the land to suit their needs, some citizens expressed a desire to preserve the wilderness. They feared the harmful effects humans could have on the natural world.

Such fears were heightened by reports from travelers who had come from the European continent. These travelers told of landscapes devastated by farming and building, as well as pollution clouding the water and air in the newly industrialized western Europe. They warned Americans to avoid the same fate. Throughout the nineteenth century came the earliest expressions of what would become the environmental movement: concerns about conserving natural resources, preserving and protecting areas of wilderness, and controlling industrial pollution.

A number of visual artists and authors in the nineteenth century called attention to the wonders of nature and the extraordinary beauty of the American landscape. George Catlin (1796–1872) had been trained as a lawyer but abandoned that career to spend his life painting scenes of Native Americans and wildlife in the Midwest and on the western plains. Awed by the magnificence of the western landscapes, Catlin expressed a concern about the preservation of these lands. During a trip to the Dakotas in the 1830s, he suggested the idea of the government setting aside and protecting land for use as a national park. This idea was realized forty years later with the establishment of Yellowstone National Park in Wyoming.

Admiration for the American wilderness was also expressed by artists in the Hudson River School, a group of painters who created landscapes

Artist George Catlin painted scenes of the American West, including this scene of a buffalo hunt. THE LIBRARY OF CONGRESS.

of New York's Hudson River Valley as well as the Catskill and Adirondack Mountains. Many of the Hudson River artists wished to connect natural beauty with godliness. This idea was also expressed in the writings of American poet and philosopher Ralph Waldo Emerson (1803–1882). In his works, he encouraged people to live in harmony with nature. One of Emerson's students, Henry David Thoreau (1817–1862), spent more than two years living alone in a cottage on Walden Pond in Massachusetts. From that experience, Thoreau wrote *Walden; or, Life in the Woods,* a classic of early environmental writing that praised a simple life in true harmony with nature.

The first conservationists

The term "conservationist" refers to a person who wishes to save and protect natural resources or wilderness areas. But conservationists have differed throughout the years over the purposes of such preserved areas.

Some conservationists take a purist approach to the cause, believing that areas of natural beauty should be preserved as they are, with minimal human intervention. These activists believe that such areas should be protected from development by businesses even if they are rich with natural resources that could be used to build homes or produce electricity. Others promote conserving wilderness areas for human recreation, including hiking, boating, fishing, and hunting. Still others believe that protecting nature and promoting business interests can be compatible. For example, humans can develop the land, exploit its resources, and live on it while still conserving it. As long as the land is managed carefully, a policy described as wise use, it can be used for long-term economic gain as well as for human recreation. The tension between these various types of conservationists has continued through the generations.

George Perkins Marsh (1801–1882) was an extremely influential naturalist, lawyer, diplomat, and politician. He was elected to several terms in the U.S. Congress, and he served as an ambassador abroad. Marsh traveled all over the world, and wherever he went he made keen observations of the natural world. In 1864 he published *Man and Nature; or, Physical Geography as Modified by Human Action.* In the work, he warned that abuse of the land could cause permanent damage. Marsh noted the harm caused when humans upset the delicate balance of nature, pointing out, for example, that killing certain insect-eating birds resulted in a huge increase in the numbers of unwanted insects. This idea of the interconnectedness of nature, widely accepted today, was relatively new in Marsh's time. Considered by some to be the father of the modern American conservation movement, Marsh awakened people to the importance of protecting natural resources. Humans will inevitably have an impact on nature, Marsh explained; it's simply a question of whether that impact is positive or negative.

Another critical figure in the early days of the conservation movement was John Muir (1838–1914). Born in Scotland, Muir was raised in an intensely religious household in the United States. He spent most of his adult life traveling through wilderness areas of North America and South America, from Alaska down to the rain forests near the Amazon River. Muir spent many years studying Yosemite Valley in California, theorizing that the towering land forms there had been carved by glaciers. The theory was disputed at the time but has since been supported by much scientific evidence. Muir also made several trips to Alaska to study glaciers, making a significant contribution to the understanding of glacial activity.

President Theodore Roosevelt (left) and John Muir stand on Glacier Point in Yosemite Valley in California. Both men were devoted to preserving natural areas for future generations to enjoy.
NATIONAL ARCHIVES AND RECORDS ADMINISTRATION (NARA).

In the late 1880s, Muir showed a journalist the destruction taking place from sheep grazing and other activities in Yosemite. The series of magazine articles that followed united the public in a call for government protection of the natural beauty of Yosemite. In 1890 that area was designated Yosemite National Park. Muir campaigned for the creation of several other national parks as well. He formed friendships with powerful people, including U.S. President Theodore Roosevelt (1858–1919; served 1901–09), who went on to enact a number of policies protecting American wilderness and wildlife. In 1892 Muir and several colleagues founded the Sierra Club to try to "do something for wildness and make the mountains glad," as quoted on the *Sierra Club* Web site. Muir's numerous books and hundreds of magazine articles have influenced many students of the environment since his day. His work awakened people to the idea of wilderness areas as national treasures that should always be protected.

Like John Muir, George Bird Grinnell (1849–1938) was a naturalist and conservationist who spent much of his life traveling throughout the American West. He devoted many years to studying and spending time with western Native American tribes. He wrote several influential books about these tribes and served as an advocate for Native Americans. Grinnell was an owner and the editor of *Forest and Stream,* a magazine for those who hunted, fished, and loved the great outdoors. After a trip to the Yellowstone area, Grinnell became alarmed at the widespread destruction of game animals there. Thus, he dedicated himself to the issue of wildlife conservation. He also worked to protect bird species, establishing the Audubon Society in 1886. Named for renowned naturalist John James Audubon (1785–1851), the national society struggled financially, but local offshoots flourished. Eventually, the organization became the National Audubon Society in 1905.

Grinnell's concern for wildlife conservation led to his involvement in the formation of the Boone and Crockett Club in 1887. An organization for conservationists and outdoorsmen, the club included Theodore Roosevelt among its ranks. The members of this club wanted to promote certain standards among hunters, limiting the number of animals that could be taken at one time and preventing the wholesale slaughter of wild creatures. They pointed out that unethical hunting practices would drastically reduce the populations of many animals. In addition, these conservationists appreciated the beauty of an untamed landscape and wished to preserve areas of wilderness for future generations. Grinnell played a significant role in the passage of an 1894 law prohibiting the killing of game in national parks. He was also largely responsible for the establishment of Montana's Glacier National Park in 1910. His dedication to the nation's parks was recognized in 1925 when he became president of the National Parks Association.

The conservation president President Theodore Roosevelt loved hunting and camping and cared deeply about preserving areas of wilderness. Known to some as the "conservation president," Roosevelt relied heavily on the counsel of his environmental advisor, Gifford Pinchot (1865–1946). A forestry expert, Pinchot advocated conservation of all natural resources. Both Pinchot and Roosevelt believed that wise use of such resources would benefit citizens, industries, and the environment itself. During his presidency, Roosevelt brought millions of acres of woodlands under the protection of the U.S. Forest Service. In addition, he set up fifty federal wildlife refuges, places where wilderness areas are managed and protected. Wildlife refuges are havens for animals, including many endangered species, and they attract many human visitors as well. In some refuges, people can hunt and fish. Although these activities may seem contradictory to the purpose of a wildlife refuge, hunting and fishing are carefully regulated in these protected areas to avoid excessive damage to animal populations. Many conservationists promote hunting as beneficial to some habitats, helping to keep certain animal populations from growing too large. Allowing hunting in such areas, some argue, helps maintain a healthy wildlife population.

Roosevelt also promoted the passage of the 1906 Antiquities Act and proceeded to stretch that law to protect places of great natural beauty. The Antiquities Act was intended primarily to protect areas of archaeological interest (sites that might yield artifacts from the past) from thieves. But Roosevelt used this law to protect a wide variety of sites. For example, he used the law to designate the Grand Canyon in Arizona and many other sites as national monuments. A number of such monuments were later made into national parks, thereby protecting them from business interests and making them available for the general public to view and enjoy. Roosevelt increased interest in the conservation movement by emphasizing the importance of preserving wilderness areas for the benefit and enjoyment of current and future generations.

Aldo Leopold: wilderness advocate Aldo Leopold (1887–1948), an influential conservationist, helped to introduce to the public the idea of preserving wilderness areas that would be free of human development. These areas would include no roads, no buildings, just natural wilderness. His theories about conservation altered considerably throughout his life. As a young man, Leopold worked for the U.S. Forest Service for many years. Although some national forests were designated as protected wilderness areas, others were set aside for the logging industry or for private ranchers to use as grazing lands for cattle. Leopold initially supported such uses of federal lands. Yet after many years of educating himself about all aspects of the environment, he began to write and speak publicly about a shift in his thinking. He came to support the idea of preserving some wilderness areas not for logging, grazing, or human recreation, but simply as beautiful, untamed wilds. Leopold was a founder of the Wilderness Society (1935), an organization that, years later, was instrumental in the passage of the Wilderness Act of 1964, which in part established such primitive areas.

Leopold also experienced a shift in his beliefs regarding hunting and wildlife conservation. He believed at one time in his life that the populations of certain predatory animals, like wolves, should be minimized so that the populations of their prey, like deer, could flourish. A large deer population, he felt, would be a positive development for hunters. His studies of wildlife led him to dispute such theories, however. He concluded that predators served a useful function, helping to keep a healthy balance in their habitats. For example, without wolves to keep the deer population of a given area in check, the number of deer steadily grew. The deer then had trouble finding enough food to eat, encountering problems like disease and hunger. The deer consumed so much of the plant life in their attempt to survive that other plant-eating animals began to have trouble finding enough to eat.

Leopold helped familiarize people with the term "ecology," in part through his course on wildlife ecology at the University of Wisconsin. Ecology refers to the study of the relationship between an organism and the entirety of its surroundings. In his writings and speeches, Leopold heralded a new direction for the conservation movement. He approached his study of nature from a scientific perspective, helping to attract scientists from various disciplines to the subject. In turn, this helped make the conservation movement more legitimate in the eyes of the general public. *A Sand County Almanac and Sketches Here and There,* a well-known collection of his essays released a year after his death, was a powerful influence on the public's thoughts about the environment. Using sound scientific principles as the basis of his theories, Leopold helped people see that many different facets of the environment are connected to and dependent upon one another.

The movement's early years

After President Roosevelt left office, protection of the environment became a lower priority for the government. The nation's involvement in and recovery from World War I (1914–18) and the Great Depression (1929–41) made environmental protection seem less important to many citizens. Membership in conservation organizations continued to grow, however, and activists continued to fight for protections. A 1934 law required all adult hunters of ducks and other water fowl to purchase a federal duck stamp. The duck stamps served as annual hunting licenses, with 98 percent of the purchase price benefiting national wildlife refuges. The duck stamp program continued into the twenty-first century.

During its first seventy years of existence, the program raised more than $500 million to purchase more than 5 million acres of wildlife habitat. The stamps are bought each year not just by hunters but by art lovers, nature lovers, and others who wish to contribute to the preservation of wildlife areas and wetlands.

The man behind the passage of the duck stamp law, J. N. "Ding" Darling (1876–1962), also made his mark on the conservation movement in other ways. He helped organize local conservation clubs into a group that became the National Wildlife Federation (NWF). In the early twenty-first century, the NWF was the largest environmental organization in the nation, with more than four million members. Some of the members are hunters, but many more are simply people who appreciate and want to protect the natural world.

After World War II (1939–45), the United States entered a period of economic prosperity and rapid progress. Science and technology were revered by Americans, many of whom believed that few challenges existed that could not be addressed by scientific advancements. Automobiles became affordable to a greater number of people. This led to the expansion of the nation's roadways and an increase in demand for gasoline. A postwar baby boom and a surge in immigration meant an explosion in the nation's population. To accommodate the population increase, suburbs expanded rapidly, sprouting up on lands formerly used for farming. More and more products purchased by consumers were disposable rather than reusable, with convenience being the primary goal. By the end of the 1950s, some of the negative effects of these changes became apparent. Citizens became increasingly concerned about the dangers posed to humans by such hazards as air and water pollution.

Silent Spring Several key publications at that time raised awareness of the emerging environmental movement, a movement that had grown out of and expanded upon the older conservation movement. These works were particularly influential among college students, a segment of the population that continued to play a decisive role in the movement throughout the next several decades. One such publication was Leopold's *A Sand County Almanac and Sketches Here and There*. Another was the first ecology textbook, *Fundamentals of Ecology*, published in 1953. The single most influential environmental book released at that time, however, was *Silent Spring*, written by Rachel Carson (1907–1964).

A fogger machine sprays the pesticide DDT through residential streets while people watch from their porches in 1949. At one time, people thought that DDT was not harmful to humans, only to disease-causing insects. THE LIBRARY OF CONGRESS.

Released in 1962, Carson's *Silent Spring* aroused a storm of controversy. She wrote of the harmful effects of long-lasting pesticides, like dichloro-diphenyl-trichloroethane (DDT), which had been used to control pest insects, like mosquitoes and lice, in many countries. Farmers used DDT to control insect damage to their crops. The pesticide was also used in parts of the world where insects spread dangerous diseases, like malaria and typhus. DDT was praised for saving millions of lives and was hailed for its lasting effectiveness. But it remained poisonous long after it had been sprayed.

Carson, an aquatic biologist, had worked for the government and written books about the environment. She became interested in the potential dangers of insecticides after hearing reports of birds and fish being harmed by the chemicals. She researched the subject for several years before publishing *Silent Spring*. Writing in a passionate, poetic style, Carson explained that DDT and other long-lasting pesticides had become part of the food chain. The chemicals, remaining on plants and in water after sprayings, were ingested by small animals, which were then eaten by larger animals, including humans. Carson pointed out that these so-called pesticides killed not only harmful insects like mosquitoes but also creatures that were not pests, such as bees, fish, and birds.

Using such poisons in large quantities without knowing exactly what the long-term effects would be for humans and other animals was foolish, according to Carson. Later discoveries about these ill effects showed that Carson was right to worry. She had expressed concern about DDT's affect on birds' reproductive systems. Other scientists confirmed that exposure to DDT devastated the reproductive abilities of certain birds, particularly those that fed on DDT-infested fish. The toxic chemical weakened their ability to make strong eggshells.

Carson also pointed out that insects developed resistance to many pesticides, which would lead to the ongoing development of ever-stronger chemicals to kill these pests. She suggested that most farmers could apply far less of the pesticides to their crops and still reap the chemicals' benefits. She also promoted the notion of farmers controlling pest insects by introducing their natural enemies, such as birds or other insects, to their fields.

Even before its release, *Silent Spring* drew harsh criticism from several areas. The chemical companies that manufactured pesticides objected for obvious reasons: Carson's claims threatened their profits. Government officials, scientists, professors at agricultural colleges, and public-health officials also criticized Carson's book. She had dared to question the scientific community and raised difficult questions that most people preferred not to confront. Her critics dismissed her book as the work of an alarmist and hysteric. Some observers note that these critiques were likely based on her gender. She was a female scientist working in a profession comprised mainly of men.

Carson wrote *Silent Spring,* as well as her other best-selling books on nature, in a dramatic, even poetic style. Her opponents pointed to this style, and her lack of a Ph.D. degree, as evidence that Carson was not a legitimate scientist. In spite of the opposition to it, *Silent Spring* had a tremendous impact on the general public. Many people began to think for the first time of the potential harm to the environment brought on by chemicals. In addition, many people began to make the link between their own health, and that of future generations, and the health of the natural world. Published at a turbulent time in American history, when unrest existed over the Vietnam War (1954–75), women's rights, and civil

Rachel Carson, the biologist who warned people about the damaging effects of pesticides like DDT, takes children on a walk in the woods near her home to observe nature. ALFRED EISENSTAEDT/TIME & LIFE PICTURES/GETTY IMAGES.

rights for African Americans, *Silent Spring* made a strong impression on the public.

Carson died in 1964, less than two years after her book was released. She did not live to see the significant developments in environmental protection over the following years. These actions included the banning of DDT in the United States in 1972 and the establishment of the federal Environmental Protection Agency in 1970.

Environmental events of the 1960s

Throughout the 1960s, the young environmental movement gained steam, raised up by growing support from the public and several new pro-environment laws. In 1964 Congress passed the Wilderness Act, which is designed in part to protect certain natural areas from the interference of human beings. Designated wilderness areas are free of roads and permanent structures; no cars or other motorized vehicles are allowed. Even bicycles are forbidden. People can walk the trails and camp out within a wilderness area, but the basic idea is for visitors to experience an unspoiled wilderness without leaving any trace of their presence.

In the mid-1960s, a government plan to construct a dam spurred environmentalists to action and infuriated many citizens. In 1966 the Sierra Club waged war with the federal government when it learned about plans to build a dam and flood the Grand Canyon. The government's plan involved the construction of a dam to produce hydroelectric power, electricity generated by the force of flowing water. Under the leadership of executive director David Brower (1912–2000), the Sierra Club ran a series of highly effective full-page advertisements in the *New York Times* protesting these plans. After these advertisements appeared, the Internal Revenue Service (IRS) suspended the Sierra Club's tax-exempt status, which meant that donations to the organization were no longer tax-deductible. Brower felt certain that the Sierra Club's public protests of the government's plans to flood the Grand Canyon had led directly to this suspension, though the government denied it. Rather than discourage donations, however, this move by the IRS had the opposite effect. Membership in the Sierra Club grew rapidly and so did the organization's power. Two years later, the government abandoned its plan to flood the Grand Canyon.

During the 1960s, one issue that came to the forefront of public awareness was overpopulation. Paul Ehrlich, a founder of the organization Zero Population Growth, wrote *The Population Bomb*. In the book, he raised alarm about the rapidly expanding global population. In addition to aggravating problems such as poverty, disease, and homelessness, population explosions also put tremendous stress on the environment. The needs of a growing population—including food, housing, schools, clothing, and other products—would require an increase in construction, an expansion of farmland, and greater production of consumer goods. All of those things have negative consequences for the natural world, including an increase in air and water pollution. A troubling symbol of the nation's polluted waters arose in 1969. At that time, the Cuyahoga River, a tributary of Lake Erie that runs through Cleveland, Ohio, caught fire because it was so polluted by chemicals from nearby industrial plants.

Kids Who Made a Difference

Significant environmental support in the United States and elsewhere has come from young people. Many kids study environmental issues in school and are inspired to become involved in the movement. The book *Acting for Nature: What Young People around the World Have Done to Protect the Environment*, written by Sneed B. Collard III, details the ways kids from all over the world have tackled environmental problems in their communities.

At the age of twelve, Andrew Holleman of Chelmsford, Massachusetts, learned of a developer's plans to build a new neighborhood on the site of a wilderness area near his home. Andrew often visited this area to walk through the woods, fish in the stream, and enjoy the quiet pleasures of nature. He decided to try to do something to stop this new development. He began with a visit to his local library, where he learned of a law in Massachusetts prohibiting development of wetlands. He then discovered that more than half of the future site of this new neighborhood was classified as wetlands. Andrew and others in his community wrote letters to politicians, filed petitions, and alerted the media to the situation. After many months, Andrew's fight had been won. The developer backed out of the plan to develop the wetlands.

In 1992, a toxic spill into the Ebro River in northeastern Spain made the water unusable for humans and deadly for the fish and other creatures living in the water. Two thirteen-year-old girls who lived nearby and loved spending time on the banks of the river felt a sense of mourning for the river. Judith Pérez and Miriam Burgués Flórez decided to take action. They planned a march for their school and another school in a nearby town and set about making posters and devising slogans. As the students concluded their march, they were surprised to be joined by hundreds of parents, teachers, and additional students. The march drew attention from the press, and Judith and Miriam capitalized on that publicity to secure meetings with politicians and other officials. Cleanup of the Ebro began soon afterward. Many of the citizens in the nearby communities had a new appreciation both for the river and for the ability of ordinary citizens to effect change.

The Endangered Species Act One of the most significant issues of the environmental movement has been the fight to protect animal and plant species from becoming extinct. A species is a group of related animals or plants that can breed with one another. Animals from one species cannot mate and produce offspring with animals from a different species. Throughout the history of life on Earth, new species have evolved and many existing species have become extinct, which means that every member of that species has died off. As populations have grown in the United States and humans have taken over more and more territory and industries have expanded, numerous animal and plant species have been rapidly driven to extinction or nearly so.

As residential neighborhoods expand farther and farther out from a city center, animal and plant habitats are destroyed to make way for homes, schools, and businesses. In addition, chemical pollution from such sources as factories and cars has dirtied the air, water, and land. Such pollution not only harms humans but also vast numbers of fish, birds, mammals, and other organisms. Some species, when their habitat is damaged or their food source is diminished, can simply go elsewhere and adapt to the change. Other species require a specific type of environment or food and cannot survive if their habitat is destroyed. Such species face a far greater threat of extinction.

In an attempt to slow down the rate of extinction, Congress passed the Endangered Species Preservation Act in 1966. However, this law only applied to fish and wildlife, and only to species native to the United States. The Endangered Species Conservation Act, passed in 1969, broadened coverage to offer greater protection to larger numbers of animals. The 1969 law, for example, extended protection to crustaceans and mollusks; crustaceans include shrimp and lobster, and mollusks include clams, oysters, and mussels.

Another law passed in 1973, the Endangered Species Act, further strengthened protections for endangered species. The law established two distinct categories for animals in jeopardy: endangered and threatened. According to the Web site of the U.S. Fish and Wildlife Service, the agency that runs the endangered species program, "An 'endangered' species is one that is in danger of extinction throughout all or a significant portion of its range. A 'threatened' species is one that is likely to become endangered in the foreseeable future." In addition, the act broadened coverage to include U.S. and foreign species, as well as all species of animals and plants that had been determined to be threatened or endangered. Although some changes were made to the 1973 law in subsequent years, the basic provisions were still in effect in the early twenty-first century.

The Endangered Species Act protects the listed animals and plants by making it illegal to harm their habitat; to kill, injure, or capture any of them; to buy or sell them; or to transport them across state or national boundaries. In addition, the law requires government agencies to work toward an endangered species' recovery, and it allows federal agencies to acquire land for that purpose. The work of federal agencies, in combination with the efforts of such nongovernmental organizations as the World Wildlife Fund, has had a significant impact on several species. The bald eagle, which is the symbol of the United States, has increased its numbers

The Endangered Species Act protects creatures such as the bald eagle, which was still listed as "threatened" in mid-2006.
ROBERT J. HUFFMAN/FIELD MARK PUBLICATIONS.

in many parts of the United States. It still faces considerable threat due to loss of habitat, but its status has improved from endangered to threatened.

Although the Endangered Species Act has helped many species, it has also been criticized for not doing enough. The process of placing a species on the endangered list is very thorough and therefore takes a long time. Once a species is on the list, it may take additional months or even years to develop a recovery plan. Without such a plan, the fate of the species will not improve. The Endangered Species Act has also been criticized for doing too much, developing protections for a species even when those protections may have a negative impact on the economy of a community. Some people feel that species should only be protected if it can be done without harmful consequences for humans. In other words, if protecting a species means a loss of jobs because a new housing development cannot be built, or a loss of income because people are prevented from fishing in a certain area, then that species should not be protected.

A heated debate has raged over logging of the old-growth forests in the Pacific Northwest, home to many animal and plant species. Some have argued that parts of these forests, which include trees that are several hundred

A Fragile Balance

An ecosystem is a community of plants and animals that live in balance with one another. Examples of an ecosystem are a desert, a pond, or a forest. The balance in an ecosystem can be quite delicate. Changes to the environment, including the introduction or disappearance of a species, can devastate an ecosystem. Within an ecosystem, different plants and animals perform different functions. Scientists don't always know what each species' function is, but they have observed several examples illustrating that when something upsets the balance in an ecosystem, far-reaching and unexpected consequences can develop.

During World War II, for example, brown tree snakes were brought to the island of Guam from the Solomon Islands. The population of these snakes grew quickly, and they ate vast quantities of birds. It wasn't long before they had driven three species of birds into extinction. When the bird population decreased, the insects that had been those birds' food source flourished. The explosive growth of the insect population has resulted in the widespread destruction of plant life on Guam.

An attempt to manipulate an ecosystem in Africa to increase the fish population in a lake backfired. Officials believed that taking Nile crocodiles out of an African lake would result in an increase of fish in that lake for people to eat. To their surprise, they found that the number of edible fish actually began to decrease after the crocodiles were removed. It turned out that when the crocodiles were in the lake, they ate a number of inedible fish, known as "trash" fish. When the crocodiles were gone, the trash fish increased in number and ate tremendous amounts of food fish, leaving less for the people of the region to eat.

Nature is filled with abundant examples of wide-ranging negative consequences for an ecosystem thrown out of balance. Predicting the outcome of a disruption in an ecosystem can be quite difficult. Many environmentalists feel that human beings have an obligation to preserve all that they can in the natural world to help maintain the balance.

---

years old, should be cut down for timber. Others have declared that these old-growth forests are a national treasure. They note that destroying them would result in a great loss for humans as well as cause the devastation of certain species, including the threatened northern spotted owl.

Several amendments have been made to the endangered species law since 1973 that have weakened it, including a provision that allows a special high-level government committee to decide if a particular endangered species should be saved when its protection conflicts with human needs. Many environmentalists worry that such provisions will lead to widespread extinctions, with unforeseen and possibly negative consequences for all living creatures. A number of scientists have pointed out that human beings are part of habitats. Thus, if the soil, water, or air is too polluted for one animal species to thrive, then it most likely is too polluted for humans as well.

Earth Day, 1970

Many people mark the beginning of the environmental movement by the celebration of Earth Day in 1970. That year, and every year since, two Earth Days have been celebrated. One Earth Day, first celebrated on March 21, 1970, was designed to celebrate the wonders of the natural world and warn of abuses to its fragile ecosystems. An ecosystem is a community of plants and animals that live in balance with one another. This Earth Day is generally known as International Earth Day. It is also referred to as the equinoctial Earth Day because it is celebrated on the vernal equinox, the day in March that marks the beginning of spring in the Northern Hemisphere. On that day, the hours of daylight are roughly equal to the hours of darkness. This balance of day and night inspired the organization to plan an annual celebration to focus on the importance of maintaining Earth's delicate balance. In addition, the vernal equinox seemed an appropriate day to celebrate the Earth as spring is a time of rebirth and renewal. International Earth Day was first suggested by activist John McConnell (1915–) in the fall of 1969 in San Francisco, California. McConnell obtained the support of the United Nations (UN), which continues to mark the day each year with the ringing of the UN Peace Bell.

A number of countries as well as several communities in the United States celebrate International Earth Day on the vernal equinox each year. But throughout much of the United States, Earth Day is celebrated annually on April 22. This event originated on April 22, 1970, about a month after McConnell's Earth Day. The April 22 Earth Day was initiated by Gaylord Nelson (1916–2005), a Democratic senator and environmental activist from Wisconsin. From the beginning of his career in the U.S. Senate in the early 1960s, Nelson had worked to bring environmental issues to the top of the national agenda. During 1969 Nelson created a nationwide grassroots event to educate citizens about environmental problems and to celebrate the natural wonders of the planet. April 22 was chosen as the date in part because it coincided with Arbor Day, a tree-planting holiday begun in the late 1800s. In addition, Nelson chose that date because he hoped that college students would play a major role in Earth Day activities. He knew that by April 22, students would be done with spring break and not yet studying for final exams.

Inspired by the success of "teach-ins" conducted primarily by university students across the country to raise opposition to the Vietnam War, Earth Day was planned as a string of events throughout the nation. As quoted in *USA Today*, Nelson stated that he "wanted a demonstration by

President Bill Clinton (left) and Vice President Al Gore remove debris in conjunction with Earth Day in 1996 at C&O Canal in Great Falls, Maryland. AP IMAGES.

so many people that politicians would say, 'Holy cow, people care about this.'" People did care, and some twenty million participants joined in local events to show their concern. Two thousand colleges and universities, about ten thousand primary and secondary schools, and citizens in hundreds of communities across the country held celebrations, demonstrations, educational seminars, and local cleanups of rivers and parks. The U.S. Congress closed for the day so politicians could participate in local events. Earth Day succeeded so well because "it organized itself," Nelson once said according to *USA Today*. "The idea was out there and everybody grabbed it." The widespread citizen participation in Earth Day festivities sent a clear signal to the government: a significant environmental movement had arisen, and the people were demanding change.

The 1970s: The Green Decade

During the 1970s, key changes regarding the environment emerged from the federal government. The gains made by the environmental movement during this period led some to dub the 1970s as the Green Decade. The Environmental Protection Agency (EPA) was established in 1970 to regulate pollution affecting air, water, and land. Before the EPA, no federal agency had existed that could coordinate the nation's approach to cleaning up polluted areas. The EPA was faced with trying to clean up the messes that had been made in generations past as well as setting policy that would make for a cleaner future.

Congress passed a number of significant environmental laws during the 1970s. The Clean Air Act of 1970 called for the EPA to regulate the emission of airborne contaminants. The purpose of the law was to reduce pollutants in the air that could cause harm to human beings and to the environment. Two years later, in 1972, the Federal Water Pollution Control Act was passed. After a number of amendments were added to it in 1977, the law became known as the Clean Water Act. This law required individuals and companies to obtain permits before releasing any pollutants into a body of water. It also placed limits on the amount of toxic substances that could be released into water by plants or factories. The goals of the Clean Water Act included making waterways clean enough for humans to use for recreational activities like swimming and fishing.

Other laws passed during the 1970s attempted to reverse the damage that had been done to the natural world. These laws included regulations on pesticides, noise pollution, and toxic substances. Several new laws in the 1970s offered protections to creatures of the land and sea. The National Parks and Recreation Act of 1978 greatly expanded the land to be preserved as wilderness areas in national parks.

Two major oil shortages in the 1970s contributed to an energy crisis that added a new facet to the emerging environmental movement. Energy required for heating and cooling homes, schools, and businesses accounted for a significant percentage of all the energy consumed in the United States. More and more citizens began focusing on ways to conserve energy. New homes featured better insulation and more energy efficient windows. New appliances boasted greater efficiency as well. As gas prices rose, many drivers began conserving gas by driving less, carpooling or taking mass transit, or investing in a car that could squeeze more miles out of each gallon of gas.

Love Canal Despite the positive steps taken by citizens and lawmakers during the 1970s to protect the environment, a number of alarming incidents occurred during that era. Such happenings reminded Americans that environmental dangers still lurked and that problems remained to be solved.

In 1978 a Niagara Falls, New York, neighborhood known as Love Canal began making headlines for the fight its residents were waging against the government and a large corporation. The neighborhood, including hundreds of homes and an elementary school, had been constructed on top of a former toxic waste dump that had been used by the city of Niagara Falls and by a company called Hooker Chemical. Residents, unaware of the former use of their land, had long noticed the unpleasant smells and unusual substances that occasionally seeped up into their yards and basements. After a local paper reported that the homes and school had been built over a chemical waste site, resident Lois Gibbs began a petition drive in the neighborhood to get the school board to close the elementary school. She believed that the buried chemicals were causing harm to residents. In an essay on the *EnviroArts: Orion Online* Web site, Gibbs recalled going door to door, collecting signatures: "It became apparent, after only a few blocks of door knocking, that the entire neighborhood was sick. Men, women, and children suffered from many conditions—cancer, miscarriages, stillbirths, birth defects, and urinary tract diseases."

Soon the New York Department of Health began to investigate the site. It was determined that 239 families close to the dump site had unsafe levels of chemicals in the air inside their homes and in their yards. Those families were soon evacuated at the government's expense, but the hundreds of remaining residents, farther from the waste site but still in contaminated areas, had to wage a lengthy battle for relocation. Love Canal residents worked together to pressure lawmakers and political candidates, protesting at political conventions, granting interviews to news outlets, and publicly challenging candidates regarding their positions on toxic-waste cleanup. The state and federal governments eventually agreed to relocate all of the Love Canal families and to begin cleaning the site.

A young activist in the Love Canal neighborhood protests the fact that residents' homes were built on the site of a former toxic waste dump—a fact that had not been disclosed to homeowners until after health problems surfaced. AP IMAGES.

The Love Canal disaster prompted the U.S. Congress to pass a law in 1980 known as Superfund, which set up a toxic-waste cleanup program for the nation's most polluted sites. The Superfund law further dictated that the party responsible for the toxic waste had to pay for its cleanup. Based on the Superfund law, the U.S. government sued Hooker

Chemical's parent company, Occidental Chemical Corporation, which eventually was forced to pay the U.S. government more than $125 million for cleanup of the site. Occidental also had to pay nearly $100 million to New York State and $20 million to settle a class-action lawsuit the residents had filed. Although the Superfund law seemed to provide a framework for the nation's worst polluters to pay for toxic-waste cleanup, it has proven to be a law that is difficult to enforce, and therefore has aroused considerable controversy. Loopholes in the law have allowed many corporate polluters to avoid responsibility for cleanup, and many sites remain toxic while complicated court cases go on for extended periods.

Three Mile Island Another incident in the late 1970s served to heighten citizens' anxiety about hazards to their health and that of the environment. It was an accident at the nuclear power plant known as Three Mile Island. Nuclear energy comes from a controlled chain of nuclear reactions, described as such because they take place in the nucleus of an atom. These reactions generate tremendous power and can be an effective energy source as well as an incredibly powerful weapon. The energy generated at nuclear power plants provides massive quantities of electricity, but nuclear reactions also generate a great deal of harmful radioactive waste. People are exposed to small levels of radioactivity in everyday life, from X rays, for example, or microwave ovens, or from naturally occurring radioactivity in Earth's crust. Exposure to significant levels of radioactivity, such as the levels existing in spent nuclear fuel, causes problems for all living beings. Humans exposed to high levels of radiation can develop a number of cancers as well as heart disease and genetic disorders that can then be passed on to future generations.

The radioactive waste generated at nuclear power plants can remain dangerous for time periods ranging from a few days to thousands of years. Such waste must be stored very carefully until it is no longer radioactive. The difficult question of how and where to store this waste has plagued the nuclear energy industry and has worried citizens since the earliest days of nuclear power plants. Another grave concern is the possibility of an accident at a nuclear power plant. One of the primary problems that could result from a malfunction at a nuclear power plant is the release of harmful levels of radiation. Such an incident could have devastating consequences for all organisms within a certain distance of the power plant, and the harmful effects can last for many years.

During the 1970s, nuclear energy was championed by some as the solution to the nation's energy problems. Advocates praised nuclear energy because it was abundant and could potentially be produced inexpensively. Only after the incident at Three Mile Island did concerns about the safety of nuclear power become widespread. Early in the morning on March 28, 1979, a series of problems, including worker error, design flaws, and equipment malfunction, occurred at the Three Mile Island nuclear power plant near Harrisburg, Pennsylvania. The result was a partial meltdown of the core of the nuclear reactor and the release of massive quantities of radioactive waste into the containment building, a thick-walled structure that housed the reactor and was designed to hold in any leaked waste.

As government officials and the company that operated the plant investigated the extent of the problem, nearby residents lived in fear that the accident would lead to disaster. After a few days, the problems at the plant were brought under control, though citizens learned that some radiation had escaped into the atmosphere. No deaths were directly attributed to the Three Mile Island incident, but some reports have shown a higher rate of cancer among residents living close to the plant. The unit where the accident occurred was permanently shut down, and much of the leaked radioactive waste was removed for storage elsewhere. Cleanup of the site officially ended in 1993, with the total cost adding up to almost one billion dollars.

Although the Three Mile Island incident was not nearly as disastrous as it could have been, it did have a chilling effect on the nation. In addition, public support for nuclear power dropped dramatically. The government instituted a long list of improvements designed to heighten the safety of nuclear power plants and the effectiveness of plant workers. These changes made nuclear power safer, but they also increased the cost of constructing new plants. In addition, attempts to build new plants met with stiff opposition from local residents fearful of another accident. As a result, no new nuclear power plants have been authorized for construction since the Three Mile Island incident.

Complexities of the late twentieth and early twenty-first centuries

The 1970s saw an abundance of environmental laws and massive growth of the environmental movement. Every initiative undertaken by the movement, however, was fought by corporations seeking to protect their business interests. Improving the air and water quality meant that a number of industries had to spend money to reduce their polluted waste. Saving endangered species sometimes meant that a strip mall or housing project could not be built, or that the logging industry had to cut down fewer trees. During the 1980s and 1990s, big business exerted ever greater pressure on the government to loosen environmental regulations. At the same time, as scientists grew increasingly knowledgeable about global environmental problems, new issues surfaced that many experts felt severely threatened the health of the planet. The American environmental movement faced tremendous challenges, including educating the public about complex scientific theories, seeking cooperation across international borders to solve global environmental problems, and facing down the pressures of large corporations and, in some cases, a government opposing their efforts.

In the 1980s President Ronald Reagan (1911–2004; served 1981–89) generally sided with big business on environmental issues, believing that the government should impose fewer regulations on corporations. During his time in office, Reagan presided over budget cuts for environmental research and the EPA, and he worked to minimize antipollution restrictions for industry. The Reagan administration favored the use of public lands for logging or mining rather than preserving such land as wilderness areas. Disturbed by the government's policies, millions of citizens became active in the environmental movement, swelling the ranks of numerous organizations. Increased participation in the environmental movement helped to show lawmakers that many citizens took such issues very seriously. However, opposition to environmental initiatives was strong enough that accomplishments came about only after a long struggle.

Acid rain One of the significant issues that became the subject of much debate in the 1980s was acid rain. Back in the 1950s, scientists had discovered that, in some regions, the surfaces of some buildings and statues were being eroded by air pollutants. In addition, certain bodies of water had been affected by these pollutants, causing the deaths of fish and other water creatures. They traced these problems to a higher-than-usual level of acid in the rain falling in these areas. Rainwater is normally slightly acidic. But experts learned that air pollution, primarily sulfur dioxide from coal-burning power plants and secondarily nitrogen oxides from car exhaust, resulted in unhealthy levels of acid in precipitation, including rain, sleet, snow, and fog. Acid can also appear in the atmosphere in "dry" form, in gases and dust.

Whether wet or dry, acid can be carried great distances by the wind. In the United States, the prevailing winds move from west to east, resulting in a far greater concentration of acid rain in the northeastern

Greenscamming and Other Deceptions

As more and more people began to identify with the goals of the environmental movement in the 1980s and 1990s, many businesses developed creative ways to improve their image or to trick the public into thinking they supported environmental causes. A number of businesses that have been under fire for pollution or other harmful activities have hired public-relations firms to help them craft an environmentally friendly appearance. Such companies spend a great deal of money on advertising and marketing campaigns that emphasize minor concessions they have made to the environmental cause. For example, they might print materials on recycled paper, while ignoring major violations, such as dumping toxic waste. This tactic is known as greenwashing, after the term "whitewash," which refers to covering up something unpleasant.

Another tactic commonly used by anti-environmentalists is to create an organization with a name that sounds environmentally friendly but is actually opposed to environmental policies. This approach is known as greenscamming. These organizations sometimes choose a name or logo very similar to that of an established environmental group to create confusion. Such names are intended to sound like the name of a group that would promote conservation or perhaps wildlife protection. Instead, such organizations are often politically conservative groups designed in part to weaken endangered species or other environmental laws.

In his book *The Environmental Movement*, Laurence Pringle describes a type of greenscamming known as astroturf, a name taken from the artificial grass used in sports arenas. This term refers to groups that pretend to be grassroots organizations, meaning their members are ordinary citizens. In fact such groups are composed of powerful lobbyists or business executives with an anti-environmental agenda. For example, a group in the early 1990s called People for the West! sought to make more public land, such as parks, available for mining or for grazing livestock. Pringle points out that, in 1992, twelve of the organization's thirteen directors were executives in the mining industry.

The term "greenscamming" also refers to politicians who present themselves as pro-environment during election season (by participating in a local cleanup, for example, or distributing campaign literature touting the importance of protecting the environment) and then vote to weaken environmental laws once in office. Some anti-environmental businesses promote a green-friendly image by donating money to a local community project or to an environmental group. Such money is considered well spent if it convinces the public that this company helps to protect the natural world.

As schools have increased environmental education programs, businesses have sought to counteract these programs by distributing their own materials to students. Oil companies, electric utilities, and chemical companies are among many industries that have created programs for schools that deliver information about an environmental topic from the perspective of that industry. Such materials are offered free of charge, a gift few public schools would turn down. Consumers Union, the publisher of *Consumer Reports* magazine, examined more than one hundred examples of corporate-created materials. Pringle wrote of the results of this study, which found that "about 80 percent contained blatant bias [obvious prejudice], commercial pitches, inaccuracies, or often all three."

states. Densely populated areas were also affected due to the high number of cars being driven there. In some high-elevation areas in the Northeast, the acid content of lakes and ponds rose dangerously. Many aquatic creatures and plants did not survive, causing a subsequent decline in the wildlife that fed on those organisms. Forests were affected as well, with many trees dying or unable to reproduce.

During the 1980s, environmental groups as well as some local and state governments pushed for pollution controls that would reduce the acid levels in rainwater. They met with considerable opposition by several industries, including coal-mining companies, utility corporations that burned coal to produce electricity, and car manufacturers. Such opponents claimed that not enough was known about the causes of acid rain to begin solving the problem. An additional complication to reducing acid rain was the regional nature of the problem. Some areas of the United States were heavily affected while others were not. In some cases, the industries producing the most pollution were not located in the regions most affected, and those industries were reluctant to pay to resolve a problem in another locale.

After many years of pressure on both sides, lawmakers amended the Clean Air Act in 1990, forcing industries to reduce emissions of pollutants such as sulfur dioxide. With the help of the Environmental Defense Fund and other organizations, a number of creative solutions were devised to help companies reduce harmful pollutants without excessive cost. Within a few years, sulfur dioxide emissions were reduced, though emissions of nitrogen oxides continued to pose a problem. Newer car models emit fewer pollutants, however, and as time goes by, fewer and fewer older models are on the roads. Acid rain continues to be an issue, but it has been surpassed in the public awareness by other pressing environmental hazards.

Ozone depletion Among the most widely debated environmental issues in the late twentieth and early twenty-first centuries has been the depletion of the ozone layer. A thin layer of ozone is concentrated in the stratosphere, about twelve to twenty miles above Earth's surface. Ozone, which is a form of oxygen, performs an important function by filtering out harmful ultraviolet rays from the sun. Without the ozone layer, radiation from the sun would make life on Earth an impossibility.

During the 1970s, scientists discovered that, in some parts of the world, the ozone layer had begun to thin. They suspected this thinning might be the result of emissions from human activity, and two American

Although environmental activists warn of the dangers of air pollution, not all pollutants are preventable and caused by humans. For example, when Mount St. Helens started to erupt again in 2004, it became Washington State's biggest source of air pollution, sending sulfur dioxide into the air and contributing to acid rain. Such pollutants also cause hazy skies, making breathing difficult for some people. © DOUG BEGHTEL/THE OREGONIAN/CORBIS.

chemists, F. Sherwood Rowland (1927–) and Mario Molina (1943–), theorized that a chemical compound known as chlorofluorocarbons, or CFCs, could be the culprit. CFCs were used in a number of products, from aerosol spray cans to styrofoam to refrigerators and air conditioners. Rowland and Molina showed that CFCs could be broken down by ultraviolet light, an action that released chlorine. Chlorine would then destroy ozone molecules. Furthermore, it was determined that the CFCs that had been released into the air stayed in the stratosphere for as long as one hundred years, with the total amount building up year after year.

More and more scientists supported Rowland and Molina's theory, and activists began pressuring the U.S. government to ban the use of CFCs. In 1985 scientists discovered an alarming thinning of the ozone, or an ozone hole, as it's commonly called, over Antarctica, indicating that the ozone layer was depleting faster than originally calculated. Depletion of the ozone layer, by allowing greater amounts of ultraviolet light to reach Earth's surface, leads to an increase in skin cancer, immune system problems, and cataracts, which are vision-obscuring films that cover the lens of the eye. Scientists have warned that ultraviolet rays can cause significant damage to other life forms as well.

In spite of vigorous protests from CFC-producing industries, 150 nations eventually signed the Montreal Protocol, which called for CFCs to be gradually phased out. Ozone depletion continued throughout the 1990s, though scientists expected the dramatic reduction in the use of CFCs worldwide to slow down the depletion rate considerably.

Global warming Perhaps the most controversial and hotly debated environmental issue of the late twentieth and early twenty-first centuries is global warming. The scientific theory behind global warming states that an atmospheric increase of certain gases that result from human activity—like carbon dioxide, methane, and CFCs—has begun to cause a warming of Earth's climate. The sun's rays heat Earth's surface, and then that heat is radiated back into the atmosphere. Certain trace gases in the atmosphere, known as greenhouse gases, trap the energy from that heat and warm the atmosphere. Several greenhouse gases, like water vapor and carbon dioxide, occur naturally; others have been generated or markedly increased by human activity. The burning of coal, oil, wood, and natural gas adds massive quantities of carbon dioxide to the atmosphere. The fueling of cars, trucks, and jets; the operation of manufacturing plants; and the logging of forests all result in increases in carbon dioxide and other greenhouse gases.

Most scientists believe that the increased presence of greenhouse gases will lead to a small but significant climate change. Even a slight change in Earth's average temperatures can have a far-reaching impact. Sea levels around the world have risen over the past half-century, and further increases in temperature could cause a greater rise, resulting in the flooding of coastal regions. Many scientists point to global warming as the cause of an increase in the number and severity of hazardous weather events like hurricanes, tornadoes, and floods. Some regions might benefit from higher temperatures, while others would suffer from excessive heat and drought. Global warming's long-term effects on Earth's ecosystems are not yet known, though scientists generally agree that it would benefit all life on Earth to slow down the current pace of global warming.

Forest fires release CO_2 into the atmosphere, which contributes to greenhouse gases. Some scientists are concerned that global warming could lead to more forest fires as the climate warms and areas become drier than normal. © 2004 KATHLEEN J. EDGAR.

Industries responsible for the production of greenhouse gases have waged a public-relations war against prevailing theories on global warming. They have hired their own scientists to dispute the generally accepted evidence of the rate of climate change, causing confusion for the general public about whether global warming is an issue at all. Most scientists do believe that the rate of temperature change is a cause for alarm. A number of nations around the globe have agreed, banding together to sign the Kyoto Protocol in 1997. This agreement calls for all participating nations to cut their hazardous emissions gradually over the course of several years. President George W. Bush (1946–; served 2001–) announced his opposition to the Kyoto Protocol after becoming president in 2001. President Bush stated that he opposed the protocol because he felt it was a flawed agreement, but his administration failed to present an alternative. The United States is the leading source of carbon dioxide emissions, accounting for approximately 25 percent of the total.

Fossil fuels One proposed way to decrease greenhouse gases and other harmful emissions is to reduce the world's dependence on fossil fuels, which include coal, natural gas, and oil. Fossil fuels provide about 90 percent of all commercial energy used throughout the world. These energy sources are used for fueling cars, trucks, and airplanes; for heating and cooling homes; and for providing power to homes, businesses, and factories. These energy sources are called fossil fuels because they were formed millions of years ago from the fossilized remains of plants and animals.

One of the primary concerns regarding fossil fuels is that there is a limited supply of each: once they have been used up, they are gone forever. In addition, fossil fuels are connected to serious environmental problems. Mining for coal can have a devastating impact on the landscape, leaving scars like deep holes and mountains with their tops shaved off. Coal mining also produces toxic waste that pollutes waterways. And the burning of coal, primarily used to produce electricity, releases massive amounts of harmful gases, like carbon dioxide and carbon monoxide, as well as toxic metals, like mercury, into the atmosphere. Mercury can collect in water, build up in fish, and cause serious health problems in animals all the way up the food chain, including humans. Burning coal also releases large amounts of radioactive elements into the atmosphere.

Drilling for oil can cause damage to land and ocean habitats. The main concerns about oil, however, come from the dangers of transporting it and the harmful effects of burning its by-products, primarily gasoline. High-profile oil spills have illustrated the massive damage that oil can cause to wildlife and to entire ecosystems. And the harmful emissions from gas-burning engines of cars and trucks constitute the largest source of air pollution in U.S. cities. Natural gas, while generating fewer harmful emissions when burned, poses problems similar to that of oil. Drilling for natural gas can be destructive to wildlife habitats, and burning natural gas results in emissions of carbon dioxide, carbon monoxide, and methane.

***The Exxon Valdez* oil spill** A number of major oil spills have devastated waterways and shores throughout the world. One of the most infamous oil spills took place on March 24, 1989, when the *Exxon Valdez* oil tanker collided with Bligh Reef in Alaska's Prince William Sound. Part of the Gulf of Alaska, Prince William Sound is an area of extraordinary natural beauty. The rich wildlife of the area includes numerous shore birds, fish, whales, and sea otters.

The Exxon Valdex *oil spill in 1989 caused massive destruction to the environment. Here, rescue workers try to save sea otters, covered in oil, from the contaminated waters of Prince William Sound.* © BETTMANN/CORBIS.

When the *Exxon Valdez* grounded on the reef, oil began spilling into the waters of the sound immediately. A total of eleven million gallons poured into the water. Early attempts at cleaning up the oil were slow and inefficient, and the oil slick continued to spread. Within a few days, the oil covered an area of five hundred square miles. Worse, a storm on the night of March 26 brought oil onto the shores and mixed the oil with water, causing a mixture that is much harder to clean. By the end of June, the slick covered nearly six thousand square miles.

The effects of the oil spill on wildlife were severe. Spring is the time of year when migratory birds return to Prince William Sound, and each day for weeks after the spill, thousands of birds arrived. The best efforts of volunteers could not stop the birds from landing in the oil-covered water, where their feathers became covered with oil. Once that happened, the birds could no longer fly and became vulnerable to predators. Swallowing the toxic oil also proved deadly to the creatures of the sound. The sea otters, which had once been close to extinction but had bounced back through preservation efforts, died in large numbers. Volunteers worked around the clock trying to rescue and clean affected animals, but they could only save a small fraction. Hundreds of thousands of birds died, including close to two hundred bald eagles. More than five thousand sea otters and hundreds of harbor seals also died.

After years of court battles, Exxon was ordered to pay several billion dollars for the cleanup and as a settlement for residents affected by the spill. The captain of the ship, Joseph Hazelwood, is believed by many to have been negligent the night of the spill, in large part because he left control of the ship in the hands of other officers rather than overseeing the navigation through the sound himself. He also tested positive for alcohol hours after the incident.

To the naked eye in the early twenty-first century, the waters of Prince Island Sound and the shores around it no longer showed the mark of the millions of gallons of oil spilled there in 1989. But scientists believed some areas remained contaminated. Of the dozens of wildlife species damaged by oil, several remained diminished in number following the devastation of the *Exxon Valdez* spill.

Renewable energy sources Many environmental activists and scientists have spent years exploring and promoting alternative and renewable energy sources, including harnessing wind, water, the heat of the sun, and the heat at Earth's core to produce electricity and other types of power. The power generated by the sun is called solar energy, while the power generated by Earth's core is called geothermal energy.

Another significant potential source of renewable energy is biomass, which refers to all organic material. Biomass includes plants and animals as well as products that come from these organisms, such as wood from a tree, or waste from an animal. Biomass contains energy that can be released through burning, like the heat that comes from burning wood, or through other methods. Plant crops such as corn and sugar cane, for example, can be processed and fermented to produce ethanol, a fuel that can be mixed with gasoline or used on its own to power car engines. Ethanol burns more cleanly than gasoline, emitting fewer harmful air pollutants. Another alternative fuel derived from biomass is biodiesel, which can be made from plant oils or animal fats. Biodiesel can even be made from recycled grease used to fry foods at restaurants. Any diesel engine, such as those in buses, large trucks, and many boats, can run on biodiesel, which is often blended with petroleum diesel. Like ethanol, biodiesel is cleaner than petroleum-based fuel, releasing fewer emissions that are harmful to humans and that contribute to global warming.

Even trash can be used to generate power. Some power plants, known as waste-to-energy plants, burn trash to create steam, which can then be used to produce electricity or heat for buildings. In addition, organic trash, including lawn clippings, food scraps, and animal waste, produces methane gas as it rots. That methane gas can be collected and used for energy production rather than being released into the atmosphere, where it acts as a greenhouse gas and contributes to global warming. Another potential renewable energy source involves the use of hydrogen, an element that exists in great abundance in the air and in water. Scientists continue to explore safe and cost-effective ways to convert hydrogen into fuel because burning hydrogen produces far fewer pollutants than burning other types of fuel. Often, renewable energy sources have proven to be more expensive or difficult to harness than the energy from fossil fuels, but many experts believe the limitations and dangers of fossil fuels make the use of alternatives essential.

Biodiversity Many environmentalists feel that the most pressing concern at the start of the twenty-first century is not global warming but the loss of biodiversity. Biodiversity refers to the richness of plant and animal species within an ecosystem. The term also refers to diversity within a species, or diversity among a number of different species. As the world's population continues to expand, bringing with it new homes, buildings, roads, and communities, wildlife habitats are increasingly threatened. Plant and animal species are being driven into extinction at a rapid rate, and the extinction of one species in an ecosystem can have a drastic impact on the remaining species. The irreversible nature of extinction, and the unknown effect an extinction can have on other species, has led many environmentalists to place preservation of habitat, and therefore of biodiversity, at the top of their agenda for change. The more diverse an ecosystem or a species is, the more stable it is and the greater its chances for survival.

Environmental activist Julia Butterfly Hill lived in a one-thousand-year-old Redwood tree in an effort to save it from loggers. ACEY HARPER/TIME LIFE PICTURES/GETTY IMAGES.

The many faces of the environmental movement

From its earliest days, one segment of the environmental movement has captured a great deal of publicity and attention: the radical wing. Some environmental organizations have taken an extreme approach to the issues, favoring direct confrontation with opponents as a means to effect change. For some activists, this has meant chaining themselves to trees in old-growth forests to discourage loggers from clearing that land. In 1997 a young activist named Julia Butterfly Hill (1974–) attempted to prevent logging of California redwoods by climbing 180 feet up into one of the great trees and refusing to come down. She stayed in the tree for just over two years, attracting international attention by her nonviolent approach to confrontation. Ultimately, the lumber company sold the land and the tree was saved. As a result, Hill was able to end her tree-sitting protest.

Some radical environmentalists have opted to reject nonviolence, choosing instead to draw notice to a cause through more dramatic means. Activists associated with the underground group Earth Liberation Front (ELF) set fire to several buildings at a ski resort in Colorado and to the office of a forestry company in Oregon. The organization Earth First! has also engaged in illegal acts of sabotage, targeting large companies viewed as enemies of the environment. Mainstream environmental groups, while they may agree with the goals of radical organizations, generally condemn their more extreme and illegal acts.

Many environmental activists have attempted to effect change through involvement in an ecologically motivated political party known as the Green Party. Inspired by Green parties in Europe, American activists formed a national Green movement during the mid-1980s. Many in the movement believed that the most effective way to protect the environment was to gain political power through the establishment of a national political party, a third-party alternative to the mainstream Democratic and Republican parties.

The Greens, as they are commonly known, gained national prominence during the 1996 presidential election, when they persuaded well-known consumer advocate Ralph Nader (1934–) to run as their candidate. Promoting what the Greens call "ecological wisdom" as well as other progressive political issues, Nader captured a great deal of attention but less than a million votes. Running again as the Green Party candidate in 2000, Nader earned nearly three million votes. With that election, the Greens demonstrated their potential to become an influential factor in the American political landscape, though the organization has been weakened by an internal split. As of 2001, the Greens split into two parties, the Green Party of the United States (GPUS) and the Greens/Green Party USA (G/GPUSA).

Although some environmental battles have been fought by radical fringe groups, and some by large, established, well-organized groups, a number of others have been waged by small groups of local citizens standing together to protect their communities. These local efforts, sometimes described by the nickname NIMBY (not in my backyard) have yielded numerous small victories like preserving a wildlife habitat, preventing the construction of a toxic-waste dump, and improving the quality of local waterways. The sum of all such community projects has been a substantial improvement in the health of the natural world and an increased awareness on the part of the average citizen of the impact each person can have on the environment.

The environmental movement has encountered numerous obstacles since its emergence in the 1970s. As environmental issues have become more complex, the obstacles have grown and the outlook has become less hopeful. The movement has accomplished significant change, however, substantially altering the way citizens view the world around them and live their everyday lives. New construction of homes and other buildings reflects the need for conservation, reflected in energy-saving windows and insulation as well as water-conserving toilets and showerheads. Household appliances, including refrigerators, washing machines, and dishwashers, are designed to be energy efficient as well. Recycling has become a habit with many citizens as more and more communities require that residents separate newspapers, glass, metal cans, and plastic from the rest of their garbage.

Although many environmentalists believe that car companies have not done enough, the industry has responded to concerns about harmful emissions and fossil fuels by producing cars that get better gas mileage and emit fewer pollutants. By the beginning of the twenty-first century, many automotive companies had begun production of hybrid cars that are powered by gasoline and electricity and use far less gas than traditional cars. The challenges facing the environmental movement in the new century are great, but many believe that the cause has won an important struggle because it has raised the general public's awareness of the importance of protecting the fragile balance of life on Earth.

For More Information

BOOKS

Blashfield, Jean F., and Wallace B. Black. *Oil Spills.* Chicago: Children's Press, 1991.

Brower, David, and Steve Chapple. *Let the Mountains Talk, Let the Rivers Run.* New York: HarperCollins, 1995.

Carson, Rachel. *Silent Spring.* Boston: Houghton Mifflin, 1962.

Collard, Sneed B., III. *Acting for Nature: What Young People around the World Have Done to Protect the Environment.* Berkeley, CA: Heyday Books, 2000.

Ehrlich, Paul. *The Population Bomb.* New York: Ballantine Books, 1968.

Fisher, Marshall. *The Ozone Layer.* New York: Chelsea House Publishers, 1992.

Josephy, Alvin M., Jr. *500 Nations: An Illustrated History of North American Indians.* New York: Knopf, 1994.

Leopold, Aldo. *A Sand County Almanac and Sketches Here and There.* New York: Oxford University Press, 1949.

Marsh, George Perkins. *Man and Nature; or, Physical Geography as Modified by Human Action.* New York: Scribner, 1864.

National Wildlife Federation. *Pollution Problems and Solutions.* Philadelphia: Chelsea House Publishers, 1999.

Odum, Eugene Pleasants. *Fundamentals of Ecology.* Philadelphia: Saunders, 1953.

Pringle, Laurence. *The Environmental Movement: From Its Roots to the Challenges of a New Century.* New York: HarperCollins, 2000.

Thoreau, Henry David. *Walden; or, Life in the Woods.* Boston: Ticknor & Fields, 1854.

Willis, Terri, and Wallace B. Black. *Endangered Species.* Chicago: Children's Press, 1992.

WEB SITES

America's National Wildlife Refuge System. http://refuges.fws.gov/ (accessed on May 28, 2006).

"The Endangered Species Program." *U.S. Fish and Wildlife Service.* http://www.fws.gov/endangered/ (accessed on May 28, 2006).

"Energy Kid's Page." *Energy Information Administration.* http://www.eia.doe.gov/kids/index.html (accessed on May 28, 2006).

Environmental Literacy Council. http://www.enviroliteracy.org/index.php (accessed on May 28, 2006).

"Former Wis. Senator, Earth Day Founder, Gaylord Nelson Dies" (July 3, 2005). *USA Today.* http://www.usatoday.com/news/washington/2005-07-03-nelson-obit_x.htm?csp=34 (accessed on May 28, 2006).

Gibbs, Lois Marie. "Learning from Love Canal: A 20th Anniversary Retrospective." *EnviroArts: Orion Online.* http://arts.envirolink.org/arts_and_activism/LoisGibbs.html (accessed on May 28, 2006).

"John Muir: A Brief Biography." *Sierra Club.* http://www.sierraclub.org/john_muir_exhibit/frameindex.html?http://www.sierraclub.org/john_muir_exhibit/life/muir_biography.html (accessed on May 28, 2006).

U.S. Environmental Protection Agency. http://www.epa.gov/ (accessed on May 28, 2006).

The Gay Rights Movement

In the history of social reform movements in the United States, some crusades have brought about revolutionary change for a particular group in society, altering the lives of the people in that group as well as changing the views of society overall. The gay rights movement has brought about such a change. Over a period of several decades, members of the gay community have gone from lives cloaked in secrecy to open and proud declarations of their sexual orientation. The gay rights movement has also accomplished significant legal victories, helping to overturn laws that punish a gay lifestyle as well as working to establish legal protections for gay people.

The term "gay" refers specifically to men who are romantically and physically attracted to other men. Often the term is also used to encompass a larger community that includes lesbians, women who are attracted to other women, and bisexuals, people who are attracted to both genders. The term "homosexual" is another way of describing a person attracted to people of the same gender, while the term "heterosexual," or "straight," describes a person attracted to people of the opposite gender. Often linked with the gay community are transgendered individuals, a description that covers a broad range of people who generally express their gender in ways that differ from conventional expectations. A transgendered person, for example, might be a man who has had surgery to become a woman, or it may refer to a woman who cross-dresses as a man.

Unlike other groups in society who have been oppressed because of race or gender, gay men and lesbians can hide their sexual identities, leading outwardly straight lives in which they pretend to be attracted to those of the opposite sex. Keeping a gay identity hidden is often referred to as living "in the closet." The act of revealing to family, friends, and coworkers one's identity as a gay man or lesbian is known as "coming out of the closet," or simply "coming out."

WORDS TO KNOW

AIDS: Acquired immunodeficiency syndrome; a disease related to a severely compromised immune system, leaving the body unable to defend against infection.

bisexual: A person who is romantically and physically attracted to both men and women.

civil union: A legally recognized relationship, usually between two people of the same sex, that offers many of the same legal rights and benefits as marriage.

coming out: The act of revealing to others one's sexual orientation, which had previously been hidden.

cross-dresser: A person who wears clothing typical of the opposite sex; also described as a "transvestite."

gay: A man who is romantically and physically attracted to other men; also sometimes refers to the broader gay community including lesbians and bisexuals.

heterosexual: A person who is romantically and physically attracted to people of the opposite sex.

HIV: Human immunodeficiency virus; the virus that causes AIDS.

homosexual: A person who is romantically and physically attracted to people of the same sex.

lesbian: A woman who is romantically and physically attracted to other women.

straight: A person who is heterosexual or attracted to members of the opposite sex.

transgendered individuals: A range of people, including transsexuals and cross-dressers, who express gender in ways that differ from conventional expectations.

transsexual: A person who has changed his or her biological gender through surgery and/or hormone treatment.

Early attempts to organize

Homosexuality has existed in various forms throughout history. Different societies have displayed varying levels of acceptance. In numerous cultures across many generations, homosexual relationships have been viewed as immoral and illegal, and gay men and lesbians have been prosecuted as criminals. For most of American history, same-sex relationships were not well tolerated. The message sent to gays and lesbians was that their sexual orientation was wrong—a mental illness, a perversion, a sin against nature and God. Many gay men and lesbians believed this message and worked hard to change their attraction to the same gender. Others lived double lives, keeping their homosexuality a secret, unwilling to be prosecuted or harassed simply for being themselves.

In the United States, tolerance of gay men and lesbians has risen and fallen throughout the twentieth century in keeping with the overall social and political mood of the nation. Midway through the century, the nation was beginning a period of post–World War II (1939–45) prosperity while at the same time experiencing unprecedented vulnerability due to the escalating Cold War (1945–91) with the Soviet Union. (The Cold War was a period of hostilities between the United States and the Soviet Union, in which propaganda and threats were used rather than military confrontation.) Capitalizing on this sense of national anxiety, Senator Joseph McCarthy (1908–1957) rose to fame for his relentless crusade against a supposed Communist conspiracy in the American government and military. McCarthy also targeted homosexuals.

Amid this atmosphere of paranoia and fear, generated in large part by McCarthy but perpetuated by many in the federal government, gay men and lesbians were seen as a threat to national safety and to American culture. Widespread concern about the so-called dangers of homosexuality led to a national "witch-hunt" throughout much of the 1950s and 1960s, with police forces and government agencies dedicating tremendous resources to the investigation and arrest of people described as "sexual perverts."

In several large cities, an active gay and lesbian social scene had arisen in spite of the fact that many states had laws preventing the public gathering of and sale of alcohol to homosexuals. Such laws forced many gay bars and nightclubs to go "underground," meaning they operated in secrecy. The police often raided gay bars during the 1950s and 1960s, making numerous arrests. In exchange for an evening of entertainment and socializing, a person arrested during such a raid could pay a high price: being beaten by the police, for example, or being exposed as gay by a newspaper photograph depicting the raid. Exposure for some people meant the loss of a job, friends, even a spouse.

In the wake of this police harassment and government persecution, several gay rights organizations were established during the 1950s. The Mattachine Society, founded in Los Angeles in 1950, was the first such group. The Mattachine Society was formed by a small group of men, including renowned activist Harry Hay (1912–2002). A gay man and a communist, Hay is considered by many to be the father of the modern gay rights movement. The Mattachine Society, named for a secret society of French performers during the Renaissance era, was designed to help defend the rights of homosexuals. The society was also envisioned as an organization for the gay masses that would help create a distinct, alternative culture for gay people.

Considered by many to be the father of the modern gay rights movement, Harry Hay (left) sits with his partner, John Burnside, in their San Francisco, California, home in 2002. AP IMAGES.

Hay promoted the idea of the Mattachine Society as a "homophile" organization, a term that embraced gay men as well as those who supported gay rights. Hay viewed the gay community as a separate cultural identity. Within a few years, the leadership of the Mattachine Society had changed. Hay and other founders were ousted by more conservative members who dismissed the notion of gay culture as distinct from the larger society. The new leaders wanted to blend in with society, and they feared that the communist backgrounds of Hay and other founders would disturb mainstream Americans and harm the gay rights movement.

Although the Mattachine Society was primarily an organization of gay men, the San Francisco-based Daughters of Bilitis (DOB) was founded exclusively for lesbians. Established in 1955 by Del Martin and Phyllis Lyon, two prominent lesbian activists and a longtime couple, the Daughters of Bilitis was initially intended as a social club and an outlet of expression for lesbians. The DOB later became more politically

Phyllis Lyon (left) and Del Martin hold up their marriage certificate in San Francisco, California, in 2004. Although same-sex marriage certificates were issued in San Francisco from February 12 to March 11, 2004, the California Supreme Court later voided such marriages. © KIM KULISH/ CORBIS.

active, agitating for civil rights and attempting to educate the larger culture about the lesbian community.

DOB chapters arose in numerous cities throughout the United States. The group's publication, *The Ladder,* became an influential periodical. The DOB never reached the membership levels of the national men's organizations, but it became the standard imitated by numerous lesbian organizations that followed. Like many gay and lesbian organizations of that era, the name of the group did not convey to the general public that it was a lesbian organization. The name came from a book of lesbian-themed French poetry by Pierre Louÿs called *Songs of Bilitis.* Only those involved in the lesbian community would understand the significance of the DOB's name.

The 1960s: The modern gay rights movement begins

On some levels, the 1960s, particularly in the early years of the decade, were characterized by conservative politics and conformist social practices. On other levels, however, a revolution was brewing on several fronts. The civil rights movement had made significant gains and radically altered the lives of African Americans in the South. The women's movement had begun its campaign for liberation and equal rights. The student-led antiwar movement gained steam in the latter part of the decade, staging passionate protests against the Vietnam War (1954–75). The youth movement rejected the values of the older generation and embraced a back-to-basics peace-and-love lifestyle. In the midst of the turmoil of the 1960s, the gay rights movement built an ever-larger following and became an increasingly vocal force for social change.

During the 1950s, several of the early gay rights organizations had modest goals and a conservative approach. Their members wanted to work within the system to gain greater acceptance for gay men and lesbians. They did not wish to attract too much attention or stir up agitation in the larger society. The protests that took place during the 1960s were generally civilized and polite; the protesters were well dressed and even-tempered. During these early years, the gay rights movement was known as the homophile movement, a term emphasizing the emotional aspect of same-sex love rather than the sexual aspect. The homophile movement sought freedom for gay men and lesbians in a manner that would allow them to blend in with society.

By the late 1960s, the movement was evolving and becoming more radical. Many gay rights activists at that time wanted to revolutionize society, expanding the notions of human sexuality to accommodate more than just the traditional man-woman model. Gay liberation was a primary goal of that era: creating a new society that would allow gays and lesbians to freely express and celebrate their love. At the same time, some activists, while still working toward overall liberation, began shifting their focus to obtaining basic civil rights for gays and lesbians.

From the beginning, one of the fundamental goals of American gay rights activists has been to repeal, or overturn, laws in numerous states that make gay sexual activity a crime. In 1961 Illinois became the first state to make such activity legal when taking place between consenting adults. Many gay activists spent many years working one state at a time to overturn all such laws. Their diligence paid off in large measure. By the

Franklin Kameny: Gay Rights Pioneer

Although he may not have achieved the widespread fame of Harry Hay and others, Franklin Kameny (1925–) was one of the leading pioneers of the gay rights movement. Kameny did not set out to become a gay rights activist. His passion from early childhood was astronomy. After earning a master's degree and doctorate from Harvard, he began working as an astronomer for the U.S. Army Map Service. In 1957 he was arrested on a "morals charge," which was code for suspected homosexual behavior. As a result, Kameny was fired from his job. A 1953 executive order prohibited hiring or employing homosexuals in the federal government. Kameny protested his firing and the ban on gays by suing the government, the first openly gay person to do so. He filed a petition with the U.S. Supreme Court, which, in 1961, refused to hear his case.

Kameny never again worked as an astronomer, devoting himself instead to gay rights activism. In late 1961 Kameny and a friend founded the Washington, D.C., chapter of the Mattachine Society. Unlike many other gay leaders during that period, Kameny encouraged confrontation with public figures and such direct action as protest marches and demonstrations. Kameny and the Washington Mattachine Society organized the first gay rights march at the White House in the spring of 1965. He was instrumental in the organization of annual gay rights marches on July 4 in Philadelphia, Washington, D.C., and New York between 1965 and 1969. For Kameny and the other marchers, such public declarations of their support for gay rights at a time when most gay men and lesbians remained invisible took tremendous courage.

Kameny met each of many obstacles in his activist career with determination. His dedication paid off in a number of ways. His fight to reverse the ban on homosexuals in the federal government was won in 1975. He helped launch the effort to persuade the American Psychiatric Association to remove homosexuality from its official list of mental illnesses, which was achieved in 1973. He helped write legislation that, in 1993, reversed Washington, D.C.'s law that outlawed gay forms of sexual activity. Kameny is credited with coining the 1968 slogan "Gay is good," a phrase inspired by that of the later stages of the African American civil rights movement, "Black is beautiful."

In 1971 Kameny became the first openly gay person to run for national office. He sought to be elected as the District of Columbia's nonvoting representative in Congress. He lost the election but continued for many decades to be closely involved in the Washington political scene. He was a co-founder of the National Gay Task Force, which later became the National Gay and Lesbian Task Force (NGLTF). He also helped establish, in the mid-1970s, the Gay Rights National Lobby, which became the Human Rights Commission (HRC).

In their book *Out for Good: The Struggle to Build a Gay Rights Movement in America*, Dudley Clendinen and Adam Nagourney quote Kameny's guiding philosophy: "If society and I differ on something, I'm willing to give the matter a second look. If we still differ, then I am right and society is wrong; and society can go its way so long as it does not get in my way. But if it does, there's going to be a fight. And I'm not going to be the one who backs down."

mid-1970s, almost half of the states had decriminalized private sexual activity among gay men and lesbians.

Early on, gay rights activists realized that increasing their political power was essential to their success. During the 1960s several activist groups began trying to attract the notice of politicians and legislators as well as trying to get gay men and lesbians elected to public office. They demanded to be recognized as an oppressed minority that was being unfairly denied civil rights. In 1965 pioneering activist Franklin Kameny (1925–) organized the first gay rights demonstration at the White House. Kameny was also instrumental in the planning of annual marches taking place in such cities as Philadelphia, New York, and Washington, D.C., between 1965 and 1969.

Key organizations and alliances As the 1960s progressed and the activist spirit spread throughout the nation, a few key organizations helped gay rights activists form into a fledgling movement. One such group, the Society for Individual Rights (SIR), was founded in 1964 in San Francisco, which was and continues to be the heart of gay rights activism. SIR was intended as a political and social club for gay men and lesbians. SIR sponsored numerous social events, including dances and parties, while also establishing bowling leagues, exercise groups, art classes, and more for gays and lesbians. In 1966 SIR opened a gay community center, the first of its kind. The organization played a crucial role in creating a sense of community and togetherness among the many and varied people it served.

Another important step in the formation of a gay rights movement involved partnerships with religious groups. The general opposition to homosexuality on the part of organized religion offered justification for widespread discrimination and even, some contended, violence toward gay men and lesbians. The establishment in late 1964 of the Council on Religion and the Homosexual (CRH) resulted from an alliance between several sympathetic Protestant ministers and gay rights groups in San Francisco. The CRH hosted a gay New Year's Eve ball at the end of 1964. It was a daring move during a period when police routinely raided gay bars and nightclubs, arresting same-sex couples for such violations as hugging or hand-holding. On the night of the ball, the police came out in great numbers, harassing the guests. The ministers of CRH charged the police with intimidation and hostility toward the law-abiding citizens attending the ball. Publicity surrounding the incident aroused the anger of many citizens who disapproved of the police actions. With the support of the ministers, the gay and lesbian community earned a newfound respect, and police harassment gradually decreased.

A few years later, the Reverend Troy Perry founded the Metropolitan Community Church (MCC) in Los Angeles, the first gay church in the nation. Perry had been a Pentecostal preacher who had twice been removed from the ministry because he was gay. At first, he had believed his religion's teachings that homosexuality was a sin. However, Perry eventually came to feel that he and others like him were worthy of God's love. Wanting to share this message with others, Perry began conducting church services in his living room in the autumn of 1968. The MCC soon moved to another building, and then another, eventually buying and remodeling an old building in 1971. Within two years, antigay arsonists burned the church to the ground. But even such violent acts could not slow the growth of the MCC, which soon spread to cities all across the nation.

The Reverend Troy Perry founded the Metropolitan Community Church (MCC) in Los Angeles, California, which was the first gay church in the United States. GREY VILLET/ TIME & LIFE PICTURES/GETTY IMAGES.

Stonewall During the summer of 1969, a pivotal event took place at a gay bar in New York City that many people later defined as the true starting point of the modern gay rights movement. Although the movement had been brewing for many years, it was the incident at the Stonewall Inn that sent a current of outrage and righteousness through the gay community, ushering in a period of intense political and social activism.

As it had been many nights before, the Stonewall Inn on Christopher Street in New York's Greenwich Village was crowded with gay men, lesbians, and transgendered people. And, as had happened many nights before, the police raided the Stonewall Inn in the early morning hours. Officers ejected customers and arrested the least accepted segment of the gay community: the drag queens, or men dressed as women. But this time, rather than quietly accepting the humiliation and fear of such a raid, the crowd turned angry and rebellious. Punches were thrown, followed by a torrent of stones and bottles, and the spontaneous outbreak of violence turned into a full-fledged riot. Word quickly spread through Greenwich Village, and hundreds of local gays and lesbians showed up to join in the fighting. The police were forced to retreat within the bar, and it took riot-control police several hours to disperse the crowd.

The next night, hundreds of protesters returned to the Stonewall Inn, renewing the riots from the night before. The crowds chanted slogans like "Gay power!" and again threw bottles and stones at the police. The riots continued for several more nights. Many activists came to believe that when the Stonewall riots ended, the movement began. For the people at Stonewall, the feelings of injustice and anger over the police raid were not new. What was new was the sense of strength and power experienced during the riots. Many people realized that the gay community could be a significant force for social change. They felt that the time had come to demand equal treatment and to express gay pride.

Within a few weeks of the Stonewall riots, the changes in the gay community became apparent. The Gay Liberation Front (GLF) was founded in July of 1969, the first gay rights organization to use the word "gay" in its name. The GLF was soon followed by the Gay Activists Alliance (GAA), which later became the Gay and Lesbian Activists Alliance. A number of gay newspapers arose in the wake of Stonewall, increasing the sense of community and improving avenues of communication among gays and lesbians. Almost immediately, various gay rights factions began arguing about what Stonewall meant and what should happen next. Conservative gay leaders urged people to refrain

Thousands of gays and lesbians march at the first Christopher Street Liberation Day parade in New York City in 1970.
© JP LAFFONT/SYGMA/CORBIS.

from future violence and do nothing more to alienate mainstream society. A growing number of gay men and lesbians, however, rejected this notion, feeling that they had been patient long enough.

The 1970s: Victories and setbacks

The energy generated among gay activists by the Stonewall riots spilled over into the 1970s, a decade of social and political breakthroughs. On June 28, 1970, thousands of people gathered to commemorate the one-year anniversary of Stonewall by marching in the Christopher Street Liberation Day parade in New York. Smaller parades took place at the same time in other cities as well. The last Saturday in June became the date for annual celebrations of gay pride.

American Social Reform Movements: Almanac

The gay rights movement in the 1970s devoted itself primarily to gaining political power and civil rights. During those years a number of states repealed laws that criminalized gay sexual activity, and many communities enacted antidiscrimination laws to protect gay rights in areas such as employment and housing. Efforts to achieve recognition for gays and lesbians within the Democratic Party met with gradual success. At the 1972 Democratic National Convention, five of the delegates were openly gay. That number jumped to seventy-seven by 1980, and in 1984 gay civil rights became an official item on the party's agenda.

Activists also worked tirelessly to get gay and lesbian candidates elected, convinced that having the gay community represented in political bodies would be an effective means to change. In 1974 an openly gay candidate named Kathy Kozachenko was elected to the Ann Arbor, Michigan, city council. That same year Elaine Noble, a lesbian from Massachusetts, was elected to her state legislature. Other openly gay politicians followed. Although their numbers did not reflect the proportion of gay men and lesbians in society, they had made an important beginning.

One of the most significant victories for the gay rights movement involved a concession from the nation's mental health professionals. After a lengthy battle on the part of Franklin Kameny and other gay activists, the American Psychiatric Association (APA) removed homosexuality from its official list of mental disorders in 1973. Gay activists had focused a great deal of energy on changing the official views of the nation's psychiatrists and psychologists because they felt that a medical diagnosis of homosexuality as a mental illness provided the basis for society's persecution of gays.

Some therapists had subjected a number of gay men and lesbians to extreme methods to persuade them to abandon homosexuality. Patients were forced to undergo treatment methods like receiving electric shocks while reading about gay behavior or being given nausea-causing drugs while viewing erotic images of people of the same sex. Gay activists viewed such treatment as torture and made it their mission to transform psychiatry's basic views on homosexuality. The APA was later joined in this decision by other medical organizations, including the American Psychological Association and the American Medical Association.

Although the 1970s marked a period of abundant victories for gay rights, the period was also distinguished by significant turbulence within the movement. Tensions between gay men and lesbians mounted, with many lesbians feeling that gay men were even less sympathetic to their cause than straight men. Conflicts developed between gay rights groups that were more moderate and those that were radical. Problems also arose between lesbian feminists and straight feminists. Some members of the women's movement, including noted leader Betty Friedan (1921–2006), felt that it was a mistake to allow lesbians to have a role in the women's movement, fearing their presence would alienate too many people and weaken their progress. Lesbian feminists argued that their role was essential. In 1971 the National Organization for Women (NOW), a major force in the women's movement, formally acknowledged that the feminist agenda should address civil rights for lesbians.

Steadfast—and violent—opposition In addition to tensions within and among gay organizations, the movement also experienced setbacks from outside forces during the 1970s. In 1977, in response to a gay rights ordinance banning discrimination that passed in Florida's Dade County, entertainer and political conservative Anita Bryant (1940–) led a campaign to overturn it. She was joined by many religious conservatives, including the Reverend Jerry Falwell (1933–), an evangelical preacher and right-wing political activist. Bryant, with her Save Our Children campaign, spread the notion that gay men and lesbians recruited young people to convert them to homosexuality. According to Bob Moser in "Holy War," published on the Southern Poverty Law Center's Web site: "'Homosexuals cannot reproduce,' Bryant often said, 'so they must recruit. And to freshen their ranks they must recruit the youth of America.'" Her campaign was successful, and a referendum in Dade County overturned the gay civil rights ordinance.

Bryant's success led to similar victories in other communities, including St. Paul, Minnesota; Wichita, Kansas; and Eugene, Oregon. In addition, California state senator John Briggs proposed a referendum that would ban gay men and lesbians from teaching in public schools and would prohibit teachers from making any positive comments regarding homosexuality. Briggs's proposal was defeated, but he did garner significant support. Bryant's antigay crusade had some positive impact on the gay rights movement, re-energizing activists. That summer, 75,000 people showed up for the Christopher Street Liberation Day march in New York, and 300,000 attended the annual gay pride parade in San Francisco.

San Francisco, a haven for gay men and lesbians and a center of gay rights activity, was the scene of one of the movement's most infamous

Harvey Milk, the first openly gay man to be elected to public office in San Francisco, was murdered in 1978 by former colleague Dan White, who later killed himself. AP IMAGES.

and shocking incidents. Harvey Milk (1930–1978), the first openly gay man to be elected to public office, was voted onto San Francisco's board of supervisors, akin to a city council, in 1977. After moving to San Francisco in 1972, Milk had established himself as a talented and dedicated community leader. He helped the heavily gay Castro neighborhood organize economically and politically, and he established relationships between the gay community and organized labor. Just eleven months after assuming his position as a city supervisor, Milk was assassinated. After the passage of a gay rights ordinance that had been introduced by Milk, fellow city supervisor and political conservative Dan White resigned in protest. On November 27, 1978, White snuck into the city hall and made his way to the mayor's office. He fatally shot Mayor George Moscone, seen as a friend of the gay rights movement, and then walked down the hall and killed Milk.

At White's trial, his lawyer argued that White had been suffering from a type of temporary insanity the day of the crimes. In what came to be known as the "Twinkie defense," the lawyer claimed that White was severely depressed and that his condition had been aggravated because he had consumed an excess of junk food. Instead of receiving a conviction for premeditated murder, White was handed a guilty verdict for the lesser crime of manslaughter. He was sentenced to seven years in prison.

Gay activists in San Francisco reacted with outrage to White's light sentence, pouring into the streets to express their frustration. The resulting "White Night" riots led to approximately one million dollars in damage to city property. San Francisco police struck back by raiding the Castro neighborhood, damaging gay businesses and assaulting people on the street. As for White, he was released on parole after about five years in jail. He committed suicide in 1985.

The 1980s: The AIDS decade

The 1980s brought a new and unexpected enemy, a plague that dramatically altered the gay rights movement and the nation as a whole. A mysterious disease, displayed in some patients as a rare type of cancer called Kaposi's Sarcoma and in others as a deadly pneumonia, emerged in the early 1980s. Doctors and scientists quickly realized that the disease seemed most often to afflict gay men. Initially called gay-related immune deficiency (GRID), the disorder was later renamed acquired immunodeficiency syndrome, or AIDS.

By 1982 doctors did not know exactly how AIDS was transmitted, but they noticed that it also afflicted intravenous drug users and people who frequently received blood transfusions. Scientists later learned that a virus, labeled the human immunodeficiency virus, or HIV, causes the body's immune defenses to weaken until the body can no longer fight off infections. The final stage of HIV is AIDS. HIV is transmitted primarily through unprotected sex with an infected person, but it can also be acquired through tainted blood transfusions and the sharing of contaminated needles. Scientists also learned that an infected pregnant woman can pass HIV on to her baby.

Despite the fact that anyone can get AIDS, the disease quickly became associated with the gay community. Many people, fearful of this new epidemic, lashed out against gays and lesbians. Discrimination against those afflicted with AIDS, based largely on ignorance of how the disease was spread, led many homosexuals to lose their jobs, their housing, and sometimes their friends.

The politically conservative administration of President Ronald Reagan (1911–2004; served 1981–89) was extremely slow to react to the AIDS crisis. Reagan did not publicly address the crisis until 1987. By that time, more than 20,000 Americans had died of the disease. The government initially allocated very little money for AIDS research and social services. In the absence of governmental assistance, gay activist groups mobilized quickly, turning their attention from gay civil rights to protecting the community from a deadly assault. The AIDS crisis was so severe during the 1980s that the gay rights movement in large measure became the AIDS activist movement.

The Gay Men's Health Crisis (GMHC), founded by author and activist Larry Kramer (1935–) in 1982 in New York, was the first organization created to deal with AIDS. That same year, an organization known as the Kaposi's Sarcoma Research and Education Foundation formed in San Francisco. Two years later, the group renamed itself as the San Francisco AIDS Foundation. These and other AIDS-related organizations provided medical and emotional support for those afflicted with AIDS. In addition, they educated people about the transmission of the disease and the best ways to minimize the risk of contracting it. The GMHC and others also attempted to have a political impact, protecting AIDS victims from discrimination.

Gay Activists March on Washington

Following the example of the African American civil rights movement, the gay rights movement held massive marches on the nation's capital. They wanted to show the government the size and strength of their movement. Several gay activists began discussing the idea for a march on Washington during the late 1970s, but support for the idea was not widespread. Some community leaders felt it would be unwise to pour time and money into a march when they had so many pressing concerns. Across the United States, gay activists were waging battles to pass gay rights ordinances or to keep existing laws from being repealed. A national march was not high on their priority list. Also, some leaders worried that it would be disastrous for the movement if they staged the march and few showed up.

San Francisco city supervisor and gay rights activist Harvey Milk supported the idea of a march. When Milk was assassinated in 1978 by a conservative former city supervisor, the gay community was stunned. Soon after Milk's death, the idea of a march on Washington was revived, with many people viewing it as Milk's legacy. The March on Washington for Lesbian and Gay Rights was scheduled for October 14, 1979. Turnout exceeded expectations. Coming from all over the United States and several other countries, some 100,000 demonstrators arrived in Washington, D.C. Just ten years after the Stonewall riots, the gay rights movement had developed into a major social and political force.

In 1986 the U.S. Supreme Court outraged the gay community. In the case *Bowers v. Hardwick*, the court ruled that states had the right to enact laws prohibiting gay sexual activity. The verdict indicated that gays and lesbians were not entitled to privacy and that it was acceptable to apply a different legal standard to homosexuals. Shocked by the ruling and frustrated by the government's slow response to the AIDS crisis, many gay leaders began discussing a second national march.

The second march on Washington for Lesbian and Gay Rights occurred on October 11, 1987 with more than 500,000 participants. The march coincided with the first public display of the AIDS Memorial Quilt, a project consisting of thousands of cloth panels, each one crafted in memory of someone who died of AIDS. The vast size of the quilt showed the far-reaching impact and human toll of the disease.

The next march on Washington was held on April 25, 1993. The March on Washington for Lesbian, Gay, and Bi Equal Rights and Liberation occurred soon after President Bill Clinton took office. Clinton was viewed as being far more sympathetic to gay issues than Ronald Reagan and George H. W. Bush had been. Even the name of the march, which for the first time included the presence of bisexuals, reflected the movement's advances. An estimated one million people participated, setting a record as the largest demonstration at that time in U.S. history. Major news media featured the event in front-page articles; *Newsweek* magazine devoted its cover story to the march. Events were planned to coincide with the march, including workshops, conferences, and efforts to lobby Congress.

A fourth march on Washington (2000) occurred amid objections from many gay rights leaders. Although previous marches were planned by a broad coalition of gay rights activists and organizations, the 2000 Millennium March on Washington for Equality was organized by two large mainstream gay rights groups: Human Rights Campaign and Universal Fellowship of Metropolitan Community Churches. Many gay rights leaders complained that the group of organizers did not reflect the diversity of the gay rights movement, stating that the event relied too heavily on corporate sponsorship. Some objected to the emphasis on entertainment over political action. Some gay rights groups refused to participate, so attendance was much lower than the previous march. About 200,000 people participated. A financial scandal that emerged later further cemented the view of the Millennium March as ill-conceived and poorly planned.

ACT UP By the mid-1980s, some gay activists felt that the existing AIDS organizations had lost some of the activist spirit and were not doing enough to effect change. In 1987 Kramer, having been forced out of the GMHC and wishing to inject the AIDS movement with more radicalism, formed the AIDS Coalition to Unleash Power, or ACT UP. The group addressed issues such as education and AIDS prevention, but its primary mission was to protest the actions of the government, doctors, and drug companies, pressuring these groups to make treatments more accessible to AIDS patients. Although no cure for AIDS had emerged, drug companies had begun to develop effective medicines to treat the disease, prolonging life for those infected. But these medicines were

In 1991 members of ACT UP march in Kennebunkport, Maine, where then-President George H. W. Bush's family vacations. They are protesting the president's AIDS policy and demanding access to life-saving drugs for all people suffering from the disease.
DIRCK HALSTEAD/TIME & LIFE PICTURES/GETTY IMAGES.

extremely expensive, and the process for developing new medicines was lengthy and complicated.

ACT UP staged flashy, disruptive demonstrations on Wall Street and other seats of American power in an attempt to focus attention on the AIDS crisis and improve AIDS patients' chances of survival. ACT UP, with chapters throughout the United States and in other countries as well, proved to be an effective means to social change. ACT UP raised awareness about the disease among ordinary citizens and forced the powerful drug companies and government agencies to confront the crisis. The problem of accessibility to AIDS drugs was not solved in the 1980s and in fact continued into the twenty-first century.

In the United States, the development of a new treatment in the mid-1990s, called protease inhibitors, gave HIV/AIDS victims a far better chance of prolonging their lives. According to the U.S. Food and Drug Administration (FDA): "Protease inhibitors block the protease enzyme that HIV needs in order to make new viruses. When protease is blocked, HIV makes copies of itself that cannot infect new cells." After protease inhibitors were introduced, the death rate from AIDS fell by nearly 50 percent. But in poor countries, particularly many African nations, the epidemic swelled to disastrous proportions with most victims unable to afford the necessary treatment. AIDS activists continue to appeal to drug companies and international governments to make inexpensive medicines available to all.

Community awareness projects A key goal of AIDS activists was to raise awareness of the disease as a crisis affecting everyone, not a disease limited to the gay community. In the early 1990s, a group of artists in New York City created a simple symbol that anyone could display to show support for HIV/AIDS victims: a red ribbon. The ribbon project quickly became a massive phenomenon and an extremely effective way for ordinary citizens to make an activist expression. At high-profile awards shows, the red ribbon adorned the tuxedo lapels and high-fashion gowns of nearly every celebrity. Political candidates showed support for the AIDS movement by pinning on a red ribbon. Millions of people sported red ribbon pins, T-shirts, and caps. The red ribbon became such a powerful symbol that other causes adopted the idea: pink ribbons showed support for breast cancer research and treatment, for example, while yellow ribbons showed support of U.S. troops fighting in Iraq.

AIDS activists also sought to put a human face on AIDS, enabling people to go beyond the statistics heard in news reports and realize the impact of the loss of so many people to the disease. The gay community in particular has been devastated by AIDS. A vast number of gay men and lesbians who were adults during the 1970s and 1980s either dealt with infection personally or lost friends or loved ones to AIDS. The AIDS Memorial Quilt, begun in San Francisco in 1987 and maintained by the NAMES Project, serves as a memorial for individual victims of AIDS as well as a visual demonstration of the vast number of people killed by the disease. As of the summer of 2005, the quilt consisted of nearly six thousand squares, sewn together into 12-foot-square blocks, with each square created by friends or family members in memory of someone who died of AIDS. Portions of the quilt are continually on display in numerous locations, and even a small fraction of the entire project takes up a tremendous amount of space. The size of the quilt, as well as the moving messages of love and sadness on each square, give viewers an idea of the human cost of the disease.

Beyond AIDS: The 1990s and the twenty-first century

Although AIDS activism continued to be a significant aspect of the gay rights movement into the 1990s, the advances being made in treatment of the disease lessened the sense of urgency and made room for a host of new battles and initiatives.

Gays in the military The presidential candidacy of Bill Clinton (1946–; served 1993–2001) offered new hope to gay activists. A supporter in some respects of gay rights, Clinton promised to end the ban on gays and lesbians in the U.S. military if he were elected. Once Clinton was in office, however, he backed down in the face of deep opposition by military leaders and political advisers. Many of Clinton's opponents argued that allowing gay men and lesbians into the military would undermine the values of the armed forces and weaken the bonds of combat units. It was suggested that heterosexual soldiers would be so uncomfortable fighting and working alongside gay soldiers that the effectiveness of the unit would be severely compromised. Clinton proposed a watered-down version of his original plan, a policy that came to be known as "don't ask, don't tell."

Under this new law, recruiters and commanding officers were forbidden from asking new recruits and soldiers if they were gay, and the soldiers did not have to reveal their sexual orientation. However, the law allows commanders to launch an investigation into any service member suspected of homosexual behavior and to discharge those who are found to engage in such behavior. Several thousand service members were discharged under this law in its first decade. The "don't ask, don't tell" policy did nothing to improve the status of gays in the military. Only deeply closeted gay men and lesbians could hope for a military career, and harassment and discrimination of suspected homosexuals continued to be a problem.

In some cases, harassment led to violence. In 1999 Private First Class Barry Winchell was beaten to death with a baseball bat while lying in his bed at Fort Campbell in Kentucky. For months Winchell had been the victim of harassment and gay-bashing by fellow soldiers who suspected he was gay. But if Winchell filed any complaints, he could have faced an investigation into his sexual orientation and a possible discharge from the military.

Hate crimes Hate crimes, illegal acts motivated primarily by hatred of a particular group of society, have always been a problem for the gay community. Initially hate crime legislation created a special category of crimes committed against a person or property because of that person's race, religion, or national origin. During the 1980s, gay rights activists began campaigning to have hate crime laws apply to sexual orientation and gender identity as well. Such campaigns were met with resistance by many people who were reluctant to create any special legal categories that supported the rights of gays and lesbians.

A number of high-profile instances of gay hate crimes in the 1990s persuaded many people that it was necessary to include sexual orientation in hate crime laws. Among these crimes was the murder of Brandon Teena (1972–1993), a biological female who had been passing as a boy since her/his teenage years. When Teena's true identity was discovered in a small Nebraska town in 1993, two young men raped and later murdered the person they had assumed was a man. Teena's story was recounted in a 1997 documentary, *The Brandon Teena Story,* and a 1999 feature film, *Boys Don't Cry.*

Another murder that made national headlines occurred in 1998. Gay college student Matthew Shepard (1976–1998) was beaten to death by two young men in Laramie, Wyoming. The two men pretended to be gay to draw Shepard out of a bar one night. They drove him to a field across town, beat him with the butt of a pistol, and tied him to a fence, leaving him for dead. Shepard was not discovered until the next day, and he died in the hospital a few days later. Shepard's story inspired the play and the film *The Laramie Project.*

The trials of the men who killed Shepard received major media attention. Many gay and lesbian activists as well as antigay groups flocked to the town and held demonstrations. Members of a highly conservative church traveled to Wyoming, where they protested by holding signs saying that God hated gays and that Shepard was in hell. Gays and friends of Shepard countered the conservative protests by dressing as angels. Wearing bed sheets, they spread their angel wings to try to block the anti-Shepard demonstrators. Ultimately, the two men who murdered Shepard were sent to prison.

The publicity surrounding such violent attacks on gays encouraged various lawmakers to consider adding sexual orientation to hate crime legislation. More than half of American states include sexual orientation in their hate crime legislation. A few states also specify that offenses

Gay activist Ellen Degeneres speaks at a vigil for Matthew Shepard, a gay student who was brutally murdered in Wyoming in 1998. BRAD MARKEL/ GETTY IMAGES.

against transgendered individuals qualify as hate crimes. A federal hate crime law, passed in 1994, mandates an additional penalty for those convicted of hate crimes, but sexual orientation and gender identity are not included in this law. Supporters of hate crime legislation suggest that a more extreme punishment is warranted for hate crimes because they send a message of intimidation and violent threat that goes beyond the individual victim and into his/her community as well.

Gay marriage One of the most controversial and important battles fought by gay activists in the 1990s and into the twenty-first century was the quest for legal, same-sex marriage. For many years, gays and lesbians have fought for same-sex marriage to be permitted. The desire for legalized marriage stems in part from a couple's wish to be recognized by society as a legitimate, committed partnership in much the same way that heterosexual married couples are. Legalized marriage also has several practical and legal benefits. If a person becomes very ill, it is far easier for a legally recognized spouse to care for that person and to make decisions about health care than it would be for an unmarried partner. In addition, the law gives many tax benefits to married couples that unmarried couples do not receive. Companies that provide health insurance to their employees often offer coverage for spouses, but many do not extend coverage to unmarried partners.

In matters involving child custody, gay couples are at a distinct disadvantage. If a married woman gives birth to a child, her husband is automatically granted the rights of a parent even if he is not the biological father. When a lesbian in a committed relationship gives birth, her partner has no parental rights and often cannot obtain these rights through adoption or other legal arrangement. Gay couples face many obstacles to adopting children under any circumstances, and legalized same-sex marriage would remove many such barriers.

During the 1990s, small steps were taken in the direction of legalized same-sex unions, though these minor victories often have been weakened or reversed by later initiatives. In the early twenty-first century, same-sex marriage remains extremely controversial and is strongly opposed by significant segments of society, particularly conservative religious groups. In 1993 and 1996 Hawaiian courts ruled that denying same-sex citizens the right to marry violated the state's equal rights provisions. Before these rulings could be applied, however, the state legislature proposed an amendment to Hawaii's constitution to prevent gay marriage, and voters overwhelmingly approved it. Legislators additionally wrote a law specifying that marriage was an act taking place between a man and a woman. A similar series of events took place in Alaska during the late 1990s.

One of the biggest victories in the battle for legalized same-sex marriage took place in Vermont. In 1999 Vermont stopped short of allowing gay couples to receive a marriage license, but it did institute the notion of a civil union between same-sex couples. A civil union granted gay couples the same rights in Vermont as married heterosexual couples, including child custody, worker compensation, and family leave. In addition, ending a civil union requires the same legal process as the dissolution of a marriage.

A few years later, the Massachusetts Supreme Judicial Court went one step further, declaring that same-sex marriage was legal in that state. The state legislature immediately began trying to draft an amendment banning gay marriage, but in the meantime, the court ruling stood. Beginning on May 17, 2004, same-sex couples could obtain marriage licenses, participate in a marriage ceremony, and enjoy all the rights of being a legally married pair. The law only applied to Massachusetts citizens, however. The Republican governor, Mitt Romney, pointed to a 1913 law that prevented out-of-state couples from being married in Massachusetts. Although many couples happily took advantage of the new ruling, gay activists feared the right to marry would be short-lived, overturned by a constitutional amendment as soon as voters had the opportunity to vote on the issue.

Several other states have addressed the gay marriage issue, with mixed results. Some states have instituted domestic partnership laws, which give some of the rights of marriage to same-sex couples. Well over half of the American states, however, have passed "defense of marriage" acts, which explicitly state that marriage can only take place between a man and a woman. These laws also forbid the recognition of a same-sex marriage or civil union that took place in another state. Such laws were similar to federal legislation passed in 1996, signed by President Clinton, denying federal rights to same-sex couples regardless of the legal status of their union in their home state. The federal Defense of Marriage Act (DOMA) marked the first time the U.S. government had defined marriage, a task formerly left up to each state.

Legal protections: A constant battle Throughout the history of the movement, gay rights activists have had little success obtaining federal civil rights protections. But activists have achieved substantial gains in obtaining such protections at the state and local level. Over the years, many cities and states have passed ordinances and statutes protecting the civil rights of the gay community. These ordinances offer protection from discrimination in such areas as housing, employment, credit, education, and public accommodations, like restaurants, hotels, and public transportation. In other words, a gay person cannot be fired, denied housing or

In 2004 members of various religious organizations voice their approval of same-sex marriage outside the House Chamber at the Statehouse in Boston, Massachusetts. The protesters are letting it be known that not all religious people are against such marriages. AP IMAGES.

credit, or evicted from a hotel because he or she is gay. Such laws give gay men and lesbians legal backing if they are discriminated against, and they also indicate a general acceptance of the gay community.

In a number of communities, anti-discrimination laws are extremely controversial. Opponents, primarily political and religious conservatives, feel that such an ordinance sends a message of approval of the gay and lesbian lifestyle. In many cases, the passage of anti-discrimination laws is soon followed by a voter referendum (when an issue is put on the ballot to be decided by registered voters) that overturns the ordinance. Some cities' anti-discrimination ordinances are rendered powerless when a statewide referendum bars "special" rights for the gay community. Although the existing anti-discrimination laws have improved the lives of millions of gay men and lesbians, the ever-changing political climate offers no guarantees that such protections will last.

One of the most fundamental legal rights the gay community has sought is the legalization of gay sexual activity in every state. About half of the states had overturned laws banning such activity by the mid-1970s, but others held firm to the notion that, even between consenting adults, gay sex was immoral and should be illegal. Periodically, a case would come before the U.S. Supreme Court that held the potential to make all such antigay laws in the United States unconstitutional. Time and again, the rulings upheld the state's rights to make these decisions. In 2003, however, with the case *Lawrence v. Texas,* the U.S. Supreme Court ruled that it was unconstitutional to make private sexual activity between two adults illegal when the people are of the same sex, and legal when the people are of the opposite sex.

The *Lawrence* decision was a significant victory. Even in states with laws that made gay sexual activity a crime, few people had been prosecuted for violating these laws in recent years. But the declaration that such laws were unconstitutional signaled an unprecedented acceptance of gay and lesbian lifestyles. Furthermore, the fact that the court ruled it was unfair to penalize gay couples for certain activity but not straight couples seemed to open the door for future rulings promoting gay civil rights.

One community among many One of the most significant changes at the end of the twentieth century was a dramatic increase in the visibility of gay men, lesbians, and bisexuals in American culture. Despite continued discrimination and harassment, the gay community, due to its major role in politics and American culture, transformed the perception of gay men and women from a group on the margins of society to that of a community integrated with society as a whole.

Gay, lesbian, and bisexual characters in major movies and television series became increasingly common throughout the 1990s and into the twenty-first century. A growing number of singers and musicians, particularly women, proclaimed their homosexuality and found that their careers were unaffected when they "came out." Novels published by gay and lesbian authors, many specifically addressing gay subjects, appeared on best-seller lists. In the early twenty-first century, several cable TV shows depicted gays and lesbians not as minor characters but as the central players. Cable networks devoted entirely to gay and lesbian programming arose in the early 2000s.

Increasing numbers of openly gay politicians have been elected to political office. Longtime U.S. Representative Barney Frank came out in 1987 and was re-elected numerous times after that. In some communities,

In 2005 the film Brokeback Mountain *told the story of two cowboys who fall in love. Although some religious groups urged people to boycott the film due to its gay theme,* Brokeback Mountain *starring Jake Gyllenhaal and Heath Ledger was nominated for an Academy Award for best picture.* BUREAU L.A. COLLECTION/CORBIS.

gay high schools and gay youth centers have been established. Although many mainstream religions continue to oppose the gay lifestyle, others have made significant accommodations, embracing gay men and lesbians as part of the religious community and, in some cases, as part of the religious leadership.

Just a few decades ago, many gay people were forced to live invisible lives. Their homosexuality was despised, feared, and judged immoral by many, and they were confined to the fringes of society. By the start of the twenty-first century, the situation had altered dramatically. During the presidential campaign of 1992, Bill Clinton courted the gay community, acknowledging their significance to society and actively seeking their vote. No presidential candidate had done that before. Although many believe that Clinton's record on gay issues fell short of his promises, his embrace of the community showed the growing strength of the national awareness for gay concerns. As quoted in *Out for Good,* Clinton spoke to a large crowd of gay men and lesbians during the campaign, expressing his appreciation for their contributions: "We cannot afford to waste the capacity, the contributions, the heart, the soul, and the mind of the gay and lesbian Americans." Clinton went on to proclaim, "What I came here today to tell you in simple terms is, I have a vision [for America], and you're part of it."

For More Information

BOOKS

Clendinen, Dudley, and Adam Nagourney. *Out for Good: The Struggle to Build a Gay Rights Movement in America.* New York: Simon & Schuster, 1999.

D'Emilio, John. *Making Trouble: Essays on Gay History, Politics, and the University.* New York: Routledge, 1992.

Kranz, Rachel, and Tim Cusick. *Gay Rights.* New York: Facts on File, 2000.

Marcus, Eric. *Making History: The Struggle for Gay and Lesbian Equal Rights.* New York: HarperCollins, 1992.

Roleff, Tamara L., ed. *Gay Rights.* San Diego, CA: Greenhaven Press, 1997.

WEB SITES

The AIDS Memorial Quilt. http://www.aidsquilt.org/ (accessed on May 28, 2006).

"CDER Report to the Nation: 2003." *Center for Drug Evaluation and Research, U.S. Food and Drug Administration.* http://www.fda.gov/cder/reports/rtn/2003/rtn2003-1.HTM (accessed on May 28, 2006).

glbtq: An Encyclopedia of Gay, Lesbian, Bisexual, Transgender, and Queer Culture. http://www.glbtq.com/ (accessed on May 28, 2006).

"History of the GLBT Movement in San Francisco." *Shaping San Francisco.* http://www.shapingsf.org/ezine/gay/ (accessed on May 28, 2006).

Moser, Bob. "Holy War" (Spring 2005). *Southern Poverty Law Center Intelligence Report.* http://www.splcenter.org/intel/intelreport/article.jsp?aid=522 (accessed on May 28, 2006).

Where to Learn More

Books

Altman, Linda Jacobs. *Slavery and Abolition in American History.* Berkeley Heights, NJ: Enslow Publishers, 1999.

Bardham-Quallen, Sudipta. *AIDS.* Farmington Hills, MI: Kidhaven Press, 2005.

Bausum, Ann. *With Courage and Cloth: Winning the Fight for a Woman's Right to Vote.* Washington, DC: National Geographic, 2004.

Behr, Edward. *Prohibition: Thirteen Years That Changed America.* New York: Arcade, 1996.

Berkeley, Kathleen C. *The Women's Liberation Movement in America.* Westport, CT: Greenwood Press, 1999.

Carson, Claybourne, et al., eds. *The Eyes on the Prize: A Civil Rights Reader.* New York: Penguin, 1991.

Carson, Rachel. *Silent Spring.* Boston: Houghton Mifflin, 1962.

Clendinen, Dudley, and Adam Nagourney. *Out for Good: The Struggle to Build a Gay Rights Movement in America.* New York: Simon & Schuster, 1999.

Cohen, Marcia. *The Sisterhood: The True Story of the Women Who Changed the World.* New York: Simon & Schuster, 1988.

Collard, Sneed B., III. *Acting for Nature: What Young People around the World Have Done to Protect the Environment.* Berkeley, CA: Heyday Books, 2000.

Colman, Penny. *Strike! The Bitter Struggle of American Workers from Colonial Times to the Present.* Brookfield, CT: Millbrook Press, 1995.

Covey, Alan, ed. *A Century of Women.* Atlanta: TBS Books, 1994.

Currie, Stephen. *Life of a Slave on a Southern Plantation.* San Diego, CA: Lucent Books, 2000.

Dumbeck, Kristina. *Leaders of Women's Suffrage.* San Diego, CA: Lucent, 2001.

Dunn, John M. *The Civil Rights Movement.* San Diego, CA: Lucent Books, 1998.

Fisher, Leonard Everett. *The Schools.* New York: Holiday House, 1983.

Fisher, Marshall. *The Ozone Layer.* New York: Chelsea House Publishers, 1992.

Flagler, John J. *The Labor Movement in the United States.* Minneapolis: Lerner Publications, 1990.

Flexner, Eleanor. *A Century of Struggle: The Woman's Rights Movement in the United States.* Cambridge, MA: Belknap Press, 1996.

Freedman, Russell. *Kids at Work: Lewis Hine and the Crusade against Child Labor.* New York: Clarion Books, 1994.

Fremon, David K. *The Great Depression in American History.* Springfield, NJ: Enslow Publishers, 1997.

Frost, Elizabeth, and Kathryn Cullen-DuPont. *Women's Suffrage in America: An Eyewitness History.* New York: Facts on File, 1992.

Gates, Henry Louis, and Cornel West. *The African-American Century: How Black Americans Have Shaped Our Country.* New York: Touchstone Books, 2000.

Gaughen, Shasta, ed. *Women's Rights.* San Diego, CA: Greenhaven Press, 2003.

Gerdes, Louise I. *Globalization: Opposing Viewpoints.* Detroit: Greenhaven Press, 2006.

Haley, James, ed. *Prisons.* Detroit: Thomson Gale, 2005.

Hampton, Henry, and Steve Fayer. *Voices of Freedom: An Oral History of the Civil Rights Movement from the 1950s through the 1980s.* New York: Bantam, 1990.

Harness, Cheryl. *Rabble Rousers: 20 Women Who Made a Difference.* New York: Dutton Children's Books, 2003.

Katz, William Loren. *Breaking the Chains: African American Slave Resistance.* New York: Aladdin, 1990.

Kent, Zachary. *World War I: 'The War to End Wars.'* Berkeley Heights, NJ: Enslow Publishers, 1994.

King, Martin Luther, Jr. *Letter from the Birmingham Jail.* San Francisco: Harper San Francisco, 1994.

Kranz, Rachel, and Tim Cusick. *Gay Rights.* New York: Facts on File, 2000.

Meltzer, Milton. *Poverty in America.* New York: William Morrow & Co., 1986.

Meltzer, Milton. *There Comes a Time: The Struggle for Civil Rights.* New York: Landmark Books, 2001.

Mondale, Sarah, and Sarah B. Patton, eds. *School: The Story of American Public Education.* Boston: Beacon Press, 2001.

Murolo, Priscilla, and A. B. Chitty. *From the Folks Who Brought You the Weekend: A Short, Illustrated History of Labor in the United States.* New York: New Press, 2001.

Olson, Lynne. *Freedom's Daughters: The Unsung Heroines of the Civil Rights Movement from 1830 to 1970.* New York: Scribner, 2002.

Powledge, Fred. *Free at Last? The Civil Rights Movement and the People Who Made It.* Boston: Little, Brown, 1991.

Rebman, Renee C. *Prohibition.* San Diego, CA: Lucent, 1999.

Reef, Catherine. *Working in America.* New York: Facts on File, 2000.

Roleff, Tamara L., ed. *Gay Rights.* San Diego, CA: Greenhaven Press, 1997.

Scherer, Randy. *The Antiwar Movement.* San Diego, CA: Greenhaven Press/ Thomson Gale, 2004.

Sullivan, Larry E. *The Prison Reform Movement: Forlorn Hope.* Boston: Twayne Publishers, 1990.

Tackach, James. *The Abolition of American Slavery.* San Diego, CA: Lucent Books, 2002.

Ward, Geoffrey C. *Not for Ourselves Alone: The Story of Elizabeth Cady Stanton and Susan B. Anthony.* New York: Alfred A. Knopf, 1999.

Weatherford, Doris. *A History of the American Suffragist Movement.* Santa Barbara, CA: ABC-CLIO, 1998.

Wexler, Sanford. *The Civil Rights Movement.* New York: Facts on File, 1999.

Willis, Terri, and Wallace B. Black. *Endangered Species.* Chicago: Children's Press, 1992.

Winters, Paul A., ed. *The Civil Rights Movement.* San Diego, CA: Greenhaven Press, 2000.

"The World Bank Group." *Worldmark Encyclopedia of the Nations, Vol. 1: United Nations.* 11th ed. Farmington Hills, MI: Thomson Gale, 2004.

Web Sites

"Africans in America." *Public Broadcasting Service (PBS).* http://www.pbs.org/ wgbh/aia/home.html (accessed on July 31, 2006).

The AIDS Memorial Quilt. http://www.aidsquilt.org/ (accessed on July 31, 2006).

EarthDay.gov. http://www.earthday.gov/ (accessed on July 31, 2006).

"The Endangered Species Program." *U.S. Fish and Wildlife Service.* http:// www.fws.gov/endangered/ (accessed on July 31, 2006).

Federal Bureau of Prisons. http://www.bop.gov (accessed on July 31, 2006).

The Gilder Lehrman Center for the Study of Slavery, Resistance, and Abolition. http://www.yale.edu/glc/ (accessed on July 31, 2006).

Global Warming: Kids Site. United States Environmental Protection Agency. http://www.epa.gov/globalwarming/kids/index.html (accessed on July 31, 2006).

"An Introduction to the Woman's Suffrage Movement." *National Women's History Museum.* http://www.nmwh.org/exhibits/tour_1.html (accessed on July 31, 2006).

"The Martin Luther King Jr. Papers Project." *Stanford University.* http://www.stanford.edu/group/King/mlkpapers/ (accessed on July 31, 2006).

Military Families Speak Out. http://www.mfso.org/ (accessed on July 31, 2006).

"Temperance and Prohibition." *Ohio State University Department of History.* http://prohibition.osu.edu/ (accessed on July 31, 2006).

U.S. Environmental Protection Agency. http://www.epa.gov/ (accessed on July 31, 2006).

Weisbrot, Mark. "Globalization: A Primer." *Center for Economic and Policy Research.* http://www.cepr.net/publications/global_primer.htm (accessed on July 31, 2006).

Wittner, Lawrence S. "Have Peace Activists Ever Stopped a War?" (2006). *ZNet.* http://www.zmag.org/content/showarticle.cfm?ItemID=9543 (accessed on July 31, 2006).

Index

Italic type indicates the volume number. Illustrations are marked by (ill.).

M

N

U

V

W